GHOSTS

Ghosts

Deconstruction, Psychoanalysis, History

Edited by

Peter Buse
and
Andrew Stott

First published in Great Britain 1999 by
MACMILLAN PRESS LTD
Houndmills, Basingstoke, Hampshire RG21 6XS and London
Companies and representatives throughout the world

A catalogue record for this book is available from the British Library.

ISBN 0–333–71143–2 hardcover
ISBN 0–333–71144–0 paperback

First published in the United States of America 1999 by
ST. MARTIN'S PRESS, INC.,
Scholarly and Reference Division,
175 Fifth Avenue, New York, N.Y. 10010

ISBN 0–312–21739–0

Library of Congress Cataloging-in-Publication Data
Ghosts : deconstruction, psychoanalysis, history / edited by Peter
Buse and Andrew Stott.
p.   cm.
Includes bibliographical references and index.
ISBN 0–312–21739–0 (cloth)
1. Ghosts.   2. Deconstruction.   3. Psychoanalysis—History.
4. Ghosts in literature.   I. Buse, Peter, 1970–   .   II. Stott,
Andrew, 1969–   .
BF1471.G48   1998
133.1—dc21   98–34810
                                                                    CIP

Selection, editorial matter and Introduction © Peter Buse and Andrew Stott 1999
Text © Macmillan Press Ltd 1999

This book is printed on paper suitable for recycling and made from fully managed and sustained forest sources.

10   9   8   7   6   5   4   3   2   1
08   07   06   05   04   03   02   01   00   99

Printed and bound in Great Britain by
Antony Rowe Ltd, Chippenham, Wiltshire

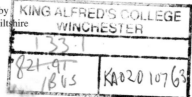

Contents

Part III Spectral Culture   201

Notes on the Contributors

Clive Bloom is Reader in English and American Studies at Middlesex University. He is the general editor of the Insights series for Macmillan and the author and editor of many books on literary theory, popular literature and cultural history, including *Cult Fiction: Popular Reading and Pulp Theory* (1996).

Christina Britzolakis is Lecturer in English at the University of Warwick. She has published articles on the 'masses' in the poetry of Pound, Eliot and Yeats, on literature and politics in the 1930s, and on modernist appropriations of *Hamlet*. She is the author of *Sylvia Plath: Rhetoric, Gender, Subjectivity* (1996).

Peter Buse is Lecturer in English at the University of Salford. He has published articles in *Textual Practice*, *Cultural Critique*, *The Journal of Dramatic Theory and Criticism* and *The European Journal of Cultural Studies*.

Steven Connor is Professor of Modern Literature and Theory at Birkbeck College, University of London. He is the author of numerous books and articles on a variety of topics including Dickens, Beckett, postmodernity and cultural value.

Natalka Freeland is Assistant Professor of English at the University of Alberta. She completed her doctoral dissertation in comparative literature at Yale University, writing on suspense fiction from Walpole to Conan Doyle.

Ken Gelder is Senior Lecturer in English and Cultural Studies at Melbourne University, Australia. His books include *Reading the Vampire* (1994) and *The Oxford Book of Australian Ghost Stories* (1994). He has recently co-edited *The Sub-Cultures Reader* (1996) with Sarah Thornton.

Jane M. Jacobs is Lecturer in Geography at Melbourne University, Australia. Her publications include *Edge of Empire: Postcolonialism and the City* (1996).

Roger Luckhurst is Lecturer in English at Birkbeck College, University of London. He has written on contemporary fiction, Derrida, deconstruction and psychoanalysis and is currently working on tele-technologies.

Willy Maley is Reader in English Literature at the University of Glasgow, and author of *A Spenser Chronology* (1994), and *Salvaging Spenser: Colonialism, Culture and Identity* (1997), and co-editor of *Representing Ireland: Literature and the Origins of Conflict, 1534–1660* (1993), *Postcolonial Criticism* (1997), and *A View of the Present State of Ireland: from the First Published Edition* (1997).

Nigel Mapp teaches at the University of Leeds. He has published widely on critical theory and continental philosophy, especially on the work of William Empson and Paul de Man.

Mandy Merck is a former editor of the film and television studies journal *Screen*. From 1988 to 1991 she produced lesbian and gay programmes for Channel 4 and the BBC. Since then she has taught at Cornell, Duke and the University of California at Santa Cruz. The author of *Perversions: Deviant Readings* (1993), she now lectures in media studies at the University of Sussex.

Ralph Noyes was Under-Secretary in the Civil Service. Honorary Secretary of the Society for Psychical Research from 1990 to 1998, he wrote a novel, *The Secret Property* (1985), and edited a collection, *The Crop Circle Enigma* (1991). He also wrote several short science-fiction stories as well as papers and articles on anomalous topics. Sadly, Ralph Noyes died in May 1998.

Ruth Parkin-Gounelas is Associate Professor of English at Aristotle University in Thessaloniki, Greece. She has published extensively in the areas of Victorian literature, feminism and psychoanalytic approaches to literature. Her book *Fictions of the Female Self* was published in 1991.

Andrew Stott is Lecturer in English Literary and Cultural Studies at the University of Westminster. He has published articles in, among other journals, *Textual Practice, Criticism, Word and Image* and *Cahiers Elisabethains*.

Acknowledgements

For their patience, we would like to thank all the contributors and especially Charmian Hearne, our editor at Macmillan. Avril Horner, Nigel Mapp and Nuria Triana-Toribio provided valuable suggestions on the Introduction, which was also presented in a slightly different form to the Northern Critical Theory Seminar at the University of Staffordshire, 6 December 1997. For countless conversations on ghostly matters, thanks are due to colleagues at the University of Wales, Cardiff, the University of Leeds, the University of Salford and the University of Westminster where we studied or taught during the development of this book.

Introduction:
A Future for Haunting
Peter Buse and Andrew Stott

I

Chances are, ghosts will make another comeback. For the time being, however, spectres, apparitions, phantoms and *revenants* have been eclipsed in the popular imagination by a rage for aliens, extra-terrestrials, conspiracy theories, Martian landings and all manner of paranormal occurrences apposite to millennial fever. In contrast, ghosts seem a little dated, paling in comparison with such sophisticated other-worldly phenomena. A solid core of psychical researchers, ghost-layers and ghost-hunters may remain, but the most dedicated enthusiasts are probably those who make their livings conducting ghost tours in medieval towns, and hosting guests in 'haunted' hotels. It is safe to say that to be interested in ghosts these days is decidedly anachronistic. Perhaps the nineteenth century, with its spiritualists, mediums, table-tilting séances, spirit-rapping, Ghost Club and Society for Psychical Research, was the most accommodating historical period for the ghosts which have fallen on hard times in the late twentieth century. And yet, it could also be argued that the nineteenth-century craze for ghosts was *already* an anachronism. If we follow Keith Thomas's compelling thesis in *Religion and the Decline of Magic*, we should properly view as anachronistic any belief in ghosts after the Reformation, which, theologically speaking (for Protestants at least), put paid to the possibility of the return of the dead by dispensing with the concept of purgatory.[1] The theological climate may have been unsympathetic, but ghosts – as Thomas concedes – have stubbornly, in one form or another, continued to appear since the Reformation, and even thrived under such anachronistic circumstances. Indeed, anachronism might well be the defining feature of ghosts, now and in the past, because haunting, by its very structure, implies a deformation of linear temporality: there may be no proper time for ghosts. It is with this possibility in mind that this book takes up a sometimes unfashionable topic.

1

Thomas dismisses contemporary ghosts on the grounds that their appearance and activities are no longer supported by a fully developed belief-system:

> although it may be a relatively frivolous question today to ask whether or not one believes in ghosts, it was in the sixteenth century a shibboleth which distinguished Protestant from Catholic almost as effectively as belief in the Mass or the Papal Supremacy.[2]

Thomas may be right about the frivolity of the question, but perhaps it is the wrong one to ask, even if the most obvious and instinctive one. Whether or not we believe in ghosts, we may nevertheless be forced to deal with them, if not in the forms of the sixteenth or nineteenth centuries. One of Sigmund Freud's 'abstract or innocent conceptual jokes' may be instructive in this context: in the shortest of jokes in *Jokes and Their Relation to the Unconscious*, Freud demonstrates the pitfalls of that satisfyingly simple question, 'Do you believe in ghosts?' The joke, from the category of 'abstract or innocent conceptual jokes', is about a man supremely confident of his rational faculties: 'Not only did he disbelieve in ghosts; he was not even frightened of them.'[3] The paradox energizing this joke captures succinctly the difficulties we encounter if we attempt to divide believers and non-believers neatly when it comes to ghosts. Freud elucidates further:

> If this joking envelope is removed, we have: 'it is much easier to get rid of a fear of ghosts intellectually than to escape it when the occasion arises.' This is no longer in the least a joke, though it is a correct and still little appreciated psychological discovery.[4]

Elsewhere, Freud reads a belief in the supernatural as a sort of vestigial trace from pre-scientific periods. For instance, in *The Interpretation of Dreams*, he says 'it would be a mistake to suppose that the theory of the supernatural origin of dreams is without its supporters in our own days', but he reminds us, in the same mode as Thomas, that this is the 'view of dreams adopted by the peoples of antiquity'.[5] According to this perspective, then, it is acceptable to treat ghosts seriously, but only if we restrict ourselves to the past tense. This attitude of indulgence towards 'the peoples of antiquity' may be the more common stance, but Freud's joke may take us down a more productive route. While proving or disproving the existence of ghosts is a fruitless exercise, it is more rewarding to diagnose the persistence of the *trope* of spectrality in culture. Spectrality and haunting continue to enjoy a powerful currency in language and in thinking, even if they have been left behind by belief.

In *Ghosts: Deconstruction, Psychoanalysis, History* we want to suspend temporarily the question of belief which dogs any discussion of ghosts. More easily said than done. Even in a 'dis-enchanted' world, ghosts are still invoked when there is some uncertainty about the believability or authenticity of an event or experience in the material world – hence phantom pregnancies, limbs, and phone calls, ghost-writers, 'a ghost of a chance', televisual ghosting, and so on. In the context of a truth test, 'ghost' and its many synonyms always provide useful metaphors when the test ends in failure. In other words, even though it is now frivolous to believe in ghosts, they cannot shrug off the spectre of belief: it is simply that now they have been consigned to the task of representing whatever is not to be believed. The equation has not changed, but now ghosts inhabit its other side. Why do ghosts continue to occupy such a prominent position in debates over the boundary between real and unreal? Why do they furnish such workable tropes of untruth? The answer lies in their relationship to reason and rationality. The current understanding of ghosts owes less to the Reformation, which denied their return from purgatory, than it does to the Enlightenment. With the advent of the Enlightenment, a line was drawn between Reason and its more shadowy others – magic and witchcraft, irrationality, superstition, the occult. In this wider activity of exclusion, ghosts of course fall very firmly in the camp of unreason and therefore become fair game for empiricists eager to demonstrate that ghosts are in fact the product of illusion or hoax, or mere hallucination. As more than one essay in this volume attests, the subsequent encounters between ghosts and empirical suspicion, though sometimes treated with the utmost sobriety by the participants, often yielded farcical results.

In recent years, cultural historians have been alert to the processes of exclusion performed by Reason on non-Enlightenment practices where ghosts found or remained in favour. These scholars of the margins painstakingly chart the histories of witchcraft and sorcery, occultism and spiritualism, giving voice to people and illuminating practices otherwise silenced or neglected by the mainstream historical record. Most relevant in the case of ghosts is the work on spiritualism, a pseudo-religion of the nineteenth century whose main tenet was the conviction that communication with the dead was possible under the proper conditions. The titles of the most well-known studies on spiritualism signal very clearly how their authors locate their subjects *vis-à-vis* the Enlightenment. Thus we have Janet Oppenheim's *The Other World* and Alex Owen's *The Darkened Room*. What these tremendous pieces of research reveal is that those who subscribed to so-called occult beliefs in Victorian England were also those in a marginal position in culture in general: spiritualism found its largest constituency among women and the working classes of the North of England, and its practices and processes gave them unprecedented access to cultural power and validation.[6] In other words, these cultural histories refute Thomas's claim that believing in ghosts after the Reformation was never more than a frivolity. However, as Oppenheim and Owen set out to redeem these isolated figures from the past, they tend to get themselves in a tangle when they are forced to give a present-day evaluation of the validity or truth-content of spiritualism. Oppenheim distances herself from her subject by distinguishing between contemporary occultism, which she dismisses as 'silliness', and its nineteenth-century antecedent:

> There is … a significant distinction between spiritualism and psychical research in the late nineteenth century and para-psychology in the late twentieth. Now, after decades of disappointments, few influential or renowned scholars endorse the claims of parapsychology. Then, a century ago, spiritualism and psychical research loomed as a very serious business to some very serious and eminent people.[7]

Owen similarly declines to pass judgement on the veracity of spirit-ualist claims, wisely 'avoiding a constant engagement with the tortuous and contentious issue of how mediumistic phenomena were produced'. She says she will treat spiritualism as an indepen-dent discursive practice with its own signifying rules:

> I deal instead with the possible meaning and significance of spiritualism as a social movement with a specific world view, one

which found expression in a unique series of symbolic practices ... this book ... presents spiritualism as a discourse – a specific historical and cultural set of beliefs and practices governed and delineated by their own rules of formulation.[8]

This is immaculate reasoning, but by treating spiritualism as a self-contained, self-propagating signifying practice, Owen in a sense lets the Enlightenment off the hook, when it too may participate in those 'symbolic practices' it establishes as other to itself.

Historical difference acts as a kind of buffer, allowing the researcher to defer a decision about the 'actuality' of spiritualist claims, and therefore avoid a potentially embarrassing contradiction.[9] These cultural historians are understandably reluctant to place themselves in the camp of the believers, for fear of losing all credibility within the camp of the sceptics, who constitute their audience and to whom they belong. In this inevitable operation, historians of the occult cannot but reproduce the terms and oppositions set out by the Enlightenment. They must ultimately confirm that there is indeed an inside and an outside of Reason, and that on the outside we find occult practices, and with them ghosts. Spiritualism may resist a dominant rationalism, they are arguing, but it is nevertheless *outside* rationalism. In *Ghosts* we want to argue, on the contrary, that not only have some 'very serious' people – as Oppenheim puts it – continued to endorse ghostly thinking in the twentieth century, but more important, that the Enlightenment never succeeds entirely in exorcising its own ghosts. Instead of saying that there is an outside of reason which has been neglected, perhaps we need to inspect the inside of reason and see how it too is haunted by what it excludes. When Stephen Greenblatt so seductively begins *Shakespearean Negotiations* with the words 'I began with the desire to speak with the dead', he is not alone among illustrious thinkers to express such a desire.[10] He is in excellent company, as Owen implies – Engels, Barrett Browning, Ruskin, Saussure, Yeats and others were all known to have attended séances; and it was Jules Michelet before Greenblatt who conceived of historiography as a discourse with the dead.[11] It will be our contention that the most sustained engagements this century with the figure of the ghost do not revolve around thinkers attending séances, but rather in the texts of what has come to be called 'theory'. This book explores how some of the forebears of contemporary theory dealt with ghostly matters and how modern theorists, the inheritors (and deformers) of the Enlightenment, find the trope of spectrality a useful theoretical tool. In this sense we are following the lead set in Jacques Derrida's recent *Specters of Marx*, where an interrogation of Marx's uneasy relationship to haunting and history opens up avenues for thinking about ghosts in the late twentieth century.

II

Occultism is the metaphysic of dunces.

Theodor Adorno[12]

This volume will argue that modern theory owes a debt to ghosts. That debt may often be unacknowledged; it may even be hotly denied, particularly by the forerunners of contemporary theory – like Marx and Freud – who wrote in an age of high empiricism and at a time when occultism was taken more seriously by their fellow thinkers. Accordingly, in his contribution, 'Spectres of Engels', Willy Maley shows how Friedrich Engels satirized spiritualism and séances from a materialist perspective, while in '"Something Tremendous, Something Elemental"', Roger Luckhurst traces Freud's flirtation with occultism and his only partial success in excluding its influence from psychoanalysis. It is easy to see why materialists in the Marxian tradition would be suspicious and sceptical about spectral matters: the realm of the phantomatic is surely not far removed from idealism. Certainly, Theodor Adorno does not restrain his scorn for horoscopes – 'astrological hocus-pocus' he calls them – and reserves some of his most venomous attacks in *Minima Moralia* for the excesses of latter-day mediums. Adorno's 'Theses against Occultism' is valuable because he does not set out simply to debunk mediums as charlatans (Engels's approach) and their spiritualist audience as straightforwardly gullible. Rather, he diagnoses the 'regression to magic' as symptomatic of the effects of late capitalism and the dominance of the 'all-encompassing exchange relationship' which in fact 'eliminates the elemental power the occultists claim to command'.[13] In other words, occultism can be seen as a vain reaction to commodity-culture, an attempt to transcend the exchange-relationship, but one which merely repeats its forms and processes. Spiritualists betray their 'regression in consciousness' in at least two aspects of their activities. First, there is the banality of their supposedly transcendental experiences: 'The mediocrity of the mediums is no more accidental than the apocryphal triviality of the revelations. Since the early days of spiritualism the Beyond has communicated nothing more significant than the dead grandmother's greetings.'[14] Second, besides the crashing mundanity of spiritualist revelations, there is the conspicuous contradiction between spiritualists' or psychical researchers' transcendent claims and their empirical methods, a contradiction addressed in different ways by Steven Connor, Clive Bloom, and Ralph Noyes in this volume. As Adorno almost gleefully points out, 'They inveigh against materialism. But they want to weigh the astral body.... The same rationalistic and empiricist apparatus that threw the spirits out is being used to reimpose them on those who no longer trust their own reason.'[15] Adorno's suspicion about the conservative nature of spiritualism makes 'Theses against Occultism' a useful companion-piece to the recovery work done by historians like Owen and Oppenheim, but it does not tell the whole story. In a more strictly philosophical vein, Adorno himself had a vexed set of negotiations with the opposition between the transcendental and the empirical, a tension explored in relation to both Adorno and Derrida by Nigel Mapp in his essay 'Spectre and Impurity: History and the Transcendental in Derrida and Adorno'. Equally, one of Adorno's contemporaries, Walter Benjamin, found the notion of 'phantasmagoria' productive in describing the experience of modernity, as Christina Britzolakis shows in 'Phantasmagoria: Walter Benjamin and the Poetics of Urban Modernism'.

Freud's paper 'Repression', from 1915, provides an excellent example of how a text operating very much within a rationalistic discourse can have recourse to a ghostly tropology without subscribing wholeheartedly to 'astrological hocus-pocus'. In this paper Freud gropes towards articulating the workings of a psychical mechanism hitherto unrecognized: the process whereby an instinctual impulse must be rendered 'inoperative' because of the distress it will cause the subject if it is not dealt with. Irreconcilable with other wishes and desires in the conscious system, the offending ideational content is banished to the unconscious. Freud acknowledges '[i]t is not easy in theory to deduce the possibility of such a thing as repression.'[16] In other words, he is about to propose a counter-intuitive or seemingly illogical concept. Nor is there any finality about repression, for, like the unconscious, with which it is closely aligned, repression undergoes many vicissitudes and continues to have effects in the conscious. The repressed may be gone, but it also comes back. Freud describes it thus:

> Not only is [repression], as we have just shown, *individual* in its operation, but it is also exceedingly *mobile*. The process of repression is not to be regarded as an event which takes place *once*, the results of which are permanent, as when some living thing has been killed and from that time onward is dead; repression demands a persistent expenditure of force.[17]

In order to explain his difficult new concept, Freud alludes to the habits of ghosts, although he never spells it out, to be sure. But he is very clear that to understand repression, we must think beyond any simple organic distinction between the living and the dead. The notion of the return, or repetition ('repression is not to be regarded as an event which takes place *once*') is paramount. As Ralph Noyes points out in his essay, one of the defining features of ghosts is their capacity to return, and for Freud, who is trying to elaborate a temporal structure in which past, present, and future are inter-implicated rather than autonomous, the return is indispensable. The return, of course, is not necessarily a happy event, but one in which the stakes are high: 'The ambivalence which has enabled repression through reaction-formation to take place is also the point at which the repressed succeeds in returning. The vanished affect comes back in its transformed shape as social anxiety, moral anxiety and unlimited self-reproaches.'[18] We could not hope for a more eloquent definition of haunting, which in this case is also a definition of contradiction and social conflict. Whereas Adorno suggests dabbling in ghosts is politically disabling, the theory of repression implies that the realm of the political functions in an extraordinarily ghostly fashion.

At least some of this is old news to literary critics and theorists who have been writing about Gothic fiction, the Uncanny and the literature of the fantastic for many years.[19] Literature has always been a more accommodating place for ghosts, perhaps because fiction itself shares their simulacral qualities: like writing, ghosts are associated with a certain secondariness or belatedness. Accordingly, in *Ghosts* we dedicate an entire section to the phantoms of fiction and film, with papers which take on board some of the more recent spectral insights of deconstruction and psychoanalysis. Freud himself found literature a productive way to talk explicitly about issues only implicitly touched on in essays like 'Repression'. His most notable treatment of literary matters is in 'The "Uncanny"' where he makes an unusual foray into the realm of aesthetics in order to address what he sees as a neglected aspect of the reading experience, that is, 'that class of the frightening which leads back to what is known of old and long familiar'.[20] He notoriously fails to arrive at a satisfactory final definition of the Uncanny, but along the way he links it with the experience of *déjà vu*, with the idea of the double, with the loss of the eyes, with an inability to distinguish between the animate and inanimate, with repetition and with death. Freud's inability to pin down the Uncanny is a hazard of the project, because, as he says, 'the word is not always used in a clearly definable sense, so that it tends to coincide with what excites fear in general'.[21] As a result, the Uncanny has proved a flexible, if frightening, concept, a useful tool when writing about literature. The essays in this volume on fiction and film accordingly all draw either explicitly or implicitly on Freud's notion.

Ruth Parkin-Gounelas, Natalka Freeland, Mandy Merck, and Ken Gelder and Jane Jacobs all address in one way or other the question of property or possession. They hint that where there are disputes over property, we find ghosts, or that where we find ghosts, there are bound to be anxieties about property. As much is already implied by Freud in 'The "Uncanny"' where he points out that the meanings of *heimlich* (the homely, the familiar) and *unheimlich* (the uncanny, the strange, the hidden) tend to dovetail. The familiar and secure is always haunted by the strange and unfamiliar, while the unfamiliar often has a troubling familiarity about it. The experience of the Uncanny might be summed up as that moment when the seemingly natural reveals itself to be cultural after all. Property, as Freeland puts it, is 'frightening and dangerous, conjuring fears of ghosts rather than circulating freely and without history as in the bourgeois ideal' (p. 157, *infra*). Whether property is a Gothic ancestral home, a Romantic heroine's inheritance, a loft space in downtown Manhattan, or a sacred site in Australia, it is never free of ghostly vicissitudes, contrary to all rhetoric of propriety and possession which would exorcise past struggles over it. It is entirely appropriate, then, that Freud likened the repressed idea to an unwelcome house-guest.[22] If these chapters on the Uncanny and property privilege literature and cinema, it is because literature has always been the Uncanny site *par excellence*,

while, as Mandy Merck points out, not only has film been historically identified as a spectral medium, but 'the ghost motif is
virtually as old as cinema itself' (p. 168, *infra*). In *Ghosts* we juxta-
pose these literary and cinematic papers with papers on theory and
history because we want to avoid the tendency, inherent in studies
of the literary fantastic, to restrict ghosts to a genre (Gothic) or a
representational medium (fiction or film). Rather, we want to
consider fiction simultaneously with psychoanalysis and deconstruction.

III

In *Specters of Marx*, Derrida claims that 'there has never been a
scholar that really, and as a scholar, deals with ghosts'.[23] By this
remark, we are sure that he does not wish us to believe that scholars
have never tried to prove the truth or otherwise of uncanny apparitions or ghostly occurrences. Indeed, Derrida's complaint is that
the scholar will *only* seek to determine matters of supernatural
veracity, positioning him or herself at a distance from the apparition, and attempt '*to make or let* a spirit *speak*'.[24] By not 'dealing' with
ghosts, Derrida argues that traditional scholarship asks questions of
the ghost only with the intention of ontologizing it, or interpellat-
ing it from the necessary distance of scholarly 'objectivity'. This, he
believes, constitutes an avoidance of spectrality, since to figure the
ghost in terms of fact or fiction, real or not-real, is to attribute to it a
foundational ground, either a positive or negative facticity that the
notion of ghostliness continually eludes. It is this elusiveness that
should be addressed, and so, for Derrida, a pseudo-concept like
spectrality looks very much at home among the motifs that have
been central to deconstruction for many years.

The relevance of a trope of spectrality to deconstruction is clear.[25]
Ghosts are neither dead nor alive, neither corporeal objects nor
stern absences. As such, they are the stock-in-trade of the
Derridean enterprise, standing in defiance of binary oppositions
such as presence and absence, body and spirit, past and present,
life and death. For deconstruction, these terms cannot stand in
clear, independent opposition to one another, as each can be
shown to possess an element or trace of the term that it is meant to
oppose. In the figure of the ghost, we see that past and present
cannot be neatly separated from one another, as any idea of the

present is always constituted through the difference and deferral of the past, as well as anticipations of the future.[26] And so the liminal spirit, or to use Derrida's favoured term, *revenant*, the thing that returns, comes to represent a mobilization of familiar Derridean concepts such as trace, iteration and the deferral of presence.

The ghost as a cipher of iteration is particularly suggestive. At the beginning of *Specters of Marx*, Derrida talks about the way in which the anticipated *return* of the ghost may be mobilized on behalf of a deconstruction of all historicisms that are grounded in a rigid sense of chronology. 'Haunting is historical, to be sure', he writes, 'but it is not *dated*, it is never docilely given a date in the chain of presents, day after day, according to the instituted order of the calendar.'[27] The question of the *revenant* neatly encapsulates deconstructive concerns about the impossibility of conceptually solidifying the past. Ghosts arrive from the past and appear in the present. However, the ghost cannot be properly said to belong to the past, even if the apparition represents someone who has been dead for many centuries, for the simple reason that a ghost is clearly not the same thing as the person who shares its proper name. Does then the 'historical' person who is identified with the ghost properly belong to the present? Surely not, as the idea of a return from death fractures all traditional conceptions of temporality. The temporality to which the ghost is subject is therefore paradoxical, as at once they 'return' *and* make their apparitional debut. Derrida has been pleased to term this dual movement of return and inauguration a 'hauntology', a coinage that suggests a spectrally deferred non-origin within grounding metaphysical terms such as history and identity. This idea will be familiar from other Derridean discussions of event and causality in essays such as 'Before the Law', and 'Signature Event Context', where he argues that all committed attempts to lead us 'towards an impossible exhibition of a site and an event' can only ever stumble into iterative movements that the event has produced, but which cannot contain it in its singularity.[28] Such an idea also informs the well-known discussion of the origin of language in *Of Grammatology*, where Derrida suggests that any notion of an epiphanic 'breakthrough' initiating all subsequent intelligible verbal communication necessarily implies a chain of causality leading back to an underlying arche-system of intelligibility that permits certain sounds to be imputed with specific meanings.[29] Thus, any attempt to isolate the origin of language will find its inaugural moment already dependent upon a system of linguistic differences that has been installed prior to the 'originary' moment.

Deconstruction's ghosts, then, are considerably different from those found in the majority of fictional haunting narratives with which we have been familiar. While there are certain celebrated exceptions such as Henry James's *The Turn of the Screw*, fictional phantoms are usually banished by the imposition of closure at the end of the narrative.[30] The apparitions of *The Castle of Otranto*, for example, while never being simply explained away, nevertheless obediently evaporate as soon as the trajectories of history, legacy and property are reinstated to their rightful places. For deconstruction, a removal of all forms of haunting in the face of such awesome referential categories represents an artificial and unworkable imposition placed upon such concepts. Like the appearance of the ghost, the origin and its repetition are coterminous with one another. Thus, no signification can be unproblematically sutured to the originary context of its production, as the sign is haunted by a chain of overdetermined readings, mis-readings, slips and accretions that will always go beyond the event itself.

Deconstruction could therefore be said to explicitly work through some of the problems of ghosts that psychoanalysis tentatively and implicitly addressed. One might argue that psychoanalysis has been happier to accept the traditional 'surface' characteristics of ghosts than deconstruction, mining their powerful folkloric associations for a rich vein of analogy. As Roger Luckhurst's essay in this collection shows, Freud himself refused to rule them out, was for many years interested in the possibility of telepathy, and had his first essay published in England by the *Journal for the Society for Psychical Research*. The trope of spectrality is evident in many of the central metapsychological concepts of Freudian psychoanalysis. In addition to ideas such as the Uncanny and the return of the repressed already discussed, we might also mention the 'possessed' or inhabited melancholic, and the analysand's symptom unearthing what we might call the 'ghosts' of the past, as psychoanalytic notions which mobilize metaphors of haunting. Certainly, the classic Freudian spatialization of the human mind is somewhat akin to the internal geography of the gothic castle, in which the unconscious is conceived of as a dimly lit attic whose existence troubles the ego, and whose secrets, once known, are often terrifying.[31] For Hélène Cixous, the ghostly metaphor is used to represent the persistent shadow that constitutes the subject's relationship to death. 'Everything remains to be said on the subject of the Ghost and the ambiguity of the Return', she writes,

> for what renders it intolerable is not so much that it is an announcement of death nor even the proof that death exists, since this Ghost announces and proves nothing more than its return. What is intolerable is that the Ghost erases the limit which exists between two states, neither alive nor dead; passing through, the dead man returns in the manner of the Repressed. It is his coming back which makes the ghost what he is, just as it is the return of the Repressed that inscribes the repression.[32]

Arguably, then, the ghost has no specific theoretical function in psychoanalysis other than to feature as an expressive symptom of the phenomena that bear upon an unsettled psychic life. In his essay, 'Desire and the Interpretation of Desire in *Hamlet*', Jacques Lacan equates their appearance with a lacuna that manifests itself in the Real in the absence of a satisfactorily mediating ritual of mourning. 'This explains', he writes, 'the belief we find in folklore in the very close association of the lack, skipping, or refusal of something in the satisfaction of the dead, with the appearance of ghosts and specters in the gap left by the omission of the significant rite.'[33] The ghosts of psychoanalytic theory are predominantly symbols of lack, disquiet and unmediated tragedy. However, this is not to say that the institution of psychoanalysis is not itself haunted by the historical and clinical influences by which it was determined. In some of the more marginal writings of the movement this has been recognized, and Nicolas Abraham and Maria Torok have very successfully elaborated notions such as the 'trans-generational phantom', which Ruth Parkin-Gounelas addresses in her essay in this volume.

IV

What of the third term in our title, history? Surely ghosts are not historical in any sense other than the fact that 'historically' people have feared ghosts, reported sightings of them or dismissed them out of hand, and that our culture is immersed in centuries of super-natural belief. Ghosts, then, feature as cultural phenomena of some sociological significance; slightly less significant than a belief in

God, and slightly more significant than a belief in the prophetic effects of nail-paring. But what are the implications of applying a concept of spectrality to historiography?

Traditional history has maintained an ideal of an inert sense of the past, a past whose 'passing' can be accurately measured, and whose attributes can be quantified. It can be said that relatively recent historicisms, such as the 'New Historicism' of the past fifteen years or so, have not been happy to leave the notion of a sealed capsule of past time unchallenged. However, they too have continued to consort with the notion of isolating an actuality of past experience. Stephen Greenblatt's desire to converse with Elizabethan purgators, for example, may on first sight seem to share a Derridean openness to the iterative traces of history, but his subsequent examination of historical cause and effect shows this imagined conversation to be little more than a phonocentric fantasy, 'the dead' simply acting as shorthand for the current mortal state of the previously living people to whom he would like to talk. The 'desire to speak with the dead' does not therefore represent a negotiation or reading of the spectral traces that constitute historicity, but rather a wish to dissolve those traces into a proleptic ontology.

Ghosts are a problem for historicism precisely because they disrupt our sense of a linear teleology in which the consecutive movement of history passes untroubled through the generations. Again we return to the question of anachronism because ghosts are anachronism *par excellence*, the appearance of something in a time in which they clearly do not belong. But ghosts do not just represent reminders of the past – in their fictional representation they very often demand something of the future. The ghost in *Hamlet* is a well-known example of this. Old Hamlet arrives from the past in order to make a demand on his son's future actions. He, like many of the ghosts of later gothic and modern fictions, serves to destabilize any neat compartmentalization of the past as a secure and fixed entity, or the future as uncharted territory.

Anachronism also draws attention to the part that rhetoric plays in the construction of histories. Language is the only means we have of representing the past, and our descriptions of it are obviously formulated in an idiom that is more or less inappropriate to the time we are discussing. Through our linguistic mediation of history, therefore, we impute the existence of a historical field outside of language. Paul de Man drew attention to the way in which literary and cultural studies often mis-conceptualize the object of their study by allowing a certain trajectory of rhetoric to persuade them that there is an absolute in the object of their scrutiny. As he writes, 'In literary studies, structures of meaning are frequently described in historical rather than semiological terms. This is, in itself, a somewhat surprising occurrence, since the historical nature of literary discourse is by no means an *a priori* established fact, whereas all literature necessarily consists of linguistic and semantic elements.'[34] De Man goes on to suggest that historicism is predicated on a leap of faith that is enabled by the presence of rhetorical devices operating on the surface of the text that produce the effect both of historical movement and a *beyond* of that text. This manifests itself in the spatial metaphors of historicism that conceive of the relationship of text and context in terms of a perspectival relationship of foreground and background, one only making sense in relation to the other. The very founding principle of historicism, its imagined correspondence between the linguistic text, and the non-verbal, referential, categories outside it, is therefore the product of rhetorical movements that invite the critic to read the text, as de Man would have it, 'as a kind of box that separates an inside from an outside, [with] the reader or critic as the person who opens the lid in order to release in the open what was secreted but inaccessible inside'.[35] An awareness of the motif of spectrality, on the other hand, would involve acknowledging the fact that the sense of the past has been summoned through an iteration that takes place in the context of the present.

If we discard as unworkable the thought that the original 'event' of history programmes its subsequent understanding, we might stand accused of irresponsibly evaporating history into abstraction. However, a notion of the spectre enables us to concentrate on reading history as a series of the iterations and recontextualizations, traces and returns that constitutes our experience of it.[36] No one questions that a text can signify quite satisfactorily after it is removed from the moment of its production, but what Derrida's use of spectrality indicates is the idea that history *in general* is produced and made manifest only through the spectral iteration of those texts. Texts break with their context as soon as they leave their author to be grafted into other chains of signification quite happily without ever losing the ability to signify. Derrida argues something very similar without the aid of ghostly metaphors in his essay 'Signature Event Context', where he writes that a written sign carries with it a force that breaks with its context, that is, with the collectivity of presences organizing the moment of its inscription. This breaking force [*force de rupture*] is not an accidental predicate but the very structure of the written text.... [T]he sign possesses the characteristic of being readable even if the moment of its production is irrevocably lost and even if I do not know what its alleged author-scriptor consciously intended to say at the moment he wrote it ...[37]

However, this is not to say that the text becomes de-historicized, de-politicized or entirely alienated from external referents of any kind, it is merely that 'No context can *entirely* enclose it.'[38] According to Derrida, the history and politics of a text can be properly found in its iteration and re-inscription, *not* in the imagined fecundity of its origins. Historicism, however, seeks to close down these recontextualizations by artificially solidifying them into original contexts. Therefore, only by suppressing the more accurately 'historical' divisions and reproductions of the text that constitute the effect of its historicity, can new historicism produce its false concretions of the past.

What is the alternative to traditional historicism? Certainly not formalism, but rather a negotiation of the spectral effects of historicity as they appear in the text. Derrida has suggested that a text 'puts down roots in the *unity* of a context and immediately opens this *non-saturable* context onto a recontextualization.... The iterability of the trace ([its] unicity, identification, and alteration in repetition) is the condition of historicity – as too is the structure of anachrony and contretemps.'[39] A concept of anachronism then, can be addressed in relation to history, although in order to do so the notion of 'reading historically' has to be redefined. Anachronism is almost entirely used as a pejorative: that which disrupts chronology and makes fundamental errors of historical attribution can only be anathema to the historian whose research must not only arrange the past in an orderly, sequential fashion, but must also render patterns that can be imputed with sociological meaning. But surely all historiography necessarily harbours an inert anachronism as it ushers into the present a past that does not belong. A chronology must necessarily produce a concept of anachronism to define it and negatively keep it in place. As such, anachronism is right there at the birth of historicity. Indeed, anachronism could well be the hidden trope of historiography, which selects its objects and makes them available in a fashion that can only be incomplete and out of time. In *Specters of Marx*, Derrida makes an exemplary case of the ghost of Old Hamlet, and especially the line 'The time is out of joint'. For Hamlet, Wittenberg-educated humanist, the anachronistic burden prompts a suicidal trauma that makes him curse the fact that he should ever have been born to 'set it right'. Derrida, in contrast, takes the appearance of Old Hamlet as constitutive of time in general. He is doubtful of the possibility of any time which is not somehow 'out of joint'. Old Hamlet appears in the present, from the past, for the purposes of forming the future. For Derrida, this apparition is emblematic of the deconstructive view of time that puts into question 'a general temporality made up of the *successive* linking of presents identical to themselves and contemporary with themselves'.[40] This successive linking of presents is the time, or the theory of time, on which historiography depends. Such a time does not make room for ghosts, is on the contrary threatened by anything spectral, or, in the technical vocabulary of the historian, anachronistic. But can we rethink anachronism in terms other than simply *error*? If it is an error, is it not an error which is more often than not the 'normal' state of affairs?

Anachronism is most commonly signified or experienced through a relation to technology or fashion. Roman centurions wearing wrist-watches in Hollywood epics, or the mythical Mini-Cooper that many claim appears in *Ben Hur* are only the most obvious manifestations of the culture industry unconsciously reworking history in its own terms. Equally, we are rapidly considered 'dated' if we wear the clothing of a previous decade without the knowing licence of retro-irony, or find ourselves unable to come to terms with the latest technology. We have suggested that ghosts themselves have fallen into this kind of cultural obsolescence. Or at least the familiar chain-clanking, hair-raising, bump-in-the-night ghost has had its day for now. As Steven Connor's essay points out, if we want to find today's ghosts, we should look to the workings of telecommunications, the activities of the media, that omniscient absence-presence, in which our 'contemporary' spectrality is to be found.[41] A recently opened Viennese archive reveals that on 17 May 1911, Sigmund Freud sent an e-mail to Karl Marx saying just that.

Notes

1. Keith Thomas, *Religion and the Decline of Magic: Studies in Popular Beliefs in Sixteenth- and Seventeenth-Century England* (London: Weidenfeld & Nicolson, 1971), p. 702.
2. Thomas, *Decline of Magic*, p. 703.
3. Sigmund Freud, *Jokes and their Relation to the Unconscious, Pelican Freud Library*, Vol. 6, trans. James Strachey, ed. Angela Richards (Harmondsworth: Penguin, 1976 [1905]), p. 134.
4. Freud, *Jokes*, p. 134.
5. Sigmund Freud, *The Interpretation of Dreams, Pelican Freud Library*, Vol. 4, trans. James Strachey, ed. Angela Richards (Harmondsworth: Penguin, 1976 [1900]), pp. 60–1.
6. Janet Oppenheim *The Other World: Spiritualism and Psychical Research in England, 1850–1914* (Cambridge: Cambridge University Press, 1985); Alex Owen, *The Darkened Room: Women, Power and Spiritualism in Late Victorian England* (London: Virago, 1989). See also Logie Barrow, *Independent Spirits: Spiritualists and English Plebeians 1850–1910* (London: Routledge and Kegan Paul, 1986).
7. Oppenheim, *The Other World*, p. 3.
8. Owen, *The Darkened Room*, p. xviii.
9. R. C. Finucane reproduces this opinion at the beginning of *Ghosts: Appearances of the Dead and Cultural Transformation* (Buffalo, NY: Prometheus Books, 1989), where he writes that: 'Even though ghosts or apparitions may exist only in the minds of their percipients, the fact of that existence is a social and historical reality' (p. 1). As Finucane states, his is a general survey which collects and synthesizes a wealth of material from the classical period to the present, charting the changing appearance of ghostly manifestations.
10. Stephen Greenblatt, *Shakespearean Negotiations: The Circulation of Social Energy in Renaissance England* (Berkeley: University of California Press, 1988), p. 1.
11. Michel de Certeau writes that Michelet's historiography 'aims at calming the dead who still haunt the present, and at offering them scriptural tombs'. *The Writing of History*, trans. Tom Conley (New York: Columbia University Press, 1988 [1975]), p. 2.
12. Theodor Adorno, 'Theses Against Occultism', *Minima Moralia: Reflections from a Damaged Life*, trans. E. F. N. Jephcott (London: NLB, 1974 [1951]), pp. 238–44, p. 241.
13. Adorno, 'Theses Against Occultism', p. 239.
14. Adorno, 'Theses Against Occultism', p. 241.
15. Adorno, 'Theses Against Occultism', p. 243.
16. Sigmund Freud, 'Repression' [1915], *On Metapsychology: the Theory of Psychoanalysis, Pelican Freud Library*, Vol. 11, trans. James Strachey, ed. Angela Richards (Harmondsworth: Penguin, 1984), pp. 139–58, 145.
17. Freud, 'Repression', pp. 150–1.
18. Freud, 'Repression', p. 157.
19. The essays in this volume on fiction cite much of the relevant litera-

ture. For excellent recent overviews, see Anne Williams, *Art of Darkness: a Poetics of Gothic* (Chicago: University of Chicago Press, 1995) and Terry Castle, *The Female Thermometer: Eighteenth-Century Culture and the Invention of the Uncanny* (New York and Oxford: Oxford University Press, 1995).

20. Sigmund Freud, 'The "Uncanny"' [1919], *Art and Literature, Pelican Freud Library*, Vol. 14, trans. James Strachey, ed. Albert Dickson (Harmondsworth: Penguin, 1985), pp. 335–76, 340.

21. Freud, 'The "Uncanny"', p. 339.

22. Freud, 'Repression', pp. 152–3.

23. Jacques Derrida, *Specters Of Marx: the State of the Debt, the Work of Mourning, and the New International*, trans. Peggy Kamuf (London and New York: Routledge, 1994), p. 11.

24. Derrida, *Specters*, p. 11.

25. Nicholas Royle economically and lucidly outlines the place of ghosts in deconstruction in his 'Phantom Review', *Textual Practice* 11 (2) Summer 1997, pp. 386–98.

26. See Jonathan Culler's discussion of deconstruction's response to linear temporality in *On Deconstruction: Theory and Criticism after Structuralism* (London: Routledge, 1983), pp. 93–6.

27. Derrida, *Specters*, p. 4.

28. Derrida, 'Before the Law', *Acts of Literature*, ed. Derek Attridge (London and New York: Routledge, 1992), pp. 181–220.

29. See Derrida, *Of Grammatology*, trans. Gayatri Chakravorty Spivak (Baltimore: Johns Hopkins University Press, 1974 [1967]), pp. 242–55.

30. In *The Fantastic: a Structural Approach to a Literary Genre*, trans. Richard Howard (Ithaca, NY: Cornell University Press, 1975 [1970]), Tzvetan Todorov distinguishes between the fantastic, the uncanny, and the marvellous. While the uncanny is the 'supernatural explained' and the marvellous is the 'supernatural accepted', the fantastic is a realm of hesitation between these two choices. *The Turn of the Screw* is perhaps the most famous instance of such a hesitation, although we are more inclined to adopt Freud's terminology and to call this hesitation 'Uncanny' (pp. 72–3).

31. Sigmund Freud, *Five Lectures on Psycho-Analysis*, trans. James Strachey (London: Penguin, 1995), p. 35.

32. Hélène Cixous, 'Fiction and Its Phantoms: a Reading of Freud's *Das Unheimliche* (The "Uncanny")', *New Literary History* 7 (1976), pp. 525–46, p. 543.

33. Jacques Lacan, 'Desire and the Interpretation of Desire in *Hamlet*', *Yale French Studies* 55/56 (1977), pp. 11–52, p. 39.

34. Paul de Man, *Allegories of Reading: Figural Language in Rousseau, Nietzsche, Rilke, and Proust* (New Haven and London: Yale University Press, 1979), p. 79.

35. De Man, *Allegories of Reading*, p. 5.

36. See Jacques Derrida, 'Positions: Interview with Jean-Louis Houdebine and Guy Scarpetta', in *Positions*, ed. and trans. Alan Bass (London: Athlone, 1987), pp. 37–96, esp. 56–8.

37. See Jacques Derrida, 'Signature Event Context', in *Limited Inc.*, ed.

Gerald Graff (Evanston: Northwestern University Press, 1993), pp. 1–23, p. 9.

38.   Derrida, 'Signature Event Context', p. 9.
39.   Derrida, '"This Strange Institution Called Literature": Interview with Jacques Derrida', in *Acts of Literature*, ed. Derek Attridge, pp. 33–75, p. 63. Also, p. 64: 'There is no history without iterability, and this iterability is also what lets the traces continue to function in the absence of the general context, or some elements of the context.'
40.   Derrida, *Specters*, p. 70.
41.   See also Roger Luckhurst, '(Touching On) Tele-Technology', in *Applying: to Derrida*, ed. John Brannigan *et al.* (London: Macmillan, 1996).

Part I
Spectrality and Theory

1

Spectres of Engels

Willy Maley

The specters of Marx. Why this plural? Would there be more than one of them?[1]

1.1   BETTER DEAD THAN FRED

Friedrich Engels died in 1895. On the centenary of his death in 1995 it might have been appropriate, if anachronistic, to consider his legacy, especially in the wake of the publication of Jacques Derrida's fullest, but by no means first, engagement with Marx. It may take a hundred years for the impact of *Specters of Marx* to be felt and its implications thought through, but one thing that disappointed me was the low visibility of Engels. It seems that Derrida finds it as hard as anyone else to keep Engels in mind, or in sight, when dealing with Marxism. One could count on the fingers of two hands the references to Engels, including one hyphenated allusion to a body called 'Marx-Engels'.[2]

This was especially disheartening for me, because deconstruction is precisely that form of textual practice that one would expect to be most sensitive to the question of co-authorship. What happens between two authors? Co-authorship – itself a kind of ghost-writing, like all writing – is an unavoidable reality for all of us, yet we continue to experience difficulty in dealing with Marx's other half. Indeed, paraphrasing Derrida, one might venture the following proposition: 'There is nothing outside of co-authorship, no discourse that is not haunted by the other.' So much of Derrida's writing depends upon multiple reading heads, and although he has not, on the face of it, engaged in co-authorship, narrowly conceived, if we think in broader terms, in terms of interviews, dialogues, translations, examples, citations, iterability, double bands like those in *Glas*, or 'Living On/Borderlines', the heat-seeking missives of *The*

Post Card, or simply in terms of the medley of styles that he adopts, not to mention his constant openness to the other, then we could say that Derrida only ever co-authors. He has only ever ghost-written. Yet the signature remains singular. Thus we have Marx and Engels, Macherey and Balibar, Deleuze and Guattari, JanMohamed and Lloyd, Dollimore and Sinfield, Derrida and ... Derrida?

Still, the question of co-authorship, central to the study of Marx and Engels, seems conspicuous by its absence in *Specters of Marx*. This omission is glaring in so far as Engels is one of the most awesome spectres of Marx, one of the few who were in at the death of Marx. In his 'Speech at the Graveside of Karl Marx', delivered on 17 March 1883, Engels, coming not to bury but to praise, said: 'On the 14th of March, at a quarter to three in the afternoon, the greatest living thinker ceased to think. He had been left alone for scarcely two minutes, and when we came back we found him in his armchair, peacefully gone to sleep – but for ever'. The greatest living thinker had also ceased to live. But Engels lived on. In a letter to Sorge written the day after Marx's death, Engels had quoted Marx quoting Epicurus: 'Death is not a misfortune for him who dies, but for him who survives.'

There is a part of Marxism that is forever Engels. Engels survives, but in Derrida's *Specters of Marx* he is haunted by the *funereality* of his more famous collaborator. A ghost, Stephen Dedalus remarks in *Ulysses*, is someone who isn't there. Engels simply isn't there in so much speculation on Marx. This is understandable, and for a number of reasons. On the one hand, 'Marx', the proper name of Marx, has attached itself to, and has absorbed, other names and texts apparently independent of Marx 'himself'. On the other hand, Engels, self-effacing in the extreme, gave all tribute to Karl, so that even in the collaborative works – *The Holy Family*, *The German Ideology*, *The Manifesto of the Communist Party* – Marx apparently has the upper hand, with Engels acting as cipher, sounding-board, medium.

In 1911, the German Hegelian Johann Plenge wrote: 'Hegel continues to live in Marxism.'[3] Engels continues to live there too. Marxism is the home of the homeless. Derrida cites homelessness as one of the ten plagues in *Specters of Marx*, but home is where democracy is, as Cixous once remarked, which is to say nowhere, and indeed Derrida wants to retain Marx as the unaccommodated man, of no fixed abode, address unknown:

Marx has not yet been received. The subtitle of this address could thus have been: 'Marx – *das Unheimliche*.' Marx remains an immigrant *chez nous*, a glorious, sacred, accursed but still a clandestine immigrant as he was all his life. He belongs to a time of disjunction, to that 'time out of joint' in which is inaugurated, laboriously, painfully, tragically, a new thinking of borders, a new experience of the house, the home, and the economy. Between earth and sky. One should not rush to make of the clandestine immigrant an illegal alien or, what always risks coming down to the same thing, to domesticate him. To neutralize him through naturalization. To assimilate him so as to stop frightening oneself (making oneself fear) with him. He is not part of the family, but one should not send him back, once again, him too, to the border.[4]

And, one might add, the same goes for Engels.

There'll always be an Engels. Engels is, after all, Marx's ghostly double, the vulgar, scientific, custodian of the crypt. Primary medium of the spirit of Marx. Second guardian of the ghost of Marx, after Marx himself.[5] Freddy's nightmare weighs heavily on the brains of the living, and the mysterious disappearance of Engels – engineered by himself in the twelve years after Marx's death – is a phenomenon that has to be charted. Long before Derrida's book appeared, Terrell Carver, in the volume on Engels in the Fontana Past Masters series, wrote: 'What is lacking in the literature on Engels is a treatment of his intellectual life that is not always haunted by the spectre of Marx.'[6] That haunting continues unabated.

There is of course the long tradition of seeing Engels as just another malignant growth on the dark underside of Marxism, less harmful perhaps than Lenin or Stalin – one thinks of Engels playing Dr Watson to Marx's Sherlock Holmes – but nonetheless a figure that remains to be exorcized in order to preserve the integrity of Marx. Struggling to define Marxism, Henri Lefebvre rehearses the available options – late and early, philosophical and political (all distinctions that Derrida rejects in *Specters of Marx*, incidentally), then remarks:

which Marx? For others, Marxism is defined through the works of Marx *and* Engels. But between Marx and Engels there are notable differences, especially concerning the philosophy of nature, which was an essential consideration for Engels yet had only a subordinate importance for Marx. Thus, if one argues that Marx *and* Engels constitute Marxism, one is still left to decide which one is primary and which are the fundamental texts?[7]

The hierarchy and the canon. These have to be decided. Invariably, Engels loses out. Even when the co-authored works are the subject of discussion, it is Marx's name that is used as a synecdoche for both.

1.2   IMAGINE NO RELIGION

Fredric Jameson argues in a recent response to *Specters of Marx* that 'religion is once again very much on the agenda of any serious attempt to come to terms with the specificity of our own time'.[8] This feeds into Derrida's contention that: 'Religion ... was never one ideology among others for Marx. What, Marx seems to say, the genius of a great poet [i.e. Shakespeare] – and the spirit of a great father – will have uttered in a poetic flash, with one blow going faster and farther than our little bourgeois colleagues in economic theory, is the becoming-god of gold, which is at once ghost and idol, a god apprehended by the senses.'[9] Curiously, Engels, in an aside, once remarked: 'By the way, there exists a very close connection between alchemy and religion. The philosopher's stone has many godlike properties and the Egyptian-Greek alchemists of the first two centuries of our era had a hand in the development of Christian doctrines.'[10] Engels is disinclined, unlike Derrida, to develop what is more than an analogy.

Religion and ideology, a crucial conjunction, that is the crux of the matter. Derrida is convinced that *The German Ideology* remains haunted by the spectre of religion:

> The treatment of the phantomatic in *The German Ideology* announces or confirms the absolute privilege that Marx always grants to religion, to ideology as religion, mysticism, or theology, in his analysis of ideology in general. If the ghost gives its form, that is to say, its body, to the ideologem, then it is the essential feature [*le propre*], so to speak, of the religious, according to Marx, that is missed when one effaces the semantics or the lexicon of the specter, as translations often do, with values deemed to be

more or less equivalent (fantasmagorical, hallucinatory, fantastic, imaginary, and so on). The mystical character of the fetish, in the mark it leaves on the experience of the religious, is first of all a ghostly character.[11]

Later, Derrida emphasizes that for him 'at stake is doubtless everything which *today* links Religion and Technics in a singular configuration'.[12]

Marx and Engels may have abandoned their voluminous text 'to the gnawing criticism of the mice', as Marx put it, but the corpus as a whole remains caught up in professions of faith. In *Specters of Marx*, Derrida actually takes on board the charge that Marxism is religious and argues for a messianism without a messiah, something that has disturbed some Marxist critics.[13] Religion remains central to any discourse on Marx and Engels, whether as the great ghost with which they must struggle into the night, or as that which they are accused of creating – another doxa, another utopia, another attempt to go 'beyond the text'.

Engels had, from an early age, and in advance of his encounter with, or haunting by, Marx, a keen interest in religion, spiritualism and the supernatural. In 1839, Engels confessed that his strict religious upbringing had contributed to his protest against and eventual rejection of spiritualism. Writing to a schoolfriend, Wilhelm Graeber, Engels declared:

If I had not been brought up in the most extreme orthodoxy and piety, if I had not had drummed into me in church, Sunday School and at home the most direct, unconditional belief in the Bible with that of the church, indeed, with the special teaching of every minister, perhaps I would have remained stuck in some sort of liberal supranaturalism for a long time.[14]

Engels's progress towards atheism was slow and painful. Earlier the same year he had written:

Well, I have never been a pietist. I have been a mystic for a while, but those are *tempi passati*. I am now an honest, and in comparison with others, very liberal, supernaturalist. How long I shall remain such I don't know, but I hope to remain one, even though inclining now more, now less towards rationalism.[15]

Tempi passati. But spectres are anachronistic – they come back. Three months later, Engels's supernaturalism was showing signs of wear and tear. He no longer believed that 'rationalism purified and strengthened the religious feeling':

> I pray daily, indeed nearly the whole day, for truth, I have done so ever since I began to have doubts, but I still cannot return to your faith. And yet it is written: 'Ask, and it shall be given you'.... Tears come into my eyes as I write this. I am moved to the core, but I feel I shall not be lost; I shall come to God, for whom my whole heart yearns.[16]

I want to turn now to a text written forty years after those tears, but written, I shall argue, through those tears, as indeed the best texts are, whether in laughter or sorrow.[17]

In 1886, Engels, in his critique of Feuerbach, would write:

> Religion is derived from *religare* and meant originally a bond. Therefore every bond between two people is a religion. Such etymological tricks are the last resort of idealist philosophy. Not what the word means according to the historical development of its actual use, but what it ought to mean according to its derivation is what counts. And so sex, love and the intercourse between the sexes is apotheosised to a *religion*, merely in order that the word religion, which is so dear to idealistic memories, may not disappear from the language. The Parisian reformers of the Louis Blanc trend used to speak in precisely the same way in the forties. They likewise could conceive of a man without religion only as a monster, and used to say to us: '*Donc, l'atheisme c'est votre religion!*'[18]

Engels's impatience with Feuerbach's etymology recalls Derrida's famous footnote in *Margins of Philosophy* on the vexation caused to Marx and Engels by Stirner's etymologism in *The German Ideology*.[19] Religare – to bind. Do we stick to the letter or the spirit of the bond?[20] What binds Engels to Marx, and why has the latter been relegated? Why must Engels play second fiddle while Marxism burns?

1.3   RESUSCITATING THE CORPUS

I want to look briefly at a short text ostensibly authored solely by Engels entitled 'Natural Science in the Spirit World'.[21] Written around 1878, it was published posthumously as the third chapter of *Dialectics of Nature* in 1925. Translated into English in 1954, it hasn't been the subject of much discussion, as far as I know – at least among English Marxists – yet it is one of the most intriguing and sustained engagements with the supernatural in the corpus of Marxism, and it had a troubled birth. Engels had written to Marx on 23 November 1882 saying that he expected shortly to finish the project. Marx's death on 14 March 1883 compelled him to suspend this work-in-progress. In the preface to the second edition of *Anti-Dühring* he explains that he must busy himself with 'more urgent duties': 'I am under the obligation to prepare for the press the manuscripts which Marx has left, and this is much more important than anything else.'[22] The 1953 preface from the Marx-Engels-Lenin-Stalin Institute in Moscow comments on the unfinished nature of the manuscript:

> after Marx's death all the work of guiding the international labour movement devolved on Engels and this also demanded a great deal of his time.... After Engels's death (August 5, 1895), *Dialectics of Nature*, along with other manuscripts of Engels's, fell into the hands of the opportunist leaders of German Social-Democracy, who for a number of decades criminally kept this most valuable work hidden away, and have never published it. *Dialectics of Nature* was first published in the U.S.S.R. from photo-copies of the manuscripts. It was published in Moscow in 1925 in German with a parallel translation into Russian, and subse-quently republished several times both in the original language and in the Russian translation.[23]

It is high time, as they say, that the conspiracy of silence that has surrounded this text was broken, especially since that text alludes to another conspiracy, this time one designed to conjure away socialism through spiritualism. In breaking that silence, I shall have cause to quote at some length, letting Engels speak through me, not least of all because I believe that this particular fragment of the Marxist archive has some considerable bearing on Derrida's argu-ments in *Specters of Marx*.

Dialectics of Nature, as Pierre Macherey has pointed out, is 'a theoretical fiction *a posteriori*, wholly made up of incomplete and contradictory drafts, which can only give the illusion of a completed work at the risk of falsifying their content'. Macherey goes on to argue that

> If these philosophical texts by Engels are still of interest, as indeed they are, it is because they bear witness by their very incompleteness to the impossibility of putting materialism into dialectical form. For while the dialectic may be genuinely materialist, it is the very refutation of materialism; and if it is closely bound up with the fact of being materialist, this is precisely because it shows the impossibility of materialist knowledge, a system of knowledge concerned with materialism. The essential lesson to be drawn, then, from Engels's attempt is that it is no longer possible to be a Materialist.[24]

If *Dialectics of Nature* is 'a theoretical fiction' then it has much in common with so many other philosophical texts. The fact that it was not published in Engels's lifetime can be laid at the feet of Marx, or at his shoulder, where Engels himself stood for so many years. The spectre of Marx cast its shadow over Engels to the end, as his own work took second place to the preparation, promotion and dissemination of works by Marx, but so did *the spectre*, or *spectres*, as such. Engels, too, cast his shadow on Marx. The Eleventh Thesis on Feuerbach, so brilliantly deconstructed by Derrida in *Specters of Marx* – an interpretation that transforms what it interprets – was brought to light by faithful Fred.[25] In 1888, in the foreword to the German edition of *Ludwig Feuerbach and the End of Classical German Philosophy*, Engels writes: 'in an old notebook of Marx's I have found the eleven theses on Feuerbach printed here as an appendix. These are notes hurriedly scribbled down for later elaboration, absolutely not intended for publication, but invaluable as the first document in which is deposited the brilliant germ of the new world outlook.'[26] That germ in the appendix has caused no end of convulsions.

Étienne Balibar shares Macherey's view of *Dialectics of Nature*, seeing it as part of a process of revision undertaken in Marx and Engels's most mature writings, and thus as a product of 'late Marxism' (again, it is notable that Derrida refuses any such distinction, or any such developmental chronology):

While the first texts by Engels (and the last by Marx) are written to inaugurate and enforce Marxism, Engels's last are also written against it, because its mission, even though incomplete, has been too successful. They are written as an attempt to rectify what, in the process of constituting a Marxist orthodoxy, appears from the start to be an idealization and an ideologization of theory, as disturbing in its critical form (neo-Kantian: Bernstein) as in its materialist form (Darwinian: Kautsky). As part of this realignment, could there not also be an element of self-criticism, more or less avowed, directed not only at Engels's own writing (since Bernstein and Kautsky insist they became Marxists by reading *Anti-Dühring*) but also at the 'perverse' effects of the (available) texts of Marx, along with their omissions or excesses?[27]

Balibar comes close to Derrida when he goes so far as to say that his reading of *Dialectics of Nature* raises the question: 'Could communist-materialism not be another name for Absolute Spirit? How can one not ask oneself this question?'[28] How indeed? And should this be something from which one hides? We are still living in the age of Hegel.

1.4   MEDIUM RARE

In 'Natural Science in the Spirit World', Engels begins with a definition of dialectics 'that has found its way into popular consciousness ... expressed in the old saying that extremes meet'. Engels elaborates thus:

In accordance with this we should hardly err in looking for the most extreme degree of fantasy, credulity and superstition, not in that trend of natural science which, like the German philosophy of nature, tries to force the objective world into the framework of its subjective thought, but rather in the opposite trend, which, exalting mere experience, treats thought with sovereign disdain and really has gone to the furthest extreme in emptiness of thought. This school prevails in England. Its father, the much-lauded Francis Bacon, already advanced the demand that his new empirical, inductive method should be pursued to attain, above all, by its means: longer life, rejuvenation – to a certain extent, alteration of stature and features, transformation of one

body into another, the production of new species, power over
the air and the production of storms. He complains that such
investigations have been abandoned, and in his natural history
he gives definite recipes for making gold and performing various
miracles. Similarly Isaac Newton in his old age greatly busied
himself with expounding the Revelation of St. John. So it is not to
be wondered at if in recent years English empiricism in the
person of some of its representatives – and not the worst of them
– should seem to have fallen a hopeless victim to the spirit-
rapping and spirit-seeing imported from America.[29]

I should note in passing that Engels himself, in his old age, greatly
busied himself with expounding an interpretation of the Revelation
of St John, from an historical materialist perspective, in his essay
'On the Early History of Christianity', published in the last year of
his life, between 1894 and 1895.[30]

Engels proceeds to explore the complicity between empiricism
and mysticism, and he does so by focusing on two eminent natural
scientists seduced by such 'spirit-rapping and spirit-seeing'. First,
there is the

zoologist and botanist, Alfred Russell Wallace, who simultaneously with Darwin put forward the theory of the alteration of
species by natural selection. In his little work, *On Miracles and
Modern Spiritualism* (1875), he relates that his first experiences in
this branch of natural knowledge date from 1844, when he
attended the lectures of Mr Spencer Hall on mesmerism and as a
result carried out similar experiments on his pupils.[31]

Wallace's experiments in spiritualism are as successful as those in
zoology and botany:

He not only produced magnetic sleep together with the phenomena of articular rigidity and local loss of sensation, he also
confirmed the correctness of Gall's map of the skull, because on
touching any one of Gall's organs the corresponding activity was
aroused in the magnetized patient and exhibited by appropriate
and lively gestures. Further, he established that his patient,
merely by being touched, partook of all the sensations of the
operator; he made him drunk with a glass of water as soon as he
told him that it was brandy.[32]

Engels is not at all surprised by this, nor by the fact that Wallace 'could make one of the young men so stupid, even in the waking condition, that he no longer knew his own name, a feat, however, that other schoolmasters are capable of accomplishing without any mesmerism. And so on.' Not only is Engels unimpressed by Wallace's findings, they are quite in keeping with his theory of dialectics. Indeed, it transpires that Engels himself was no stranger to spirit-rapping or séances. He had attended a performance (or two?) in his time, and in particular on the eve of his collaboration with Marx. Engels frequented these séances as a sceptic, of course. Engels, as fate would have it, remembers the lectures of the man who exerted such an influence over Wallace:

> Now it so happens that I also saw this Mr. Spencer Hall in the winter of 1843–44 in Manchester. He was a very mediocre char- latan, who travelled the country under the patronage of some parsons and undertook magnetico-phrenological performances with a young woman in order to prove thereby the existence of God, the immortality of the soul, and the incorrectness of the materialism that was being preached at the time by the Owenites in all big towns.[33]

Here Engels puts his finger on something of great importance. Spiritualism was being conjured up as an antidote to socialist mat- erialism. In this regard, it is both ironic and appropriate that the *Manifesto of the Communist Party* opens with a warding off of the spectre of communism, a fact Derrida makes much of in *Specters of Marx*: 'Marx, unless it is the other one, Engels, then puts on stage, for the time of a few paragraphs, the terror that this specter inspires in all the powers of old Europe. No one speaks of anything anymore but this specter.'[34] Unless it is the other one. Precisely.[35]

Derrida acknowledges that while it 'is certain ... that the texts of Stirner, Marx, and Engels to which we are referring correspond – and respond – in their own time to a powerful "craze" that could summarily be called "mediumistic" ... one must not fail to rein- scribe it in a much larger spectrological sequence'.[36] In other words Engels's claim that this craze is merely a timely screen to smother socialism is not the whole story.

Engels goes on to provide a detailed eye-witness account of one of Hall's performances:

The lady was sent into a magnetic sleep and then, as soon as the operator touched any part of the skull corresponding to one of Gall's organs, she gave a bountiful display of theatrical, demonstrative gestures and poses representing the activity of the organ concerned; for instance, for the organ of philoprogenitiveness she fondled and kissed an imaginary baby, etc. Moreover, the good Mr. Hall had enriched Gall's geography of the skull with a new island of Barataria: right at the top of the skull he had discovered an organ of veneration, on touching which his hypnotic miss sank on to her knees, folded her hands in prayer, and depicted to the astonished and philistine audience an angel wrapt in veneration. That was the climax and conclusion of the exhibition. The existence of God had been proved.[37]

Engels explains his own response, and that of an unnamed colleague (Marx? This was the time of *The Holy Family* and *The German Ideology*) to Hall's display:

The effect on me and one of my acquaintances was similar to that on Mr. Wallace; the phenomena interested us and we tried to find out how far we could reproduce them. A wide-awake young boy of 12 years old offered himself as subject. Gently gazing into his eyes, or stroking, sent him without difficulty into the hypnotic condition. But since we were rather less credulous than Mr. Wallace and set to work with rather less fervour, we arrived at quite different results. Apart from muscular rigidity and loss of sensation, which were easy to produce, we found also a state of complete passivity of the will bound up with a peculiar hypersensitivity of sensation. The patient, when aroused from his lethargy by any external stimulus, exhibited very much greater liveliness than in the waking condition. There was no trace of any mysterious relation to the operator: anyone else could just as easily set the sleeper into activity. To put Gall's cranial organs into operation was a mere trifle for us; we went much further, we could not only exchange them for one another, or make their seat anywhere in the whole body, but we also fabricated any amount of other organs, organs of singing, whistling, piping, dancing, boxing, sewing, cobbling, tobacco-smoking, etc., and we could make their seat wherever we wanted. Wallace made his patients drunk on water, but we discovered in the great toe an organ of drunkenness which only had to be touched in order to cause the finest drunken comedy to be enacted. But it must be understood, no organ showed a trace of action until the patient was given to understand what was expected of him; the boy soon perfected himself by practice to such an extent that the merest indication sufficed. The organs produced in this way then retained their validity for later occasions of putting to sleep, as long as they were not altered in the same way. The patient indeed had a double memory, one for the waking state and a quite separate one for the hypnotic condition. As regards the passivity of the will and its absolute subjection to the will of a third person, this loses all its miraculous appearance when we bear in mind that the whole condition began with the subjection of the will of the patient to that of the operator, and cannot be produced without it. The most powerful magician of a magnetizer in the world will come to the end of his resources as soon as his patient laughs him in the face.[38]

Again, the burst of laughter that exercises the lungs and exorcises the living. Engels congratulates himself, and his mysterious companion, or lovely assistant, on their healthy and humorous incredulity:

While we with our frivolous scepticism thus found that the basis of magnetico-phrenological charlatanry lay in a series of phenomena which for the most part differ only in degree from those of the waking state and require no mystical interpretation, Mr. Wallace's 'ardour' led him into a series of self-deceptions, in virtue of which he confirmed Gall's map of the skull in all its details and noted a mysterious relation between operator and patient. Everywhere in Mr. Wallace's account, the sincerity of which reaches the degree of *naïveté*, it becomes apparent that he was much less concerned in investigating the factual background of charlatanry than in reproducing all the phenomena at all costs. Only this frame of mind is needed for one who was originally a scientist to be quickly converted into an adept by means of simple and facile self-deception.[39]

Engels then selects one example from Wallace's book in order to illustrate its poverty of theory and the author's predilection for 'facile self-deception':

It is certainly a strong assumption that we should believe that the above-mentioned spirits would allow themselves to be photographed, and we have surely the right to demand that such spirit photographs should be authenticated in the most indubitable manner before we accept them as genuine. Now Mr. Wallace recounts on p. 187 that in March, 1872, a leading medium, Mrs. Guppy, *née* Nicholls, had herself photographed together with her husband and small boy at Mr. Hudson's in Notting Hill, and on two different photographs a tall female figure, finely draped in white gauzy robes, with somewhat Eastern features, was to be seen behind her in a pose as if giving a benediction. 'Here, then, [writes Wallace] one of two things *are* absolutely certain. [And here Engels inserts the following note: 'The spirit world is superior to grammar. A joker once caused the spirit of the grammarian Lindley Murray to testify. To the question whether he was there, he answered: "I are"'.] Either there was a living, intelligent, but invisible being present, or Mr. and Mrs. Guppy, the photographer, and some fourth person, planned a wicked imposture, and have maintained it ever since. Knowing Mr. and Mrs. Guppy as well as I do, I feel an *absolute conviction* that they are as incapable of an imposture of this kind as any earnest inquirer after truth in the department of natural science'.[40]

Engels is unimpressed by such absolute conviction:

Consequently, either deception or spirit photography. Quite so. And, if deception, either the spirit was already on the photographic plates, or four persons must have been concerned, or three if we leave out as weak-minded or duped old Mr. Guppy who died in January 1875, at the age of 84 (it only needed that he should be sent behind the Spanish screen of the background). That a photographer could obtain a 'model' for the spirit without difficulty does not need to be argued. But the photographer Hudson, shortly afterwards, was publicly prosecuted for habitual falsification of spirit photographs, so Mr. Wallace remarks in mitigation: 'One thing is clear; that if there has been imposture, it was at once detected by spiritualists themselves'. Hence there is not much reliance to be placed on the photographer. Remains Mrs. Guppy, and for her there is only the 'absolute conviction' of our friend Wallace and nothing more.[41]

But Engels hasn't quite finished:

– Nothing more? Not at all. The absolute trustworthiness of Mrs. Guppy is evidenced by her assertion that one evening, early in June, 1871, she was carried through the air in a state of unconsciousness from her house in Highbury Hill Park to 69, Lamb's Conduit Street – three English miles as the crow flies – and deposited in the said house of No. 69 on the table in the midst of a spiritualistic séance. The doors of the room were closed, and although Mrs. Guppy was one of the stoutest women in London, which is certainly saying a good deal, nevertheless her sudden incursion did not leave behind the slightest hole either in the doors or in the ceiling. (Reported in the London *Echo*, June 8, 1871.)[42]

Having conjured away Wallace, Engels now shifts to another intellectual who believes in spirits, and who turned to spiritualism at an all-too-opportune moment, the time of the Paris Commune:

The second eminent adept among English natural scientists is Mr. William Crookes, the discoverer of the chemical element thallium and of the radiometer.... Mr. Crookes began to investigate spiritualistic manifestations about 1871, and employed for this purpose a number of physical and mechanical appliances, spring balances, electric batteries, etc. Whether he brought to his task the main apparatus required, a sceptically critical mind, or whether he kept it to the end in a fit state for working, we shall see. At any rate, within a not very long period, Mr. Crookes was just as completely captivated as Mr. Wallace. 'For some years', he relates, 'a young lady, Miss Florence Cook, has exhibited remarkable mediumship, which latterly culminated in the production of an entire female form purporting to be of spiritual origin, and which appeared barefooted and in white flowing robes while she lay entranced, in dark clothing and securely bound in a cabinet or adjoining room.' This spirit, which called itself Katie, and which looked remarkably like Miss Cook, was one evening suddenly seized round the waist by Mr Volckman – the present husband of Mrs. Guppy – and held fast in order to see whether it was not indeed Miss Cook in another edition. The spirit proved to be a quite sturdy damsel, it defended itself vigorously, the onlookers intervened, the gas was turned out, and when, after some scuffling, peace was re-established and the room re-lit, the spirit had vanished and Miss Cook lay bound and unconscious in her corner. Nevertheless, Mr Volckman is said to maintain up to the present day that he had seized hold of Miss Cook and nobody else. In order to establish this scientifically, Mr. Varley, a well-known electrician, on the occasion of a new experiment, arranged for the current from a battery to flow through the medium, Miss Cook, in such a way that she could not play the part of the spirit without interrupting the current. Nevertheless, the spirit made its appearance. It was, therefore, indeed a being different from Miss Cook. To establish this further was the task of Mr. Crookes. His first step was to win the *confidence* of the spiritualistic lady. This confidence, so he says himself in the *Spiritualist*, June 5, 1874, 'increased gradually to such an extent that she refused to give a *séance* unless *I made the arrangements*. She said that she always wanted me to be near her and in the neighbourhood of the cabinet; I found that – when this confidence had been established and she was sure that *I would not break any promise made to her* – the phenomena increased considerably in strength and there was freely forthcoming evidence that would have been unobtainable in any other way. She frequently *consulted me* in regard to the persons present at the *séances* and the places to be given them, for she had recently become very nervous as a result of certain ill-advised suggestions that, besides other more scientific methods of investigation, *force* also should be applied.' [Italics by Engels] [43]

Force is evidently a frightener of greater magnitude than science. Engels continues:

The spirit lady rewarded this confidence, which was as kind as it was scientific, in the highest measure. She even made her appearance – which can no longer surprise us – in Mr. Crookes' house, played with his children, and told them 'anecdotes from her adventures in India', treated Mr. Crookes to an account of 'some of the bitter experiences of her past life', allowed him to take her by the arm so that he could convince himself of her evident materiality, allowed him to take her pulse and count the number of her respirations per minute, and finally allowed herself to be photographed next to Mr. Crookes. 'This figure', says Mr. Wallace, 'after being seen, felt, conversed with, and photographed, *absolutely disappeared* from a small room from which there was no other exit than an adjoining room filled with spectators' – which was not such a great feat, provided that the spectators were polite enough to show as much faith in Mr. Crookes, in whose house this happened, as Mr. Crookes did in the spirit.[44]

Engels points out that Crookes's faith exceeds that even of spiritualists:

> Unfortunately these 'fully authenticated phenomena' are not immediately credible even for spiritualists. We saw above how the very spiritualistic Mr. Volckman permitted himself to make a very material grab. And now a clergyman, a member of the committee of 'The British Association of Spiritualists', has also been present at a *séance* with Miss Cook, and he established the fact without difficulty that the room through the door of which the spirit came and disappeared communicated with the outer world by a *second door*. The behaviour of Mr. Crookes, who was also present, gave 'the final death-blow to my belief that there might be "something in" the manifestations' ... And, over and above that, it came to light in America how 'Katies' were 'materialized'. A married couple named Holmes held *séances* in Philadelphia in which likewise a 'Katie' appeared and received bountiful presents from the believers. However, one sceptic refused to rest until he got on the track of the said Katie, who, anyway, had already gone on strike once because of lack of pay; he discovered her in a boarding-house as a young lady of unquestionable flesh and bone, and in possession of all the presents that had been given to the spirit.[45]

So much for Katie, a spirit only here for the present.

Engels is still not content with this ritual humiliation of the natural scientists gullible enough to be taken in by mediums. He sarcastically congratulates them on their scientific discoveries:

> Has not Mr. Crookes scientifically determined how much weight is lost by tables and other articles of furniture on their passage into the fourth dimension – as we may now well be permitted to call it – and does not Mr. Wallace declare it proven that fire there does no harm to the human body? And now we have even the physiology of the spirit bodies! They breathe, they have a pulse, therefore lungs, heart, and circulatory apparatus, and in

consequence are at least as admirably equipped as our own in regard to the other bodily organs. For breathing requires carbo-hydrates which undergo combustion in the lungs, and these carbohydrates can only be supplied from without; hence, stomach, intestines, and their accessories – and if we have once established so much, the rest follows without difficulty. The exis-tence of such organs, however, implies the possibility of their falling prey to disease, hence it may still come to pass that Herr Virchow will have to compile a cellular pathology of the spirit world. And since most of these spirits are very handsome young ladies, who are not to be distinguished in any respect whatso-ever from terrestrial damsels, other than by their supramundane beauty, it could not be very long before they come into contact with 'men who feel the passion of love'; and since, as established by Mr. Crookes from the beat of the pulse, 'the female heart is not absent', natural selection also has opened before it the prospect of a fourth dimension, one in which it has no longer any need to fear of being confused with wicked Social-Democracy.[46]

Once again the inference is that spiritualism, as well as being the last refuge of a natural scientist, is also the first port of call for anyone eager to refute materialism. Engels sums up for the prose-cution:

Enough. Here it becomes palpably evident which is the most certain path from natural science to mysticism. It is not the extravagant theorizing of the philosophy of nature, but the shal-lowest empiricism that spurns all theory and distrusts all thought. It is not *a priori* necessity that proves the existence of spirits, but the empirical observations of Messrs Wallace, Crookes, and Co. If we trust the spectrum-analysis observations of Crookes, which led to the discovery of the metal thallium, or the rich zoological discoveries of Wallace in the Malay Archipelago, we are asked to place the same trust in the spiritu-alistic experiences and discoveries of these two scientists. And if we express the opinion that, after all, there is a little difference between the two, namely, that we can verify the one but not the other, then the spirit-seers retort that this is not the case, and that they are ready to give us the opportunity of verifying also the spirit phenomena.[47]

Spectrum-analysis: that is what is at issue. Both ends of the political spectrum are haunted by ghosts. Dialectics, theory, these are the prerequisites for a materialist exorcism:

> Indeed, dialectics cannot be despised with impunity. However great one's contempt for all theoretical thought, nevertheless one cannot bring two natural facts into relation with each other, or understand the connection existing between them, without theoretical thought. The only question is whether one's thinking is correct or not, and contempt of theory is evidently the most certain way to think naturalistically, and therefore incorrectly. But, according to an old and well-known dialectical law, incorrect thinking, carried to its logical conclusion, inevitably arrives at the opposite of its point of departure. Hence, the empirical contempt for dialectics is punished by some of the most sober empiricists being led into the most barren of all superstitions, into modern spiritualism.... In fact, mere empiricism is incapable of refuting the spiritualists. In the first place, the 'highest' phenomena always show themselves only when the 'investigator' concerned is already so far in the toils that he now only sees what he is meant to see or wants to see – as Crookes himself describes with such inimitable *naïveté*. In the second place, the spiritualists care nothing that hundreds of alleged facts are exposed as imposture and dozens of alleged mediums as ordinary tricksters. As long as *every* single alleged miracle has not been explained away, they still have room enough to carry on, as indeed Wallace says clearly enough in connection with the falsified spirit photographs. The existence of falsifications proves the genuineness of the genuine ones.[48]

Engels then conjures up the biologist Thomas Huxley, who, in a letter to the London Dialectical Society dated 20 January 1869, and printed in the *Daily News* on 17 October 1871, declined an invitation to participate in the work of a committee devoted to the investigation of spiritual phenomena. 'And so', Engels concludes,

> empiricism finds itself compelled to refute the importunate spirit-seers not by means of empirical experiments, but by theoretical considerations, and to say, with Huxley: 'The only good that I can see in the demonstration of the truth of "spiritualism" is to furnish an additional argument against suicide. Better to live

a crossing-sweeper than die and be made to talk twaddle by a medium "hired" at a guinea a *séance*!'[49]

The role of medium is, I might venture to say, one not entirely incompatible with that of literary critic.

1.5   TELL-TALE MARX

Engels's treatment of Wallace and Crookes is quite in keeping with what Derrida detects in Marx: 'This hostility toward ghosts, a terrified hostility that sometimes fends off terror with a burst of laughter, is perhaps what Marx will always have had in common with his adversaries.... He will have tried to conjure (away) the ghosts *like* the conspirators of old Europe on whom the *Manifesto* declares war.'[50] For Derrida, there is no politics without an openness to ghosts. This is what distinguishes deconstruction from Marxism, this refusal to draw the line between real and non-real:

> Marx does not like ghosts any more than his adversaries do. He does not want to believe in them. But he thinks of nothing else. He believes rather in what is supposed to distinguish them from actual reality, living effectivity. He believes he can oppose them, like life to death, like vain appearances of the simulacrum to real presence. He believes enough in the dividing line of this opposition to want to denounce, chase away, or exorcise the specters but by means of critical analysis and not by some counter-magic. But how to distinguish between the analysis that denounces magic and the counter-magic that it still risks being?[51]

Derrida is here pressing a claim he made in 1980, in *The Post Card*, that *The German Ideology* – co-authored, of course – 'makes little of ... "phantoms" and "revenants"', and that for deconstruction 'this is our problem'.[52] Derrida has always spoken of Marx and of ghosts. Terry Eagleton, in his response to *Specters of Marx*, speaks in terms of a 'sudden dramatic somersault onto a stalled bandwagon'.[53] The question is: what would one have to do or say in order to call oneself a Marxist? Thirty years ago, Derrida, writing of Lévi- Strauss, asked: 'Is it sufficient to speak of superstructure and to denounce in an hypothesis an exploitation of man by man in order to confer a Marxian pertinence upon this hypothesis?'[54] In *Specters of Marx*, the spectre of what it is to be a Marxist, to speak as a Marxist, is raised again. Marx was the first post-Marxist in existence, although, if we believe Engels, he was one of those even before he died. Derrida reminds us that 'we do not have to suppose that Marx was in agreement with himself. ("What is certain is that I am not a Marxist," he is supposed to have confided to Engels. Must we still cite Marx as authority in order to say likewise?)'[55] Or again, 'what is a Marxist utterance? a so-called Marxist utterance? or more precisely: what *will be from now on* such an utterance? and who could say "I am a Marxist" or "I am not a Marxist"?'[56] Eagleton is much more sure about this than Marx or Derrida, as sure as Lévi-Strauss was.

To go quickly in conclusion. Engels, throughout his life, was obsessed with, not just the Victorian supernatural, that mediumistic craze to which Derrida refers, but, as Derrida insists, was possessed by a larger spectrological sequence, witness his work on early Christianity and on the Apocalypse of St John. The deconstruction, if one can call it that, or at least the demystification, or exposure, of the complicity between empiricism and mysticism, is Engels's undoubted strength. His weakness is in not detecting a comparable complicity in his own opposition between Marxism and religion, and between scientific and utopian socialism in particular. In 'Marxism from Scientific to Utopian', Zhang Longxi reverses Engels's opposition in *Socialism: Utopian and Scientific*, and, in a move that mirrors Derrida's charged advocacy of the messianic demand for justice in Marx, underlines the importance of the utopian strand in socialist thought, attacking Engels's naive faith in science: 'The unabashed scientism in Engels's book, the confidence in the objective laws of nature and society, the teleology of history as the unfolding of historical necessity beyond human will and consciousness, all these become highly suspect in a world of post-Hegelian philosophy and post-World War II politics.'[57] But Zhang is not one of those who seek to scapegoat Engels as the unacceptable face of Marxism:

> A convenient way to clear Marxism internally of that embarrassing Hegelian and positivist scientism is to blame it on Engels, but that seems to me an act of expediency rather than an argument of principle and good reasoning.[58]

An example of the tendency to use Engels as a take-the-blame is Gajo Petrovic's claim that the doomed Second and Third

Internationals took their cue from the self-appointed executor of Marx's will:

> Engels inspired not only the interpretation of Marx as a histor-ical materialist and economist as developed in the Second International, but also the view of Marx as a dialectical material-ist, as developed in the Third International. While he was glorifying Marx as the founder of historical materialism and the scientific political economy, and passing in silence Marx as a philosopher, Engels, in his polemics with Dühring, entered a general philosophical discussion and ventured a number of rather pretentious philosophical statements. Similarly, in ... *Dialectics of Nature*, Engels engaged in constructing a kind of a dialectical and materialist philosophy of nature. This suggests that he wanted to fill the philosophical gap he felt existed in Marx. Thus, it may be possible to say that the theoreticians of the Second International (or their majority), in their interpretations of Marx, followed Engels's explicit interpretation, while Plekhanov, Lenin, and the Third International followed (and tried to explicate) the implicit interpretation expressed in Engels's own theoretical efforts.[59]

Zhang, though critical of the anti-utopianism expressed by both Engels and Marx, finds enough of a demand for justice in their work to nevertheless contend that the shell of scientism can be shed in favour of a mystical kernel of revolutionary desire:

> Indeed, when communism has collapsed in the East, when what went on in the name of Marx and his political theory has proved to be disastrous and repressive, it is the utopian vision, the desire and hope for a more authentically human society, more than any 'scientific' approach designed to reach that land of prophecy through class struggle and the dictatorship of the proletariat, that may yet sustain our interest in Marxism and command our respect for Karl Marx as one of the great visionaries of human history.[60]

Marx, the visionary, but who is under the table that is turning and shaking in the fifth chapter of *Specters of Marx?* Why, Fred, of course. Author of the third chapter of *Dialectics of Nature*. Fred's dead, but he's coming back, and this time there's more than one.

Engels's posthumous fragment, like all ghost-busting discourse, begs the question of 'how to distinguish between the analysis that denounces magic and the counter-magic that it still risks being?'[61] 'I are' is all we as authors can ever say. It is my prepared answer when asked if I am, or have been at any time, a Marxist. There is no authorship – or membership – fully conscious to itself, or, one might add, impervious to ghost-writing, or the phantomatic and fune-real effects of co-authorship or co-othership. In 'The Heimlich Manoeuvre', Terence Hawkes writes: 'The spectre continually haunting the notion of "criticism", as described by Arnold and many others since, is that of its apparently essential *secondariness:* its status as something merely repetitive, something that is always already preceded.'[62] Interpreting for the dead. Engels once described our modern universities as Protestant monasteries. Fear and trembling are the order of the day for Marxists and communists, part of a minority dissident culture, a diasporic new international.[63] Like Eng. Lit., the literature on Marxism too often sees Engels as Hamlet's Horatio. Haunted by the spectre of Stalin, Marx is choking on his own vomit, having had his face rubbed in it, but there is still time for the Hamlet manoeuvre.[64] In the spirit of his longest surviving friend, one might say: 'Good night, sweet Prince, And flights of Engels sing thee to thy rest!'

Notes

1. Jacques Derrida, *Specters of Marx: the State of the Debt, the Work of Mourning, and the New International,* trans. Peggy Kamuf (London: Routledge, 1994), p. 3. I wish to thank FE for spiritual guidance in the preparation of this paper.
2. Derrida, *Specters of Marx,* p. 37. For some provisional responses to Derrida's intervention see Aijaz Ahmad, 'Reconciling Derrida: *Specters of Marx* and Deconstructive Politics', *New Left Review* 208 (1994), pp. 88–106; Marion Hobson, 'Dead and Read', *THES* (2 September 1994), p. 17; Graham McCann, 'Phantom of the Pop Era', *THES* (3 February 1995), p. 23; Willy Maley, 'Proletarian Poltergeist', *The Edinburgh Review* 93 (1995), pp. 223–5; Jonathan Rée, 'Shades of Politics', *New Statesman and Society* (28 October 1994), pp. 36–9.
3. Cited in Teodor Ilyich Oizerman, *The Making of the Marxist Philosophy* (Moscow: Progress, 1981), p. 19.
4. Derrida, *Specters of Marx,* p. 174.
5. On the self as host to the ghost, see Jacques Derrida, *'Fors*: the Anglish Words of Nicolas Abraham and Maria Torok', trans. Barbara Johnson, *Georgia Review,* 31:1 (1977), pp. 64–116. For other Derridean

encounters with the supernatural, see 'Telepathy', trans. Nicholas Royle, *Oxford Literary Review* 10 (1988), pp. 3–41; 'Sending: on Representation', trans. Peter and Mary Ann Caws, *Social Research* 79 (1982), pp. 294–326. For a more recent statement on hauntology, see 'The Time is Out of Joint', trans. Peggy Kamuf, in Anselm Haverkamp (ed.), *Deconstruction is/in America: a New Sense of the Political* (New York and London: New York University Press, 1995), pp. 14–38. For a non-hostile reception of Derrida's obsession with ghosts, see Derek Attridge, 'Ghost Writing', in *Deconstruction is/in America*, pp. 223–7.

6.   Terrell Carver, *Engels* (Oxford: Oxford University Press, 1981), p. 2. Nobody reads Engels these days, at least not in Eng. Lit. Christopher Caudwell quoted from *Anti-Dühring*, but that was in the old days when reading was fashionable. See Christopher Caudwell, 'English Poets: the Decline of Capitalism', in K. M. Newton (ed.), *Twentieth-Century Literary Theory: a Reader* (London: Macmillan, 1988), p. 88.

7.   Henri Lefebvre, 'Toward a Leftist Cultural Politics: Remarks Occasioned by the Centenary of Marx's Death', trans. David Reifman, in Cary Nelson and Lawrence Grossberg (eds), *Marxism and the Interpretation of Cultures* (London: Macmillan, 1988), p. 76.

8.   Fredric Jameson, 'Marx's Purloined Letter', *New Left Review*, 209 (1995), p. 98.

9.   Derrida, *Specters of Marx*, p. 42.

10.   Friedrich Engels, *Ludwig Feuerbach and the End of Classical German Philosophy* (Moscow: Progress, 1978), p. 35.

11.   Derrida, *Specters of Marx*, p. 148.

12.   Derrida, *Specters of Marx*, p. 167. See also 'The Deconstruction of Actuality: an Interview with Jacques Derrida', conducted by Brigitte Sohm, Cristina de Peretti, Stéphane Douailler, Patrice Vermeren and Emile Malet, trans. Jonathan Rée, *Radical Philosophy*, 68 (1994), pp. 28–41.

13.   See Terry Eagleton, 'Marxism without Marxism', *Radical Philosophy*, 73 (Sept./Oct. 1995), pp. 35–7, 37; Gayatri Chakravorty Spivak, 'At the *Planchette* of Deconstruction is/in America', in *Deconstruction is/in America*, pp. 240–1. For a concise formulation of this concept, see *Specters of Marx*, where Derrida speaks of 'a certain emancipatory and *messianic* affirmation, a certain experience of the promise that one can try to liberate from any dogmatics and even from any metaphysico-religious determination, from any *messianism*', p. 89.

14.   Cited Oizerman, *The Making of the Marxist Philosophy*, p. 74.

15.   Cited Oizerman, *The Making of the Marxist Philosophy*, p. 75.

16.   Cited Oizerman, *The Making of the Marxist Philosophy*, pp. 76–7.

17.   On the relationship between tears and vision, see Jacques Derrida, *Memoires of the Blind: the Self-Portrait and Other Ruins*, trans. Pascale-Anne Brault and Michael Naas (Chicago and London: Chicago University Press, 1993), pp. 126–9: 'Only man knows how to see this [*voir ça*] – that tears and not sight are the essence of the eye', p. 126.

18.   Engels, *Ludwig Feuerbach and the End of Classical German Philosophy*, p. 34.

19. Jacques Derrida, 'White Mythology: Metaphor in the Text of Philosophy', in *Margins of Philosophy*, trans. Alan Bass (Brighton, Sussex: Harvester Press, 1982), pp. 216–17, n. 13.

20. On the bond as band, tape or double-bind, see, for example, Jacques Derrida, *'Ja, or the faux-bond* II', in *Points ... Interviews, 1974–1994*, ed. Elisabeth Weber, trans. Peggy Kamuf (Stanford CA: Stanford University Press, 1995), pp. 30–77.

21. Friedrich Engels, 'Natural Science in the Spirit World', *Dialectics of Nature* (Moscow: Progress, 1954), pp. 68–82.

22. Engels, *Anti-Dühring* (Moscow: Progress, 1954), p. 15.

23. Preface to English translation of *Dialectics of Nature*, pp. 7–8.

24. Pierre Macherey, 'In a Materialist Way', trans. Lorna Scott Fox, in Alan Montefiore (ed.), *Philosophy in France Today* (Cambridge: Cambridge University Press, 1983), pp. 136–7.

25. Derrida, *Specters of Marx*, p. 50.

26. Engels, *Ludwig Feuerbach and the End of Classical German Philosophy*, p. 8.

27. Étienne Balibar, 'The Vacillation of Ideology', trans. Andrew Ross and Constance Penley, in *Marxism and the Interpretation of Cultures*, p. 175.

28. Balibar, 'The Vacillation of Ideology', p. 179.

29. Engels, 'Natural Science in the Spirit World', pp. 68–9.

30. See Friedrich Engels, 'On the History of Early Christianity', in Lewis S. Feuer (ed.), *Marx and Engels: Basic Writings on Politics and Philosophy* (Glasgow: Fontana, 1959; 1969; 1976), pp. 209–35. The Revelation of St John is parodied – by Marx – in the conclusion to *The Holy Family*, in the form of a 'Critical Last Judgement'. See *The Holy Family, or Critique of Critical Criticism: Against Bruno Bauer and Company* (Moscow: Progress Publishers, 1980), pp. 260–1.

31. Engels, 'Natural Science in the Spirit World', p. 69.

32. Engels, 'Natural Science in the Spirit World', p. 69.

33. Engels, 'Natural Science in the Spirit World', pp. 69–70.

34. Derrida, *Specters of Marx*, p. 99.

35. Elsewhere, Derrida appeals to the evidence of handwriting – a strange thing for a deconstructivist to do, in order to authenticate authorship: 'One imagines the impatient patience of Marx (rather than Engels) as he transcribes in his own hand, at length, in German, the rage of a prophetic imprecation.' *Specters of Marx*, p. 43. See also Derrida, 'Onto-Theology of National Humanism (Prolegomena to a Hypothesis)', *Oxford Literary Review* 14 (1992), pp. 3–23; 20: 'All the second volume of *The German Ideology* (manuscript in Engels's hand) aims at those who lay claim to what they call "true Socialism".'

36. Derrida, *Specters of Marx*, p. 193, n. 21.

37. Engels, 'Natural Science in the Spirit World', p. 70.

38. Engels, 'Natural Science in the Spirit World', pp. 70–1.

39. Engels, 'Natural Science in the Spirit World', p. 72.

40. Engels, 'Natural Science in the Spirit World', pp. 73–4. For a recent theoretical formulation that touches upon this new grammar of the self, see Hélène Cixous, 'Preface', Susan Sellers (ed.), *A Cixous Reader*

(London: Routledge, 1994), p. xvii: '*A* subject is at least a thousand people. This is why I never ask myself "Who am I?" (*qui suis-je?*) I ask myself "Who are I?" (*qui sont-je*) an untranslatable phrase. Who can say who I are, how many I are, which is the most I of my I's.'

41. Engels, 'Natural Science in the Spirit World', p. 74.
42. Engels, 'Natural Science in the Spirit World', pp. 74–5.
43. Engels, 'Natural Science in the Spirit World', pp. 75–6.
44. Engels, 'Natural Science in the Spirit World', p. 77.
45. Engels, 'Natural Science in the Spirit World', pp. 77–8.
46. Engels, 'Natural Science in the Spirit World', pp. 79–80.
47. Engels, 'Natural Science in the Spirit World', pp. 80–1.
48. Engels, 'Natural Science in the Spirit World', pp. 81–2.
49. Engels, 'Natural Science in the Spirit World', p. 82.
50. Derrida, *Specters of Marx*, p. 47.
51. Derrida, *Specters of Marx*, pp. 46–7. For a sophisticated and nuanced argument around exorcism that seems to me to make this point about magic and counter-magic, see Stephen J. Greenblatt, 'Shakespeare and the Exorcists', in Patricia Parker and Geoffrey Hartman (eds), *Shakespeare and the Question of Theory* (London and New York: Methuen, 1985), pp. 163–87. Greenblatt also has some sharp things to say about the staging of the supernatural, and its translation from one cultural space to another.
52. Jacques Derrida, *The Post Card: from Socrates to Freud and Beyond*, trans. Alan Bass (Chicago: Chicago University Press, 1987), pp. 267–8.
53. Eagleton, 'Marxism without Marxism', p. 35.
54. Jacques Derrida, *Of Grammatology*, trans. Gayatri Chakravorty Spivak (Baltimore: Johns Hopkins University Press, 1976), p. 120.
55. Derrida, *Specters of Marx*, p. 34.
56. Derrida, *Specters of Marx*, p. 104. For a provisional account of Eagleton's militant tendency to stand for Marx against Derrida, see my 'Brother Tel: The Politics of Eagletonism', in Stephen Regan (ed.), *The Year's Work in Critical and Cultural Theory*, Volume One (Blackwell: Oxford, 1994), pp. 270–87.
57. Zhang Longxi, 'Marxism: from Scientific to Utopian', in Bernd Magnus and Stephen Cullenberg (eds), *Whither Marxism? Global Crises in International Perspective* (Routledge: London, 1995), p. 68.
58. Zhang, 'Marxism: from Scientific to Utopian', p. 68.
59. Gajo Petrovic, 'Philosophy and the Revolution: Twenty Sheaves of Questions', in *Marxism and the Interpretation of Cultures*, p. 243. One only has to read Lenin's *Materialism and Empirio-Criticism* (1909) in order to realise how far his own conception of dialectical and historical materialism was drawn largely from Engels, as opposed to Marx.
60. Zhang, 'Marxism: from Scientific to Utopian', p. 75.
61. Derrida, *Specters of Marx*, p. 47. It is worth noting that Deleuze and Guattari seem to endorse Engels's contempt for those who actually believe 'in myth, in tragedy'. See Gilles Deleuze and Félix Guattari, *Anti-Oedipus: Capitalism and Schizophrenia* trans. Robert Hurley, Mark Seem, and Helen R. Lane (London: The Athlone Press, 1984), p. 107; p. 297. At issue here is the status of allegory and of truth, and the

limits of demythification, not to mention the metaphysical nature of such a demythification.

62. Terence Hawkes, 'The Heimlich Manoeuvre', *Textual Practice* 8:2 (1994), p. 305.

63. For an astonishing co-authored investigation of the fear and trembling induced by present-day capitalism, see Félix Guattari and Toni Negri, *Communists Like Us*, trans. Michael Ryan (New York: Semiotext(e), 1990), pp. 11–13. For a fascinating instance of a socialist acting as a medium, see E. P. Thompson's remarks concerning his approach in *The Making of the English Working Class*, in an interview cited in Richard Johnson, 'Edward Thompson, Eugene Genovese, and Socialist Humanist History', *History Workshop*, 6 (1978), p. 84: 'But the fact is, again, the material took command of me, far more than I had ever expected. If you want a generalization I would have to say that the historian has got to be listening all the time. He should not set up a book or research project with a totally clear sense of exactly what he is going to be able to do. *The material itself has got to speak through him.* And I think this happens.' (my emphasis)

64. See Jean-Paul Sartre, *The Spectre of Stalin*, trans. Irene Clephane (London: Hamilton, 1969).

2

'Something Tremendous, Something Elemental': On the Ghostly Origins of Psychoanalysis

Roger Luckhurst

I know of a doctor who had once lost one of his women patients suffering from Graves' disease.... One day, several years later, a girl entered his consulting room, who, in spite of all efforts, he could not help recognizing as the dead one. He could frame only a single thought: 'So, after all it's true that the dead can come back to life'.... The doctor to whom this occurred was ... none other than myself.[1]

There needs no ghost, my lord, come from the grave/To tell us this[2]

André Breton's 1924 Surrealist novel or document *Nadja* opens with the following statement:

Who am I? If this once I were to rely on a proverb, then perhaps everything would amount to knowing whom I 'haunt'.... Such a word means much more than it says, makes me, still alive, play a ghostly part.[3]

Breton plays on the double meaning in the proverb, shifting the emphasis from 'tell me whom you *frequent* (or: what your haunts are), and I will tell you who you are' to literalize the effect of that haunting. Discomfort attends this becoming-ghostly, for the haunting Breton has to suffer the ghost's 'blind submission to certain contingencies of time and place' and is 'doomed to retrace my steps under the illusion that I am exploring,... learning a mere fraction of what I have forgotten'.[4] His own subjectivity, now ghosted, far from masters the spatio-temporal world from a place outside it, but is constructed contingently and through a sequential forgetting; it must shadow itself, ceaselessly failing to conjure self-proximity. *Nadja* will pursue how Breton's subjectivity is constructed disjointedly through chance, accident and the uncanny encounter. As Margaret Cohen reads this opening passage: 'Breton posits ... identity as a sequence of temporally differentiated moments. The *I* becomes a series of ghosts of its contiguous experience rather than a centred self.'[5]

This shifting, ghosting subject in Cohen's formulation evidently owes much to Derrida in its conception of temporal *différantiation*, but it owes little to Derrida's specific writing on ghosts. For from '"Fors"', concerning the heterotopic crypt which lodges inside the ego and comes to haunt, up to *Specters of Marx*, the phrase 'tell me whom you haunt' would be an impossible one to employ. *You* do not haunt; *you* do not actively ghost; rather, you come *to be haunted* by another. That is, you are subjected *to* haunting, you are not the subject *of* haunting: 'This spectral someone other looks at us, we feel ourselves being looked at by it, outside of any symmetry.'[6] Given the insistence of this asymmetry, we need to re-write Breton's proverb if it is to be of use: 'Tell me whom you are haunted *by*, and I will tell you who you are.'

On the streets of Paris, Breton haunts and comes to be haunted by the enigmatic Nadja. To restore or retain any degree of subjectivity, Breton must expel, indeed exorcise, Nadja. Nearly forty years earlier, on the same streets, Freud conjured a similar exorcism: 'During the days when I was living alone in a foreign city ... I quite often heard my name suddenly called by an unmistakable and beloved voice; I then noted down the exact moment of the hallucination and made anxious enquiries of those at home about what had happened at that time. Nothing had happened.'[7] Just before this anecdote, Freud has announced: 'To my regret I must confess that I am one of those unworthy people in whose presence spirits suspend their activity and the supernatural vanishes away.'[8] But we know this is untrue, both of Freud himself and of the institution he engendered: this constitutes the subject of this essay. Even this early denial gives itself away, both in Freud's awareness of the procedure for annotating to authenticate instances of telepathic messages from *phantasms of the living*,[9] and in his oblique reference to the often rehearsed spiritualist argument of the time that the presence of sceptics prevented the return of spirits. Freud knows, then, in order not to know; a perfect instance of disavowal.

If Breton's proverb is re-written one final time to read, 'Tell me what psychoanalysis is haunted by, and I will tell you what it is', it will be to find that what haunts Freud is *haunting itself*, both in its transgressive structure and in the many contemporaneous psychologies fully imbricated in ghosts, ghost-hunting and other communications outside recognized channels.[10] And if this story has been difficult to un-cover, it is because the general category of the occult has been subject to a forgetting by the institution of psychoanalysis that would like it to have little to do with the mechanism of repression: it would wish to return to Freud's very first therapeutic treatment – to *delete* the traumatic memory in its entirety.[11] This entanglement with the occult, however, helps illuminate the ghostly origins of psychoanalysis (in *at least* two senses)[12] and may, given the temporal disadjustments attendant to spectrality effects, tell of something of the future of Freud's legacy.

Ghosts haunt borders. As in the stories of Henry James, they stand on thresholds, monitory absent presences that forbid entry, or contemptuously turn their backs; when they show their face, barring the door, it is enough to make you lose your self-presence.[13] Monitoring borders, the ghost also breaches boundaries (life versus death, presence versus virtuality), thus necessitating an anxious restatement of the border with each passage. Freud, as is often remarked, was repeatedly compelled to re-draw the limit around that which was proper to psychoanalysis, to mark out a circle and bind the inner committee to this ring.[14] External attacks were perhaps less significant than those which arrived in the sunderings of this inner circle, the Secret Committee formed to perpetuate the institution. 'On the History of the Psychoanalytic Movement', written in 1914, aimed to redraw the boundary after the loss of Adler, and the catastrophe of losing the chosen son, Jung.[15] The re-narration of the history of the origins of psychoanalysis is a compulsive activity undertaken by Freud at each departure, working also, in a logic of restitution, to attach and detach simultaneously psychoanalysis from the complex weave of filiation and disinheritance from nineteenth-century and contemporaneous psychologies. If, in 1909, Freud had opened the 'Five Lectures' with 'If it is a merit to have brought psychoanalysis into being, that merit is not mine', his 1923 footnote immediately points to 'On the

History ...' as the place 'where I assumed the entire responsibility for psychoanalysis'.[16] In 1924, 'An Autobiographical Study' sees off Adler and Jung's 'attempts against psychoanalysis', but returns anxiously to questions of origin and influence by reiterating time and again Janet's *lack* of influence; the same is done with Nietzsche.[17] By his later years Freud could dismiss the question of origin in the formulation that 'I can never be certain, in view of the wide extent of my reading in early years, whether what I took for a new conception might not be an effect of cryptomnesia.'[18] If origins are encrypted unreadably into the edifice of psychoanalysis, the trauma of Adler and Jung's deviations are erased. By 1924, it appears, these 'have blown over without doing any harm'.[19]

A short essay of 1921 recalls again the disasters of Adler and Jung, but then adds a third danger. The text begins,

> We are not destined, so it seems, to devote ourselves quietly to the extension of our science. Scarcely have we triumphantly repulsed two attacks [and here he refers obliquely to Adler and Jung] – scarcely, then, do we feel ourselves safe from these enemies, when another peril has arisen. And this time it is something tremendous, something elemental, which threatens not us alone but our enemies, perhaps, still more.[20]

This is the opening to Freud's essay 'Psychoanalysis and Telepathy', and that tremendous, elemental force is, as Freud says, the 'irresistibly strong' impetus of the occult. The third threat which haunts and liminally transgresses the proper sphere of psychoanalysis is the ghostly communication that impossibly slips tight border patrols – thoughts crossing global distances without material support, bodies walking through walls, foreign bodies coming to occupy the psyche, and, more dangerously, the conceptual field of psychoanalysis.

The 'problem' of the occult, for Freud, is precisely its uncertain place inside and outside of psychoanalysis, for the opening pages of 'Psychoanalysis and Telepathy' bewilderingly change the status of its threat virtually every sentence. The opening paragraph places the occult on the same level of danger as the secessionists; the third paragraph, however, argues for a 'reciprocal sympathy' between occultism and psychoanalysis: 'They have both experienced the same contemptuous and arrogant treatment by official science. To this day psychoanalysis is regarded as savouring of mysticism, and its unconscious is looked upon as one of the things between heaven and earth which philosophy refuses to dream of' (p. 178). 'Alliance and co-operation' seems 'plausible', but the next paragraph withdraws this sympathy again: occultists are mere 'convinced believers', holding 'superseded convictions of primitive peoples' (p. 178), whilst analysts are 'incorrigible mechanists and materialists' (p. 179) on the side of exact science.[21] This objection concerns the *subjective* dangers of interest in the occult; the next paragraph demolishes this delicate dance by switching to the *objective* danger. Freud writes:

> There is little doubt that if attention is directed to occult phenomena the outcome will very soon be that the occurrence of a number of them will be confirmed; and it will probably be a very long time before an acceptable theory covering these new facts can be arrived at.... There may follow a fearful collapse of critical thought, of determinist standards and of mechanistic science (pp. 179–80).

Suddenly, occultism is not a mere faith that, in its transparently pseudo-scientific mysticism, traduces science. Rather it is that the occult (or a portion of it) is *true*, and it is this *truth* which threatens the edifice of science and, inevitably, psychoanalysis itself. 'All these combine as motives,' Freud ends the 'Introductory', 'for withholding my remarks from a wider public' (p. 181).

These intricate assertions and retractions make all of the texts Freud wrote on the occult difficult to follow, and deliberately so. 'Dreams and Telepathy', written the next year, negates itself even as it inaugurates itself, Freud beginning: 'You will learn nothing from this paper of mine about the enigma of telepathy; indeed, you will not even gather whether I believe in the existence of "telepathy" or not.'[22] Similarly, 'Dreams and Occultism' (1933) oscillates, in a 'kettle logic', between exposing 'the secret motives of the occultist movement' as coming 'to the help of religion, threatened as it is by the advance of scientific thought', but then *incorporates* the occult within psychoanalysis, claiming its forces can only be discerned through psychoanalytic method: it is psychoanalysis alone that 'has paved the way for the assumption of such processes as telepathy'.[23]

This oscillation, marking the internal structure of the argument so clearly, also affects the very status of the essays themselves.

'Psychoanalysis and Telepathy' is signed and dated as being delivered to a meeting of the Central Executive in the Harz mountains in 1921; no such meeting took place. Only the closest followers, the inner circle, could listen to this text which announces, so secretly, the breaching of the proper sphere. Freud was to deliver three instances of occult forces in his analytic experience; he was incapable, however, of giving the full text, since his third and most important example of thought-transference was left behind, forgotten, in Vienna – a case, Freud avers, of its being 'omitted due to resistance'.[24] Once the third case had been recovered, Freud prepared the essay for publication, but the manuscript was lost, apparently irretrievably, to be discovered only after his death. Such parapraxes mark every instance of Freud's explicit dealings with the occult: 'Dreams and Telepathy' is marked as a lecture for the Vienna Psychoanalytical Society, but the minutes give no evidence of its delivery; the New Introductory lecture, like the whole text, never existed *as* a lecture; 'The Occult Significance of Dreams', intended as a new addition of the 1925 edition of *The Interpretation of Dreams* was not included, appearing only once in the *Gesammelte Werke*, before being dropped.

Ernest Jones' biography of Freud diverges only once from the Master's teachings, and this is on the issue of the occult. He ascribes (in a peculiar reversion to Victorian psychology) Freud's 'exquisite oscillation' on occultism to the aberrancy of genius, thus trying to limit its damage to individual foible.[25] Jones, however, is clearly trying to suppress the disturbances that occultism caused to the *institution*, an occult that haunts it from its very beginning. Of the close circle, Sandor Ferenczi's first psychological paper in 1899 was on mediumship, as was Jung's doctoral thesis, 'On the Psychology and Pathology of So-called Occult Phenomena' in 1902. Together, Ferenczi and Jung sought to convince Freud to 'conquer the field of occultism'.[26] Freud seemed converted by June 1911, writing to Jung (in an astonishing construction): 'I have grown humble since the great lesson of Ferenczi's experiments … I promise to believe anything that can be made to look reasonable.'[27] By 1913, Freud was visiting séances with Hans Sachs and Otto Rank in Vienna, but one spectacularly obvious fake led Freud to ask Ferenczi to withdraw his testimonial to the authenticity of the medium.[28] Ferenczi, however, gave a lecture on thought-transference to the Viennese Psycho-Analytical Association in November 1913, and their correspondence is littered with references to the topic – including a meta-correspondence on the 'negative proof' for anticipations of letters crossing between Vienna and Budapest.[29] Freud's monitory dream of his son in the trenches (fully in line with the resurgence of spiritualism and reports of phantasms of the living and the dead during the First World War) is discussed and reveals the dangers of Ferenczi's enthusiasm.[30] The incident is reported by Freud with the prefatory comment, 'I know that you are not without a secret inclination toward occult matters', to which Ferenczi replies: 'My "inclination toward occult matters" is not "secret" but rather quite obvious.'[31] Nevertheless, none of Ferenczi's many attempts to deliver papers on the subject survive into the three-volume collection of his work, although (as will be shown) constant traces remain. In the main this was due to self-censorship, but Ernest Jones, who took the protection of the Cause seriously (and successfully passed off Ferenczi's split with Freud as mental deterioration), also attempted to suppress any publication on the occult. Writing from the English context, Jones regularly warned Freud of the dangers of associating with psychical researchers. Imagine, then, Jones' consternation when, in 1925, weeks after writing a circular letter underlining the threat of association with the occult, Freud announced his conversion to belief in telepathy, helped on by Stekel's *The Telepathic Dream*[32] in 1920 and experiments with his daughter, tersely writing to Jones that this 'conversion to telepathy is my private affair'.[33]

This astonishing story can be reconstructed from the partial source of Jones' biography and the (still) incompletely published networks of correspondence. It has also been retold obliquely by Derrida in his essay, 'Telepathy'. One of his most difficult pieces, a fractured supplement of letters, 'forgotten' or 'lost' from *The Post Card* (thus repeating Freud's own acts of 'forgetting'), 'Telepathy' is written *as* 'Freud' and the issue is dealt with, as Derrida says elsewhere, 'in a more or less fictional fashion'.[34] Derrida sees the occult as an exemplary instance of liminal anxiety, psychoanalysis 'set on swallowing and simultaneously rejecting the foreign body named Telepathy, for assimilating and vomiting it without being able to make up its mind to do one or the other'.[35]

Telepathy is also used by Derrida as a lever, which, like the spectre, specifically breaches the isolation of the One, inserting a heterogeneous foreign body into the isolate ontogenetic unconscious, such that there is no coming into subjectivity without coming to be haunted by the other, voices simultaneously distant (*tele-*) and intimate (the *pathos* of touching affect)[36] housed in, even constitutive of, the unconscious: 'The truth, what I always have difficulty getting used to: that non-telepathy is possible. Always difficult that one can think something to oneself, deep down inside, without being surprised by the other, without the other being immediately informed.'[37] The unconscious is now seen as a 'kind of *je anonyme* through which passes messages which may or may not originate there'.[38]

This analysis of a liminal anxiety precisely concerning that which intricately evades or invades the *limen* around the proper of psychoanalysis is acute, but in some ways I think Derrida misreads the precise reasons for Freud's oscillation. For Freud's concern may not be that an association of psychoanalysis with the occult may drag it towards pseudo-science or the demolition of scientific precepts. It may in fact be that psychological explanations of the occult, particularly theories evinced by psychical researchers, may be *more orthodox, more rigorously close*, to the dominant psychology which is intent on expulsing Freud's thought.

This thesis can easily be demonstrated. Derrida follows Jones in speaking of the three main essays that Freud wrote on telepathy and occult phenomena, as well as referring to his comments on chance and superstition scattered throughout the oeuvre. But there is a fourth text which is ignored here. In 1912, the English Society for Psychical Research invited Freud to write a paper. No anxiety here: Freud had written delightedly to Jung the year before: 'The Society for Psychical Research has asked me to present my candidacy as a corresponding member, which means, I presume, that I have been elected. The first sign of interest in *dear old England*. The list of members is most impressive.'[39] His short essay, 'A Note on the Unconscious in Psychoanalysis' is a vital text which constitutes a first draft of his most important metapsychological paper, 'The Unconscious'. By now familiar disturbances surround this 'Note': the Editors of the *Standard Edition* show some concern about the authorship and translation of the text, forcing them to use the text from the *Proceedings the Society for Psychical Research*, but *that* context produces complex parergonal effects.

Freud outlines what the unconscious 'has come to mean in Psychoanalysis and in Psychoanalysis *alone*',[40] and this underlining is necessary because, bound within the *Proceedings*, and within that to a Special Medical Part, Freud is bordered on one side by T. W. Mitchell on Multiple Personality and on the other by Boris Sidis on

'The Theory of the Subconscious', which attacks 'Freud and his adherents' for their 'highly questionable' theories of mind.[41] What becomes clear about Freud's contribution is the aim to underscore the highly specific nature of the dynamic *unconscious*, to draw a boundary around his topography of the psyche, a distinction that is yet undermined by the contextual apparatus of its appearance in a psychical research journal. Freud, in this framing, is reduced at best to a competing psychological voice, and at worst to a fringe figure whose seemingly perverse occultation of the emerging paradigm of secondary or double consciousness departs from an orthodoxy which marks a continuum between psychology and psychical research.

This would inevitably be the case in this context, for the key founder of the SPR, Frederick Myers, who coined the term 'telepathy', and first introduced Freud into England as early as 1894, had theorized what he called the Subliminal Consciousness. In a sublime series of essays, published in the *PSPR* in the years 1891–5, Myers outlined the subliminal consciousness as a subterranean array of faculties, *continuous* with ordinary, waking consciousness, yet occluded, for the most part, and discernible only by moments of subliminal 'uprush'. Supraliminal, waking consciousness, was merely a narrow band on the spectrum of consciousness, and the unknown ends of this continuum could be used to explain anything from dreams, somnambulism, automatism, multiple personality, telepathy, and the ghost as a form of physico-mental projection of psychic energy. When William James reviewed Myers' posthumous opus, *Human Personality and its Survival of Bodily Death*, he suggested Myers 'be regarded as the founder of a new science … of the Subliminal Self, by which he colligated and co-ordinated a mass of phenomena which had never before been considered together, and thus made a sort of objective continuum of what, before him, had appeared so pure a disconnectedness that the ordinary scientific mind had either disdained to look at it, or pronounced it mostly fictitious'.[42] Freud's dynamic unconscious was explicitly opposed to the subliminal, the notion of, in effect, an unconscious consciousness, and it could be said, without exaggeration, that the lengthy refutations of split consciousness in his paper, 'The Unconscious', were directed at work which had emerged mainly from psychical research, or at least figures like Richet, William James and Myers, who easily crossed the boundary between conventional and occult concerns in psychology.

Indeed Myers, himself only recently emerging from occlusion in the history of psychology, stands at the centre of a network which proposed a divergent conception of the psyche and linked it explicitly to telepathic transfers, ghosts and phantasms of the living and dead.[43] There is only one telling distant touch of Freud on Myers: 'I understand that Myers has published a whole collection of hypermnesic dreams of this kind in the *Proceedings of the Society for Psychical Research*; but these are unluckily inaccessible to me.'[44] Freud, though, would presumably soon know that Myers' theory stood behind the phenomenal success of Théodore Flournoy's *From India to Planet Mars*, the text analysing the medium Hélène Smith, which quickly went into five editions and was widely translated whilst Freud's dream-book languished in obscurity.[45] Flournoy's ghosting of the early years of psychoanalysis, his full imbrication in the study of occult psychic phenomena, bears close enquiry: not only did Flournoy have the impudence to suggest in 1911 that 'It will be a great day when the subliminal psychology of Myers and his followers and the abnormal psychology of Freud and his school succeed in meeting',[46] but Flournoy was also the 'revered and fatherly' figure who supported Jung through his split with Freud.[47] This rival father, dashing Freud's plans for his chosen 'son', placed Myers above Freud, considering that the Subliminal Consciousness 'so much surpasses the level of ordinary scientific conceptions'.[48] Flournoy also influenced Jung to such a degree[49] that Jung in effect *repeated* Flournoy's career, moving from the psychological demystification of mediumship (Flournoy's book on Hélène gave Jung confidence in his own doctoral topic) to a 'conversion' to a belief in occult forces: as Flournoy explained ghostly materialization through a combination of telepathy and teleplasty, so Jung told Arz 'The existence of telepathy in time and space is still denied only by positive ignoramuses.'[50] Given the omnipresence of Myers behind the emergent paradigms of subliminality and double consciousness, this too might suggest one reason for Freud's antipathy to Surrealism and the dismissal of Breton, for Breton had written of 'the regrettable fact that so many are unacquainted with the work of F. W. H. Myers, *which anteceded that of Freud*' (emphasis mine).[51]

All of this opens up a whole tranche of psychoanalytic history which suggests the need for reorienting the reasons for Freud's 'exquisite oscillation' on the question of occultism. I'm suggesting that the anxiety about the occult in psychoanalysis is not simply due to its dubious scientific status: what, after all, could be more occulted at the time than the Freudian unconscious, this dynamic, structural thing, founded on the mechanism of sexual repression and 'outside', in a way still inconceivable to his contemporaries, the consciousness? Rather, Freud's anxiety is that explanations of the occult find their footing in the *orthodoxies* developing around non-physiological conceptions of psychology, an orthodoxy from which Freud is marginalized.

In 'The "Uncanny"' one source of unease is the sudden return of beliefs that one had considered surmounted by rationality. Surmounted beliefs return with a historical periodicity, such that now, in 1919, 'in our great cities, placards announce lectures that undertake to tell us how to get in touch with the souls of the departed; and it cannot be denied that not a few of the most able and penetrating minds among our men of science have come to the conclusion ... that a contact of this kind is not impossible'.[52] Freud has recourse to the upsurge of primitive animism, of the magical omnipotence of thought, to explain the power of these momentary disturbances. At one point he even suggests that resistance to psychoanalysis is a result of the fear of the 'evil eye' of the analyst, who knows more than is rationally possible: 'I should not be surprised to hear that psychoanalysis, which is concerned with laying bare these hidden forces, has itself become uncanny to many people.'[53] This is said of a technique that, from the beginning, aimed to make bodily symptoms vanish with a mere word, 'like a ghost that has been laid'.[54]

Psychoanalysis haunts people, it appears, but what is psychoanalysis haunted *by*? Perhaps the uncanny effect of the transference of thought, of the energetic hallucinatory projection that constitutes the phantasm, disturbs psychoanalysis not simply because they come to trouble the very boundaries that demarcate its proper sphere, but also because, to entertain these notions, psychoanalysis must rely on psychological conceptions it believed it had surmounted. Freud's oscillation is partly a dance with emerging orthodox psychology, that which had first ignored him, then pronounced him dead. 'Being declared dead,' Freud mused, 'was an advance on being buried alive in silence', but this uncanny living-dead psychoanalysis was itself haunted, through and through, by psychical research and its rival claims.[55]

The 1935 'Postscript' to the 'Autobiographical Study' declared 'There can no longer be any doubt that it [psychoanalysis] will survive.'[56] In its surmounting of external and internal rivals, had the occult, too, been conquered? Despite Jones' efforts to fence off the occult as the Master's foible, its forces began to infect key psychoanalytic concepts. In 1926, Helene Deutsch published 'Occult Processes Occurring During Psychoanalysis', stating: 'During psychoanalysis the psychic contact between analyst and analysand is so intimate, and the psychic processes which unfold themselves in that situation are so manifold, that the analytic situation may very well include all conditions which facilitate the occurrence of such phenomena.'[57] All of these effects, she suggests, 'are probably connected with transference' and 'seem to indicate the existence of an essential relationship between analytic intuition and the telepathic process'.[58] The journal *Imago* became host to regular disputes on this issue: Istvan Hollos, in 1933, intensified the threat by denoting *counter*transference as the locus of the telepathic transfer, the analyst's unconscious thoughts being *voiced and returned* by the reproachful analysand.[59] Hollos began to reveal the extent of his co-investigations with Ferenczi, whose infamous essay, 'Confusion of Tongues between Adults and the Child' (the text which forced the break with Freud), not only re-instated the reality of trauma, but gave the traumatized patient an 'uncanny clairvoyance'.[60] In a fragment on the theme of being dead, Ferenczi elucidated this: 'the person struck by a trauma comes into contact with death.... In the moment of the trauma some sort of omniscience about the world associated with a correct estimation of the proportion of their own and foreign powers ... makes the person in question...more or less clairvoyant.'[61] From transference and countertransference, then, Ferenczi comes to demarcate all his patients as the living dead, as those touched by powers unleashed by the 'little death' of trauma.[62]

Despite Ferenczi's apparent 'return' to seduction theory, Ferenczi and other theorists of strange analytic effects could ascribe them 'occult' powers on the basis of Freud's own writings, particularly on transference and dream-interpretation. Like the 'something elemental' of the occult, was not transference-love itself 'some elemental phenomena', the thing that drove 'women of elemental passionateness who can tolerate no surrogates'?[63] If all his women, in effect, 'decamped from me', was this not some uncanny prescience of Freud's countertransferential violence, a violence most evident to 'Dora'?[64] No wonder Freud started, when he repeats the scenario of Jensen's *Gradiva*, where 'dead' women master both 'archeologists': 'a girl entered his consulting room, who, in spite of all efforts, he could not help recognising as the dead one'.[65] Transference, like the dead, operates on an originary *coming back*: the 'stereotype plates' of first love turn everything ghostly.[66] As *The Interpretation of Dreams* stated: 'All my friends have in a certain sense been reincarnations of this first figure...: they have been *revenants*.'[67] This dream-book, which is also a ghost-book, incipiently models transference as the exorcising rational explanation for the ghost; it can confidently switch from literal to metaphorical *revenance*. But, on the other hand, the ghost keeps for itself an uncertain reserve of literal haunting: as with the dreams of dead fathers, Freud confesses 'to a feeling that dream-interpretation is far from having revealed all the secrets of dreams of this character' (p. 560). Ghosting, too, is the thematic of the dream of the dead child who speaks (p. 652), and which marks the limit of interpretation: it is the point of haunting in part that constitutes 'the dream's navel, the spot where it reaches down into the unknown' (p. 671). Once more, Freud reveals in these instances an unexpressed knowledge of the debates concerning telepathic dreams, hallucinatory projections of the living and the dead, which so fascinated the Society for Psychical Research and others: writing to Ferenczi about his monitory dream of his son's death, he wrote: 'I acknowledge that one can be far more sensitive at night', marking the dream-state as the most open to telepathic transfer (from the living and the dead), just as Myers had done.[68]

Both dream-interpretation, that 'royal road', and transference, the central device of cure, shade off into the occult, reach down into the unknown. Haunting glides between the literal and metaphoric, at once joining and separating 'proper' psychoanalysis with its outside. But the ghost, the spectre simultaneously at the edges and central to psychoanalysis, is not only a *spatial* disturbance of the limit; it also causes *temporal* disadjustments. 'What is the time and what is the history of the spectre? Is there a present of the spectre? Are its comings and goings ordered according to a linear succession of a before or after?'[69] My concern with the ghost in psychoanalysis is not simply with the ghost as interruptive witness of untold histories, as if telling this history could then lay it to rest. As Derrida suggests, the ghost intersects and divides contemporaneity with a double gesture that invaginates the past and future into the present. The occult in psychoanalysis is not solely another vector of reconfiguring Freud's indebtedness to antecedents. As Mikkel Borch-Jacobsen states: 'What is important is to re-consider what

Freud called the "pre-history" of psychoanalysis, to return to it with the suspicion that this "pre-history" belongs to a certain future of psychoanalysis rather than to a long-dead past.'[70] The future of psychoanalysis is tied up to its ghost: the ghost of Freud himself, and the ghost which ghosts this ghost.

One hundred years on from the naming of psychoanalysis, its future involves conjuring Freud's ghost to seek his word of guarantee. This, at least, is the strategy of Yerushalmi in *Judaism Terminable and Interminable*, a text whose closing fictional dialogue between the author and Freud's ghost Derrida reads at length in 'Archive Fever'. This invocation concerns the indeterminable 'Jewishness' of psychoanalysis; perhaps, too, the ghost of Freud needs conjuring because the very institution is under threat. Whilst used to invectives such as Richard Webster's *Why Freud Was Wrong*, it becomes difficult to contest texts like Patricia Kitcher's wholly sympathetic yet devastating demolition of Freud's network of misapplied consilient scientific precepts. Freud serves here merely as a catastrophic precedent for the dangers of interdisciplinarity in the new projects of cognitive psychology, a discipline intent on forgetting Freud.[71] More relevant here is the realization that after Freud's century, the ghostly impress of pre-psychoanalytic models of the psyche are returning to psychiatry, making the current reassessments of Myers, Janet and others crucial.

Today's 'ghosts' are Satanic abusers or alien abductors, the multiple personalities who split and haunt the ego in ways entirely foreign to Freud, but explicable in a revived 'double consciousness' paradigm. And if Freud is edged out, lies unacknowledged or unreferenced in these accounts, that is partly due to the explosive dispute, manufactured by Jeffrey Masson, around Freud's allegedly constitutive abandonment of the reality of seduction for the categories of 'psychic reality' and 'primal fantasy' – an insistence on the *fantasmatic* trauma.[72] The exorcism of Freud is staged both on the real trauma, and the return of nineteenth-century egoic psychologies. Azam's theory of *double conscience*, put forward in 1887 (and the text which Freud attempts to refute on the way to explaining the meaning of the unconscious 'in psychoanalysis *alone*'), models the (re)invented form of dissociation known, since 1980, as Multiple Personality Disorder.[73] Since the ego splits off, coralled outside any interchange, however disguised, between conscious, preconscious and unconscious, the Freudian 'talking cure' is inoperable: 'there is no question of remembering or verbalising an event that, quite literally [for the "main" ego], never took place'.[74] And since treatment is premised on traumatic reality there can be no imputing of unconscious elaboration to patient narratives that emerge: Satanists and multiples proliferate; abduction is systematic and widespread.

That the late-Victorian conceptions of the psyche and the ghost of psychical research have returned in barely new guises is evident in the many parallels between then and now: where mediums crossed gender and racial lines to be 'possessed' by spirit controls and 'exotic', often orientalized, spirits, so multiples repeat these transgressions; where William James noted the 'generic similarity' of spiritualist trance-utterances 'as if one author composed more than half the trance messages, no matter by whom they are authored', so the very consistency of Satanic rituals and alien abductions are upheld as proof.[75] On the wilder fringes, automatic messages from spirits are now replaced by 'channelings' from past lives and deep space, and the Society for Psychical Research's 'Census of Hallucinations', 'proving' the high incidence of visits from the dead, is matched by the UFOlogists 'Roper Poll', which statistically 'proves' the extent of alien visitation. Just as Ian Hacking notes that the host for narratives of multiple personality has shifted from spiritualism to child abuse, so our contemporary aliens are elaborated from Théodore Flournoy's analysis of Hélène Smith, medium of Geneva and onetime princess of Mars.

This uncanny echoing of the imbrication of psychology and parapsychology pre-Freud and (dare it be said?) post-Freud suggests a kind of *bracketing* around the era of the institution of psychoanalysis: its beginning and its end. Hypnosis opened the door to this bizarre occult and occulted world; Freud shut it, by claiming to found psychoanalysis on the abandonment of hypnosis. If the hypnotic technique has reopened the door once more (multiples, abuse and abductions are all 'recovered' by this technique, if not spontaneously present), the impulse may be to point to Freud's insistent warnings on the dangers of hypnotic rapport, suggestibility, unresolved transference and *fantasmatic* memory. These are the 'memories' that investigators are catastrophically invested in;[76] as Borch-Jacobsen has written, in hypnosis '"I" am *spoken by* the other, I come into the place of the other – who, by the same token, is no longer an *other* but rather "myself" in an undecidable identity of somnambulistic ego.'[77] Suggestibility, countertransference, even what William James called 'suscept[ibility] to a certain stratum of the *Zeitgeist'*, can exorcise these ghosts; Freud's topography and procedure thus *have a future*.[78] This unearthed history of psychoanalysis' dalliance with the occult, however, strengthens Borch-Jacobsen's claims that Freud never solved the *mystisch* (mystical or mysterious) power of transference or rapport. Like the navel of the dream, the relation of patient and analyst, the social-emotional tie *itself*, 'reaches down into the unknown'. And in doing so, investigators are drawn, compulsively it seems, to bridge that psychic abyss with the liminal transgressions of the ghost and the telepathic transfer. For psychoanalysis, this occult contamination cannot easily be readjusted beyond the limit, for occult concepts disadjust the notion of the limit itself.

Among the bizarraries of 'proven' spirits in Victorian psychologies, it seems to me that Freud hovered indecisively at the edges, not simply for reasons of siding with exact Science or the prudential awaiting of positivistic proof that never arrived, but because he sensed something about the ghostly that could add, incalculably, to psychoanalysis. In this, Freud is like many of his *fin-de-siècle* contemporaries, who underwent the strange experience of working with a de-mystificatory positivism that actually helped *produce* a disturbing, remystified and occulted supplement that exceeded 'rational' science.[79] If Freud did not join the scientists like Cesare Lombroso, Charles Richet and Oliver Lodge and others who sought the ghost, it was the excess of the ghost*ly* that came to haunt psychoanalysis in its most intimate procedural recesses, and used the available 'occult' frames in an attempt to articulate this excess. Perhaps, beyond the ghost, this ghost*liness* was to do with the social tie, that 'enlarged impression', as Henry James called it, 'carrying the field of consciousness further and further, making it lose itself in the ineffable'.[80] Perhaps, too, it was an ethical hesitation, a sense of the violence that the proclamation of a full mastery of psychic processes might effect. Derrida has said that we still await an ethics of psychoanalysis ('Geopsychoanalysis'),[81] and he sees the ghost as inextricably tied to this:

> The spectre weighs, it thinks, it intensifies and condenses itself within the very inside of life, within the most living life, the most singular (…) life. The latter therefore no longer has and must no longer have, insofar as it is living, a pure identity to itself or any assured inside: this is what all philosophies of life … would have to weigh carefully.[82]

It could be that it was this concern, embodied in the ghostly and the telepathic, that led Freud to write, *privately* of course, to Carrington: 'If I had my life over again I should devote myself to psychical research rather than to psychoanalysis.'[83]

Notes

1. Freud, 'Delusions and Dreams in Jensen's *Gradiva*' (1907), *Pelican Freud Library*, vol. 14, pp. 27–118, 95. References to Freud, with two exceptions, will come from the *Pelican Freud Library*, 15 vols (Harmondsworth: Penguin), and *The Standard Edition of the Complete Psychological Works of Sigmund Freud*, 24 vols (London: Hogarth Press).
2. *Hamlet*, cited Freud, *The Interpretation of Dreams* (1900), *Pelican Freud Library*, vol. 4, p. 261.
3. André Breton, *Nadja*, trans. Richard Howard (New York: Grove Weidenfeld, 1960), p. 11.
4. Breton, *Nadja*, p. 12.
5. Margaret Cohen, *Profane Illumination: Walter Benjamin and the Paris of Surrealist Revolution* (Berkeley: University of California Press, 1993), p. 64.
6. Jacques Derrida, *Specters of Marx: The State of the Debt, the Work of Mourning, and the New International*, trans. Peggy Kamuf (London: Routledge, 1994), p. 7.
7. Freud, *The Psychopathology of Everyday Life* (1901), *Pelican Freud Library*, vol. 5, pp. 324–5.
8. Freud, *The Psychopathology of Everyday Life*, p. 324.
9. The title of the first, most important two-volume collection of evidence from the Society for Psychical Research, published in 1886 by Gurney, Myers and Podmore.
10. 'Telepathy' was defined by F. W. H. Myers as 'the communication of impressions of any kind from one mind to another, independently of the recognised channels of sense' (*Human Personality and its Survival of Bodily Death*, 2 vols (London: Longmans, 1915), p. xxii). This was merely one instance (others included telaesthesia, teleplasty and phantasmogenesis) of the contact of one mind with another 'outside recognised channels'.
11. This is a reference to Maria Torok's investigations of the 'origins' of psychoanalysis, particularly 'A Remembrance of Things Deleted: Between Sigmund Freud and Emmy von N.', in Nicholas Abraham and Maria Torok, *The Shell and the Kernel*, vol. 1, trans. Nicholas Rand (Chicago: University of Chicago Press, 1994), pp. 234–48.
12. If ghosts conflate opposites (living and dead, principally), they also confuse any confident division of the literal and the metaphorical – no more so than in this essay. The 'ghostly origins' of my title might mean, metaphorically, the obscured faint traces that can be recov-

ered; on the other hand, the ghostly is to be taken literally, as concerning the disembodied spirits of the dead. Meanings proliferate beyond these two, however: I'm particularly enamoured of the definition of 'ghosting' in the *Collins* Dictionary, which reads: 'a faint secondary image ... on a television screen, formed by reflection of the transmitting waves, *or by a defect in the receiver*'. Being concerned with telepathy, that occulted channel without apparent support between sender and receiver, such ghostings should also be borne in mind. To place a ghost at the origin, as should be obvious, is to explode any originary plenitude: ghosts begin, as Derrida tells us repeatedly, by *coming back*.

13. The James stories referenced here include 'The Real Right Thing' and 'The Jolly Corner'. See T. J. Lustig's *Henry James and the Ghostly* (Cambridge: Cambridge University Press, 1994), for annotations on the persistent image of the ghost that turns its back.

14. See Phyllis Grosskurth, *The Secret Ring: Freud's Inner Circle and the Politics of Psychoanalysis* (Reading, Mass.: Addison-Wesley, 1991).

15. See Freud, 'On the History of the Psycho-Analytic Movement', *Standard Edition*, vol. 18, pp. 175–93.

16. Freud, 'Five Lectures on Psychoanalysis' (1909), in *Two Short Accounts of Psychoanalysis*, ed. James Strachey (Harmondsworth: Penguin, 1962), pp. 29-87, p. 31.

17. Freud, 'An Autobiographical Study' (1924), *Standard Edition*, vol. 20, pp. 7–74. See pp. 53, 13, 19, 30–1 and 60 respectively.

18. Freud, 'Analysis Terminable and Interminable', *Standard Edition*, vol. 23, pp. 209–53, p. 245.

19. Freud, 'On the History of the Psycho-Analytic Movement', p. 53.

20. Freud, 'Psychoanalysis and Telepathy' (1921/1941), *Standard Edition*, vol. 18, pp. 175–93, p. 177.

21. This is Freud at his most positivist: the (fake) division of his scientific self from the superstitious person is repeated in *The Psychopathology of Everyday Life*: 'The differences between myself and the superstitious person are two: first, he projects outwards a motivation which I look for within; secondly, he interprets chance as due to an event, while I trace it back to a thought' (p. 320). Freud's view that superstition and belief in spirits are survivals of primitive belief are echoing two high Victorian sources. Henry Maudsley confidently puts ghosts, spirits and omens down to 'a revival or recrudescence of a still-surviving superstition, not a new conquest of scientific thought' (*Natural Causes and Supernatural Seemings*, 3rd edn (London: Kegan Paul, 1897), p. 176); this itself is derived from Edward Tylor's discussion of spiritualism as a primitive survival in *Primitive Culture*, 2 vols (London: John Murray, 1871).

22. Freud, 'Dreams and Telepathy' (1922), *Standard Edition*, vol. 18, pp. 197–220, p. 197.

23. Freud, 'Dreams and Occultism' (1933), *Pelican Freud Library*, vol. 2, pp. 60–87, pp. 63, 85–6.

24. Freud, 'Psychoanalysis and Telepathy', Editor's note, p. 175.

25. Ernest Jones, 'Occultism', in *Sigmund Freud: Life and Work*, vol. 3

(London: Hogarth, 1957), pp. 402–36, p. 402.

26. William McGuire (ed.), *Freud/Jung Letters* (Princeton: Princeton University Press, 1974), p. 421.

27. *Freud/Jung Letters*, p. 429.

28. Eva Brabant *et al.*, *The Correspondence of Sigmund Freud and Sandor Ferenczi*, trans. Peter Hoffer, 2 vols (Cambridge, Mass.: Harvard University Press, 1993 and 1996), vol. 1, pp. 523–4.

29. *The Correspondence of Sigmund Freud and Sandor Ferenczi*, vol. 1, p. 411.

30. Oliver Lodge, physicist and theorist of the 'etheric body' as the form of the surviving spirit, for example, leapt to fame during the First World War, with his book *Raymond; or, Life and Death* (London: Methuen, 1917), which contained messages from dead soldiers.

31. *The Correspondence of Sigmund Freud and Sandor Ferenczi*, vol. 1, pp. 69–70.

32. Cf.: 'During the war I had gathered many experiences as a confirmation of the existence of telepathy. I was never inclined to believe in mysticism and was skeptical as far as metapsychological matters were concerned; but facts are facts.... What is so miraculous about telepathic dreams? We know since the discovery of radio that electric waves can be transmitted over vast distances. Can we not suppose that the brain sends out waves and that another sensitive brain may be able to receive them? I myself have had some telepathic dreams. I consider the existence of telepathy proved.' Wilhelm Stekel, *The Autobiography of Wilhelm Stekel* (New York: Liveright, 1950), pp. 224–5.

33. Cited in Jones, 'Occultism', p. 424.

34. Jacques Derrida, 'Archive Fever: a Freudian Impression', trans. Eric Prenowitz, *Diacritics* 25:2 (Summer) 1995, pp. 9–63, 56.

35. Jacques Derrida, 'Telepathy', trans. Nicholas Royle, *Oxford Literary Review*, 10 (1988), pp. 3–43, p. 43.

36. For more details on this, particularly in relation to the constant association of theorizations of telepathy with emergent tele-technologies (radio, telephones etc.), see my '(Touching on) Tele-Technology', in *Applying: to Derrida*, ed. John Brannigan *et al.* (London: Macmillan, 1996).

37. Derrida, 'Telepathy', p. 13.

38. Deborah Cook, 'Telesprache', in *Philosophy and Literature*, 11:2 (1987), pp. 292–300, p. 298.

39. *Freud/Jung Letters*, p. 396. Ferenczi was also a corresponding member. When I was in the process of researching this essay, Ralph Noyes, a member of the Society for Psychical Research, unexpectedly revealed another symptom of Freud's ambivalence to the occult: he could never quite bring himself to pay his subscription to the Society.

40. Freud, 'A Note on the Unconscious in Psycho-Analysis', *Proceedings of the Society for Psychical Research*, vol. 26 (1912), pp. 312–18, p. 312.

41. Boris Sidis, 'The Theory of the Subconscious', *Proceedings of the Society for Psychical Research*, vol. 26 (1912), pp. 319–43, pp. 334–5.

42. William James, Review of Myers, *Human Personality and Its Survival of Bodily Death*, in *Proceedings of the Society for Psychical Research*, vol. 18

(1903–4), pp. 22–33, p. 22.

43. See, for example, Adam Crabtree, *From Mesmer to Freud: Magnetic Sleep and the Root of Psychological Healing* (New Haven: Yale University Press, 1994), and Sonu Shamdasani, 'Automatic Writing and the Discovery of the Unconscious', *Spring* 54 (1993), pp. 100–31.

44. Freud, *The Interpretation of Dreams*, p. 72.

45. Théodore Flournoy, *From India to Planet Mars* (1899) (Princeton, NJ: Princeton University Press, 1994). See also Sonu Shamdasani, 'Encountering Hélène: Théodore Flournoy and the Genesis of Subliminal Psychology', in Flournoy, *From India to Planet Mars*, pp. xi–li.

46. Flournoy, *Spiritism and Psychology*, abridged and trans. Hereward Carrington (London: Harper and Brothers, 1911), p. vii.

47. See Carl Jung, *Memories, Dreams, Reflections*, trans. Richard and Clara Winston (London: Fontana, 1995), p. 186.

48. Flournoy, *From India to Planet Mars*, p. 7.

49. For more information on how Jung's central ideas of the 'mythopoeic unconscious' were indebted to Flournoy, see James Witzig, 'Théodore Flournoy – A Friend Indeed', *Journal of Analytical Psychology* 27 (1982), pp. 131–48.

50. Carl Jung, *Letters*, Selected and Edited by Adler and Jaffé, 2 vols (London: Routledge & Kegan Paul, 1973), p. 117.

51. André Breton, 'The Automatic Message', in *What is Surrealism? Selected Writings*, ed. Franklin Rosemont (London: Pluto Press, 1978), pp. 97–109, 100.

52. Freud, 'The "Uncanny"', *Pelican Freud Library*, vol. 14, pp. 335–76, p. 365.

53. Freud, 'The "Uncanny"', p. 366.

54. Freud, 'The Psychotherapy of Hysteria', *Pelican Freud Library*, vol. 3, pp. 337–93, p. 366.

55. Freud, 'On the History of the Psycho-Analytic Movement', p. 35

56. Freud, 'Autobiographical Study', p. 73.

57. Helene Deutsch, 'Occult Processes Occuring During Psycho-analysis', in George Devereux (ed.), *Psychoanalysis and the Occult* (London: Souvenir, 1974), pp. 133–46, 134.

58. Deutsch, 'Occult Processes', pp. 135, 139.

59. See George Devereux, 'A Summary of Istvan Hollos' Theories', in Devereux (ed.), *Psychoanalysis and the Occult*, pp. 199–203.

60. Sandor Ferenczi, 'Confusion of Tongues Between Adults and the Child' (1932), in *Final Contributions to the Methods and Problems of Psychoanalysis*, ed. Michael Balint (London: Hogarth, 1955), pp. 156–67, 160.

61. Ferenczi, 'Aphoristic Remarks on the Theme of Being Dead – Being a Woman', in *Final Contributions*, pp. 243–4, 243.

62. Further effects of telepathy, telegony and teleplasty are found in *The Clinical Diary of Sandor Ferenczi*, ed. Judith Dupont, trans. Michael Balint and Nichola Zarday Jackson (Cambridge, Mass.: Harvard University Press, 1988). Of one patient: 'Her hypersensitivity ... goes so far that she can send and receive "telephone messages" over

immense distance.... She suspects that even as a child she found the analyst, who is subject to similar suffering, "over a long distance", by means of telepathy, and after some forty years of aimless wandering has now sought him out' (p. 158). For how these reflections relate to the larger subject of analytic technique, see Gyorgy Hidas, 'Flowing Over – Transference, Countertransference, Telepathy: Subjective Dimensions of the Psychoanalytic Relationship in Ferenczi's Thinking', in *The Legacy of Sandor Ferenczi*, ed. Lewis Aron and Adrienne Harris (Hillside, NJ: 1993).

63. Freud, 'Observation on Transference-Love', *Standard Edition*, vol. 12, pp. 157–71, pp. 160, 167.

64. Freud, 'Remembering, Repeating and Working Through', *Standard Edition*, vol. 12, pp. 145–56, 154.

65. Freud, 'Delusions and Dreams', p. 95.

66. Freud, 'The Dynamics of Transference', *Standard Edition*, vol. 12, pp. 97–108, 100.

67. Freud, *The Interpretation of Dreams*, p. 622.

68. *Correspondence of Freud and Ferenczi*, p. 69. Cf. 'I think that there is evidence to show that many facts or pictures which have never even for a moment come within the apprehension of the supraliminal consciousness are nevertheless retained by the subliminal memory, and are occasionally presented in dreams with what seems a definite purpose', Myers, 'The Subliminal Consciousness', chapters 1 and 2, *Proceedings of the Society for Psychical Research*, vol. 7 (1891–2), pp. 298–355; chapters 3 and 4, *PSPR*, vol. 8 (1892), pp. 333–404; chapter 5, pp. 436–535; chapters 6 and 7, *PSPR*, vol. 9 (1893–4), pp. 3–128; chapters 8 and 9, *PSPR*, vol. 11 (1895), pp. 334–593; chapter 4, p. 381.

69. Derrida, *Specters of Marx*, p. 39.

70. Mikkel Borch-Jacobsen, *The Emotional Tie: Psychoanalysis, Mimesis and Affect*, trans. Douglas Brick *et al.* (Stanford: Stanford University Press, 1992), p. 44.

71. See Richard Webster, *Why Freud Was Wrong: Sin, Science, and Psychoanalysis* (London: HarperCollins, 1995), and Patricia Kitcher, *Freud's Dream: a Complete Interdisciplinary Science of Mind* (Cambridge, Mass.: MIT, 1995).

72. See Masson, *The Assault on Truth: Freud and Child Sexual Abuse*, rev. edn (London: Fontana, 1992). Another influential attack on Freud's alleged 'denial' of abuse is made by Alice Miller in *Thou Shalt Not Be Aware: Society's Betrayal of the Child* (London: Pluto Press, 1988). This dispute has produced an enormous amount of secondary literature. One excellent guide is Ann Scott's 'Feminism and the Seductiveness of the "Real Event"', in *Feminist Review*, 25 (January 1988), pp. 88–102.

73. Freud, 'A Note', p. 312.

74. Mikkel Borch-Jacobsen, 'Who's Who?: Introducing Multiple Personality', in *Supposing the Subject*, ed. Joan Copjec (New York: Verso, 1994), pp. 45–63, 51.

75. William James, *The Principles of Psychology* (1890), 2 vols (New York: Dover, 1950), p. 394. See also Budd Hopkins, *Intruders: the Incredible Visitations at Copley Woods* (New York: Ballantine Books, 1987), and

John E. Mack, *Abduction: Human Encounters with Aliens* (New York: Ballantine Books, 1994). For further discussion of these modern ghostly subjectivities, see my 'The Science-Fictionalisation of Trauma: Remarks on Narratives of Alien Abduction', *Science Fiction Studies* 25:1 (March 1998), pp. 29–52.

76. This is not to say that a severely traumatic effect does not exist in reality or have real and profoundly distressing effects, only that the narrative frames in which they *come into representability* are made available by cultural or analytic suggestion. Such a complex issue would require much more space to pursue.

77. Borch-Jacobsen, *The Emotional Tie*, pp. 49–50.

78. James, *Principles*, p. 394.

79. Compare Michael Roth's formulation: 'The increasing pace of technological change and scientific advance both explained more about the natural world and opened more mysteries in it. The development of electric power, the invention of the recording phonograph and the discovery of X-rays are only a few of the markers of what was taken to be both signs of scientific power and indices of the profound mysteriousness of nature' ('Hysterical Remembering', in *Modernism/Modernity* 3:2 (1996), pp. 1–30, p. 15). My argument here also relies on Con Coroneos' discussion of positivist science's transition from de-mystification to re-mystification at the close of the nineteenth century; a marker, for Coroneos, of the emergence of Modernism. See Con Coroneos, 'The Cult of *Heart of Darkness*', *Essays in Criticism* XLV:1 (January 1992), pp. 1–23.

80. Henry James, 'Is there Life After Death?' (1910), in *The James Family*, ed. F. O. Matthieson (New York: Knopf, 1948), pp. 602–14, 611.

81. Jacques Derrida, 'Geopsychoanalysis "... and the Rest of the World"' [1981], *New Formations* 26 (Autumn 1995), pp. 141–62.

82. Derrida, *Specters of Marx*, p. 109.

83. Cited in Jones, 'Occultism', p. 419.

3

Phantasmagoria: Walter Benjamin and the Poetics of Urban Modernism

Christina Britzolakis

Blanqui's cosmic speculation teaches that humanity will be prey to the anxiety of myth for so long as the phantasmagoria has a place in it.[1]

Fourmillante cité, cité pleine de rêves,
Où le spectre en plein jour raccroche le passant.[2]

In 1917 Max Weber, in an essay entitled 'Science as a Vocation', claimed that the essence of modernity was the disenchantment of the world, brought about by the spread of what he called 'rationalization' across all forms of social life.[3] The predominant scene of this disenchantment, according to such diverse theorists of modernity as Weber, Lukács, Simmel and Benjamin, was the modern metropolis, within which the consequences of historical change and technological innovation are actualized. The theorizing of 'modernism' in relation to 'modernity' has often appealed to the Marxist concepts of alienation and reification.[4] Yet Lukács' famous rejection of Modernism suggests that in so far as these concepts are staked on the faith that Marxist science could expunge superstition, annul the power of mythic thinking and recover a lost harmony of the particular and the general, they are inadequate to deal with the questions of subjectivity and aesthetics thrown up by modernist practice. Enlightenment notions of modernity are based on a refutation of spectres, but are haunted, as so much modernist literature attests, by the return of premodern, animistic or magical modes of thought.[5] Jacques Derrida's most recent work offers a critique of Marxist ontology, and calls for a new ontology, a *hauntology* which, far from attempting to exorcize ghosts and spectres, as Marx claimed to do, would introduce haunting into the structure of Marxist concepts.[6]

It is often said that the machine-based rhythms of metropolitan life produce a new aesthetic corresponding to a transformed perception of the urban environment as 'phantasmagoric'. In modernist texts, the metropolis becomes a theatre for the operations of dream, fantasy and memory. The notion of the 'phantasmagoria' implies a certain phenomenology of the city, among whose themes are the interpenetration between interior and exterior space, the impact of the urban crowd upon the individual psyche and the transformation of patterns of experience, including aesthetic experience, by technology. A distinctively modern temporal sensibility is characterized by a fragmentation of memory and of subjectivity which assumes a certain spectralization of subject–object relationships.

This familiar account of modernism owes much to the work of Walter Benjamin, who developed the concept of the urban phantasmagoria during the 1920s and 1930s within the context of his unfinished 'Arcades Project' on the Paris of the Second Empire.[7] The related motifs of the *flâneur*, shock, allegory and *ennui* have been enlisted in readings not only of Baudelaire, a central figure in the Arcades Project, but also of a host of other modernist writers. Indeed, they now approximate something like a repertoire of 'classic' modernist themes. For Benjamin, the key to the urban phantasmagoria was the commodity-on-display, as exemplified in the arcades. His emphasis on 'intoxication' and 'distraction' as features of urban modernism allots a central role to commodity fetishism within the historical structuring of perception. The city as poetic object resists a stable, singular perspective and demands a discontinuous, fragmented and imagistic literary form which highlights the fleeting, ephemeral character of modern metropolitan existence. While these forms of representation increasingly draw on the example of photography and film, the concept of the phantasmagoria invokes, for reasons which I shall examine, a more primitive form of spectacle: the magic-lantern shows of the nineteenth century. In this essay, I shall draw on the rich ensemble of theoretical and figurative possibilities encoded in the notion of the phantasmagoria to construct a comparative framework of inquiry into the historic conditions of possibility of modernism.

Robert Pippin has stated that modernism 'is not comprehensible unless it is viewed, first, against the background of an emerging, widely shared consensus in European high culture that the early modern hopes for a genuinely new, progressive, fundamentally better epoch had proved false'.[8] Benjamin belongs to the generation of modernists who came to maturity between 1918 and 1930. He shares their revulsion at the ideology of progress whose bankruptcy had been so dramatically revealed by the First World War, and their attempt to grasp imaginatively the forces of radical, possibly catastrophic innovation unleashed by capitalism: an attempt overshadowed, in Benjamin's case, by the rise of Nazism after 1930, which made the conditions not only of his production but of his very existence increasingly precarious. This refusal of the linear narratives of nineteenth-century historiography is stylistic as well as theoretical; as Graeme Gilloch points out, '[a] critical, redemptive reading of the city-as-text is complemented by [an] innovative, immanent writing of the text-as-city'.[9]

Benjamin's work anticipates what we would now call a semiotic approach to culture; hence its pivotal role within contemporary debates about postmodernity and history. It explores the spectral effects of exchange value at work in the everyday life of capitalist culture, engaging with both 'high' and 'low' forms of cultural production, and posing questions concerning the possibility of a modernist phenomenology, whose implications, though far-reaching, have not been engaged in any systematic way by Anglophone literary study. If modernism is often seen as polarized politically between reactionary and progressive moments (the contrast, say, between the Eliotic-Poundian cult of tradition and revolutionary Surrealism), Benjamin, who participates in both moments, tends to destabilize this opposition. His career faces Janus-like towards 'the collector' on the one hand and 'the author as producer' on the other.[10]

I cannot do justice here to the totality of Benjamin's thought, if indeed it is possible to speak of such a totality, given the fragmentary, eclectic and aphoristic nature of his writings. This essay is not concerned, as so many of his readers from Theodor Adorno onwards have been, with the task of 'redeeming' or 'correcting' this fragmentary corpus for a politics, an ethics or a metaphysics. It is, however, concerned with his aesthetics, not only in their implications for a theorization of urban modernism but as themselves part of the imaginary of urban modernism. In juxtaposing his comments on the phantasmagoria with a number of 'phantasmagoric' textual moments torn from their various contexts (T. S. Eliot's rewriting of Baudelaire in his early poems, Louis Aragon's Surrealist ethnography in *Le paysan de Paris*, and the 'Nighttown' episode of Joyce's *Ulysses*), I am, of course, proceeding in a quasi-Benjaminian way, constructing a critical configuration whose status is exploratory rather than exegetical.

PHANTASMAGORIANS I: BENJAMIN / BAUDELAIRE / ELIOT

Benjamin's theorizing of urban modernism is based upon what he calls 'a dialectical optic that perceives the everyday as impenetrable and the impenetrable as the everyday'.[11] For him, the major poetic exponent of this phenomenology of the marginal and the peripheral is Baudelaire. Much of the Arcades Project was concerned with the writings of Baudelaire, and by 1937 Benjamin was planning to compose a separate, though intimately related, study of the poet. His published essays on Baudelaire, while representing three different stages of the uncompleted Paris Arcades project, were also intended as a model of the whole.[12] Baudelaire is the archetype of the modernist poet as middle-class *flâneur*, who confronts the 'intoxicating' spectacle of mass society and whose recycling of the debris of an exhausted cultural tradition becomes a new form of heroism in the face of the loss of cultural aura.[13] For the Baudelairean *flâneur*, literary originality assumes an ironic aspect in the context of the marketplace. The city becomes the home of a peculiarly modern kind of subjectivity involving the apprehension of time as empty repetition, and the transformation (or deformation) of patterns of experience by technology. Shock becomes the basis of a new kind of poetic method based on the tearing of objects out of their usual contexts and their reassembly in new contexts. Benjamin's account of modernism and its specific subjectivity draws on his critique of the Romantic concept of the symbol and recuperation of the concept of allegory in *The Origin of German Tragic Drama* (1927). In baroque allegory, he argues, objects are drained of immanent meaning, with the consequence that they become mere material tokens, subject to the fanciful manipulations of the allegorist. In allegorical signification, the labour and artifice of the act of signifying themselves come to the fore. What Benjamin sees as 'thingifying' of language in the baroque is reborn in the art of the capitalist metropolis; as 'ever more callously the object world of man assumes the expression of the commodity', so memory increasingly becomes a species of collection.[14]

Baudelaire was equally important as an inaugurator of urban modernism for T.S. Eliot, whose early volumes *Prufrock and Other Observations* (1916), *Poems* (1920) and *The Waste Land* (1922) constitute, among other things, a rewriting of the *Fleurs du mal*. In 1930, in an introduction to Baudelaire's *Intimate Journals*, Eliot acknowledged his debt to Baudelaire. He described Baudelaire as giving 'new possibilities to poetry in a new stock of imagery of contemporary life.... It is not merely in the use of imagery of the common life, not merely in the use of imagery of the sordid life of the great metropolis, but in the elevation of such imagery to the *first intensity* – presenting it as it is, and yet making it represent something much more than itself – that Baudelaire has created a mode of release and expression for other men.'[15] The 'Unreal city' refrain of *The Waste Land* was inspired by a line from the *Fleurs du mal* – 'Fourmillante cité, cité plein de rêves, Où le spectre en plein jour raccroche le passant' – cited by Eliot in the Notes. The urban masses flowing over London Bridge appear in 'The Burial of the Dead' as a cross between the inhabitants of Baudelaire's teeming and spectral city and those of Dante's hell ('I had not thought death had undone so many').

For both Benjamin and the early T. S. Eliot, then, Baudelaire presides over the city as a theatre for the operations of memory, dream and fantasy. Benjamin's discussion of Baudelaire is informed by his reading of Bergson, also a key figure for the young T. S. Eliot.[16] In Eliot's early poems, especially 'The Love Song of J. Alfred Prufrock', 'Portrait of a Lady', 'Preludes', 'Rhapsody on a Windy Night' and *The Waste Land*, as in Benjamin's own autobiographical meditation on the city, *A Berlin Chronicle* (1932), the *flâneur*'s passage through the urban labyrinth is punctuated by moments of *ennui*, liminality, erotic fascination and repulsion, 'mixing memory and desire' ('The Burial of the Dead'). It is made up of an associative or paratactic juxtaposition of images which are simultaneously private and collective. The phantasmagoric narrative is haunted by mysterious residues and intimations of a chthonic, subterranean or submarine energy (such as the 'chambers of the sea' at the conclusion of 'The Love Song of J. Alfred Prufrock'). It traces the broken outlines of a search for the primordial beneath the contemporary, a quest to recover potentially liberating originary and pre-historical strata of experience. The ambiguous guardians of this urban labyrinth – the embodiments of its unconscious – are female, explicit or implicit prostitute figures whose seductions are crystallized in the motif of the threshold, the moment of hesitation on the stairway.[17]

What exactly is the nature of the transaction between the observer and the city in urban modernism? In Eliot's essay on Baudelaire, it is seen in terms of a 'transfiguration' or 'transformation', which turns the ordinary into the spectral, producing a figurative surplus of meaning. Benjamin stresses the extent to which this *montage* or juxtaposition of images, which fragments the sequence of classical realist narrative, is the product of the kind of attention fostered by the advertising pages of a newspaper or the traffic of a big city, which he describes as 'the disintegration of the aura in the experience of shock'.[18] The Arcades Project theorizes this fragmentation of poetic memory and subjectivity in terms of the dominance of the commodity form in metropolitan capitalist culture. Benjamin's term for the expressive character of the urban environment, whose origins he locates in the Paris of the Second Empire, is the *phantasmagoria*.

For Benjamin the prime examples of urban phantasmagoria are the arcades, which, he argues, undermined the boundaries between between interior and exterior space, transforming the street into an interior. He also applies the term to the successors of the arcades, the department stores full of novelties, and to the International Expositions, which from the mid-century until well into the twentieth century, exhibited commodities as a paean to technological progress and national pride. It becomes a metaphor for the wider process by which, in the nineteenth century, capital cities throughout Europe themselves became showcases for the commodity, advertising the promise of the new industry and technology for a new heaven-on-earth.

The phantasmagoria was one of a wide range of nineteenth-century popular visual spectacles. The word originally denoted a magic-lantern show of optical illusions, rapidly changing shape and blending with one another. Such shows were first held in the late 1790s, when phantasmagorians such as Etienne-Gaspard Robertson used this technology to produce so-called spectral or diabolical apparitions. One etymology of the word links 'phantasma' (ghost) with 'agoreuein' (to show in the market-place). The *laterna magica*, which inverted painted slides and projected them on to the screen, was the precursor of modern instruments for slide and cinematic projection. From the outset, however, the word carried powerful atavistic associations with magic and the supernatural, hinting at the demonic potential of technology.[19]

The metaphor of the magic lantern appears in a well-known passage of T.S. Eliot's 'The Love Song of J. Alfred Prufrock': 'impossible to say just what I mean! / but as if a magic lantern threw the nerves in patterns on a screen'. The culminating metaphor of the magic lantern is superimposed upon the figure of a neurological or X-ray machine.[20] The flicker of the magic lantern conveys not merely the disconnectedness of Prufrock's experiences but also their disconnection from the perceiving subject, who, like the reader, sees them projected on to a psychic screen as neurosis. The cinematic dimension of this metaphor is also exploited in 'Preludes': 'You dozed, and watched the night revealing / The thousand sordid images / Of which your soul was constituted; / They flickered against the ceiling.' The magic lantern is part of a broader phantasy of dismemberment in Eliot's early poetry (compare 'the evening ... spread out against the sky / Like a patient etherised upon a table' at the start of 'Prufrock'). Prufrock's is an anxiety of being dismembered in a language whose signs no longer correspond to the subject's intentions or emotions except in an arbitrary manner. Memory appears as a clutter of disconnected fragments of sense data, whose accumulation obstructs or aborts narrative. The magic lantern is the figure of this disjunction between language and subjectivity. Presented as a visual alternative to or transposition of the obstructed speech act – of the 'impossibility of saying just what one means' – it traces a shift from the notion of voice as expressive vehicle to that of an image-writing at once impalpable and visceral. The technological figure at once reduces consciousness to its sensory contents and inscribes an exacerbated, nerve-peeled self-reflexivity. Body, psyche and technology are transposed in a way that leaves none of these categories in a recognizable form.

Terry Castle has argued that from an initial connection with something external and public (an artificially produced illusion), the word 'phantasmagoria' now often refers to something wholly internal or subjective.[21] The shift in the word's meaning suggests the emergence of a new form of subjectivity, the opening up of an interior space or 'other stage' which is the space of the daemonic, the irrational or the unconscious. The magic lantern becomes a privileged trope in post-Romantic discourse for what Castle calls 'the spectralization or "ghostifying" of mental space'.[22] However, the phantasmagoria also belongs to an ocular rhetoric of understanding. It denotes a heightened, distorted or manipulated visibility; the apparitional quality of objects uncannily abstracted from the process of their own making, and disporting themselves in the new urban landscape of modernity. Many of the rhetorics of modernism draw on the model of photographic or cinematic montage and therefore register the impact of new visual technologies. But the High Modernist view of the city as the site of the decay of traditions, and the use of myth as a structural device, could also be seen as having a phantasmagoric aspect. In Benjamin's terms, this is a species of the activity of the collector, who in moments of historical rupture and innovation responds with a citation or borrowing from the past, often through images of classical myth or natural ritual. Cultural history, when subjected to the effects of montage, itself becomes a phantasmagoria or flicker show, as in *The Waste Land*.

Although both Eliot and Benjamin identify Baudelaire as the precursor of modernism, their readings of the *Fleurs du mal* imply diametrically opposed views of the relation between language and history. In his 1930 essay on Baudelaire, Eliot argues, in effect, that Baudelaire raises the urban landscape – in itself 'sordid' and unpoetic – to the status of symbol. He assimilates a symbolist reading of Baudelaire to a lexicon of spiritual purification and hierarchy. Baudelaire is, he argues, only superficially modern; he is opposed to mid-nineteenth-century conceptions of progress and is concerned rather with 'Sin in the permanent Christian sense'.[23] If the secular world of the city is the source of imagery 'of the first intensity', it is also a fallen realm, the demonic earthly counterpart of Augustine's City of God. Written in 1930, shortly after Eliot's conversion to Anglo-Catholicism, the essay represents something of a recoil from the modernism of his earlier poems. While paying tribute to Baudelaire as the inaugurator of urban modernism, it also attempts to put into place a certain Christianized reading of his own career. For Benjamin, by contrast, Baudelaire is not a symbolist but an allegorist whose language stages a clash of the ancient and modern, of prehistory and contemporaneity, and thereby registers the shocks of modernity. In defining Baudelaire's urban aesthetic of shock as the aesthetic of the bourgeois writer in the capitalist metropolis, Benjamin, unlike Eliot, is concerned to historicize the self-understanding of modernism.

PHANTASMAGORIANS II: ARAGON/BENJAMIN/JOYCE

From his book on the *Trauerspiel* onward, Benjamin is concerned with the uncanny power which the world of things assumes over people within certain historical and aesthetic configurations. The prehistory of modernity in the Arcades Project deploys a hybrid methodology drawing on a mixture of Marxism, anthropology, Jewish theology, Romantic metaphysics, and various aesthetic models (the baroque, Baudelaire, Proust, Surrealism). However, the central concept of the 'phantasmagoria' is based upon Marx's analysis of the operation of commodity fetishism in 'The Fetishism of Commodities and the Secret Thereof'.[24] Marx argues that the nature of the commodity as a product of human labour is obfuscated by exchange value, which invests it with an enigmatic and mysterious character, a 'phantom objectivity'.[25] This 'phantom objectivity' derives from the replacement of a relationship between people by a relationship between things.

For Benjamin, whose point of departure was, as Susan Buck-Morss points out, a philosophy of historical experience rather than an economic analysis of capital, the key to the new urban phantasmagoria was not so much the commodity-in-the-market as the commodity-on-display. In the art of Grandville, the society of commodity production surrounds itself with 'a glitter of distraction'. The ever-accelerating wastage and turnover of commodities becomes the counterpart of Nietzsche's notion of eternal recurrence. Fashion – the reign of novelty, of what he calls 'the new-as-always-the-same' – replaces rituals based on cycles of organic nature. Commodity fetishism thus informs the historical structure of perception in the modern metropolis. At the same time, and more controversially for his Marxist interpreters, Benjamin Freudianizes the commodity hieroglyph. The key to understanding Baudelaire's poetry is, he argues, the fetish: 'the fetish, with which his sensitive nature resonated so powerfully; that empathy with inorganic things which was one of the sources of his inspiration'.[26] While Benjamin's phantasmagoria obviously carries with it the idea of ideological mystification, it cannot be reduced to mere illusion.

For eighteenth-century theorists of primitive religion, such as Charles de Brosses, whose work *Du culte des dieux fétiches* Marx had read, fetishism was a debased form of mythic thinking, a savage and irrational practice which endowed material, man-made objects with divine life and power. Fetishism is inscribed, across a number of different discursive fields – anthropological, economic and psychoanalytic – as a structure of overvaluation, forgetting and disavowal. It originates in the erasure of a genesis or the obliteration of a history, and is therefore a crucial aspect of the constitution of value.[27] Jean-Joseph Goux's 1973 essay 'Numismatics' points out that Marx, Nietzsche and Freud can each be seen in different ways as engaged in a struggle against the hypostatized result of a forgotten genesis.[28]

Benjamin does not subscribe to the Weberian view of modernity as the disenchantment of the world. On the contrary, he sees the processes of nineteenth-century industrialization as culminating in a 'reactivation of mythic powers'.[29] Technology has the capacity to generate not only its own mythology, but also a collective mythological mode of perception which is compared, in some of the early notes for the Arcades Project, to a dream state. Nor does he share the revulsion of so many of the modernists against technology and the productive forces of capitalism. He is excited by the possibilities of urban dislocation and transformation of space as, in Victor Burgin's phrase, 'an erotic event in which the categorical distinctions which separate body, city and text dissolve'.[30] This view of the urban-industrial landscape as itself mythic was heavily influenced by the practice of the French Surrealists, and especially by Louis Aragon's *Le paysan de Paris* (1926), which he cited as the inspiration for the *Passagenwerk*. In his essay on Surrealism, Benjamin claims that the face of the city is 'inherently surrealistic'.[31] The Surrealist city is a topography of dream, fantasy and desire, governed by randomness and the chance encounter – what Breton calls *le hasard objectif*.[32] Like T. S. Eliot, the Surrealists inhabit an 'unreal' city. But whereas Eliot sees the city as an infernal space ('I had not thought death had undone so many') their attitude is more celebratory, embracing the technological possibilities unleashed by modernity.

In *Le paysan de Paris*, the narrator wanders, in a state of 'intoxication', through a modern city which is seen as an enchanted forest, an *ur*-city full of objects which have taken on a hallucinatory and fantastic character. In Part II of the novel, entitled 'A Feeling for Nature at the Buttes-Chaumont', the narrator describes one such encounter:

> Here are great red gods, great yellow gods, great green gods, planted at the edges of the speculative tracks along which the mind speeds from one feeling to another, from one idea to its

consequence in its race for fulfilment. A strange statuary presides over the birth of these simulacra. Scarcely ever before had man had the pleasure of seeing destiny and force look so barbaric. The nameless sculptors who erected these metallic phantoms were incapable of conforming to a living tradition like that which traced the cruciform shapes of churches. These modern idols share a parentage that makes them doubly redoubtable. Painted brightly with English or invented names, possessing just one long, supple arm, a luminous faceless head, a single foot and a numbered wheel in the belly, the petrol pumps sometimes take on the appearance of the divinities of Egypt or of those cannibal tribes which worship war and war alone. O Texaco motor oil, Esso, Shell, great inscriptions of human potentiality, soon we shall cross ourselves before your fountains, and the youngest among us will perish from having contemplated their nymphs in naphtha.[33]

The playful juxtaposition of the banal, everyday or trivial aspects of modernity with the archaic or religious constitutes what Aragon calls a 'mythology of the modern'.[34] The petrol pumps are transfigured into primitive gods, and apostrophized by the narrator as 'great inscriptions of human potential'. They are 'metallic phantoms', at once hyper-concrete and spectral. The 'mythological' nature of such objects is based not on reverence towards traditional cultural values but on the transitory, on novelty, change and motion; in this view of myth, experience is saturated by the commodity.

Like André Breton's *Nadja* (1928), *Paris Peasant* depicts an experience in which the distinction between subject and object breaks down, and the 'I' becomes a series of ghosts of its contiguous experiences. The reciprocal interpenetration of inner and outer reality in these texts announces a 'crisis of the object', paralleled by developments in the visual arts, and later to receive its theoretical formulation in Breton's essays and lectures of the mid-1930s.[35] The surrealistic 'found object' is *out of place*, removed from the systems of circulation that construct its 'normal' meaning. It needs to be seen in the context of the connections between the development of Surrealism and the emerging discourse of ethnography in the 1920s and 1930s, as represented by the journal *Documents* (1929). The Surrealist moment of ethnography has been characterized as one in which a radical questioning of norms was underpinned by an appeal to the exotic. The work becomes a playful museum and 'perverse collection' in which objects from distinct cultures undergo classification and declassification.[36] As William Pietz has pointed out, 'the surrealistic object was often constructed to be a material thing that resonated throughout all the registers (ethnographic, Marxist, psychoanalytic and modernist) of fetish discourse by appearing as a perversely anthropomorphized or sexualized thing'.[37]

Yet if Benjamin's Arcades project is informed by the Surrealist movement, he also attempts, not entirely successfully, to distance it from what he sees as that movement's shortcomings. Whereas Aragon 'persistently remains in the realm of dream', his aim is 'to find the constellation of awakening' or 'the dissolution of mythology into the space of history'.[38] In stressing the collective rather than the individual nature of the states of dream and intoxication nurtured by the modern metropolis, Benjamin would seem to be appealing to Marx's model of demystification. The temporality of urban modernity, in so far as it is generated by the 'dream worlds' of commodity culture, is mythic, for it presents as fate a state of affairs which is man-made and which can therefore be undone by human beings.

Benjamin does not denounce myth itself but the harnessing of the mythic for reaction, its alignment with the values of permanence, stasis and order. He sees the new forms of mimesis produced by technology as having a creative mythic component rooted in the mimetic capacity displayed in childhood. In an early essay, 'On the Mimetic Faculty', modernity is linked with a decay in the human capacity for producing similarities and seeing resemblances.[39] Elsewhere, however, modern techniques of reproduction are seen as opening up new and potentially revolutionary possibilities for a resurgence of mimesis through an interpenetration of body and image within perception.[40] In the early drafts and notes of Benjamin's *Passagenwerk*, the mythic elements of commodity culture – the 'dream worlds' of advertising, for instance – are seen as fixations of fantasy energy which are potentially available for social transformation. Commodity culture is a repository of 'wish images' in which, he writes, 'the new is intermingled with the old in fantastic ways'.[41] These potentially redemptive wish images are linked with 'the dreaming collective', which is the obverse or underside of the phantasmagoria. The figure of the dreaming collective has been much criticized, notably by Adorno, who saw it as undialectical and as falling into the trap of an ahistorical, mythic thinking akin to Jungianism.[42] In the later work it has a tendency, as Graeme Gilloch has pointed out, to be inverted into a pessimistic view of the urban mass as potentially totalitarian, which mirrors the catastrophic political conditions of Benjamin's own time.[43]

The connection between figures of the unconscious and those of the urban mass implicates Benjamin in a wider modernist culture. A version of the 'dreaming collective' is also present in the 'Circe' or Nighttown chapter of Joyce's *Ulysses* (1922) whose structuring draws on Strindberg's *A Dream Play* (1901), and has often been likened to the dreamlike logic of the Freudian unconscious. In Joyce's explanatory plan of the novel, the 'Linati scheme', the episode's 'technic' is classed as 'vision animated to bursting point' or 'hallucination', and its symbols as 'personification, pantheism, magic, poison, antidote and reel'.[44] This suggests that for Joyce, who in 1909 had initiated an unsuccessful scheme to open the first cinema in Dublin, the Volta, the cinematic 'reel', a technological device for the production and marketing of dreams, is central to the conception of the episode.[45]

The phantasmagoria of 'Circe' is therefore not merely a projection of the psychic worlds of Bloom and Stephen. The text's extraordinary laying-bare of the psychic apparatus – its excursion into the unconscious of Bloom and Stephen – is accompanied by a less frequently discussed excursion into the unconscious of the urban collective under imperialism; and it is upon the latter that I wish to focus here. In the Homeric parallel, Odysseus's followers are magically transformed into swine on Circe's island, and Odysseus wins over Circe with the help of a magic herb called a 'moly' which protects him against her power. The counterpart of the 'moly' or talisman is a shrivelled potato which Bloom carries with him, and which he loses and recovers in the course of the episode. This mythic-anthropological figure of the fetish is paralleled by the sexual fetishism acted out in the transvestite Bello/Bella scenario, which transforms Bloom into a woman at the mercy of the whoremistress Bella Cohen. Declan Kiberd points out that the 'mutations and reversals' of 'Circe', in which 'things often seem to assume an identity at the expense of persons', put into doubt the very idea of human individuality.[46] Animated objects participate in the dream play, as in the passage below:

BLOOM: I was just going back for that lotion whitewax, orange-flower water. Shop closes early on Thursday. But the first thing

in the morning. (He pats divers pockets) This moving kidney.
Ah!
(He points to the south, then to the east. A cake of new clean
lemon soap arises, diffusing light and perfume.)
THE SOAP:

> We're a capital couple are Bloom and I;
> He brightens the earth, I polish the sky.

(The freckled face of Sweny, the druggist, appears in the disc of
the soapsun.)
SWENY: Three and a penny, please.
BLOOM: Yes. For my wife, Mrs. Marion. Special recipe. (571)

The personification of commodities was already a commonplace of
advertising by 1904, and it is not surprising that the soap's lines
resemble an advertising jingle. In the context of the narrative, the
comical theophany of the soap has two functions. Its more immediate function is in relation to the psyche of Bloom. It follows the
semi-pornographic apparition of Molly in 'exotic' Turkish costume,
which reminds Bloom of her adulterous activities and of the sexual
failure of his marriage. The soap serves both as distraction and as
placatory offering to the sexually dominant female. It momentarily
reduces Bloom to the sum of the things he has bought during the
day, which he repeatedly enumerates and checks. At the same
time, the soap as commodity appears as a pseudo-Utopian, pseudo-
revelatory solution to social stagnation and paralysis. The notion of
the earthly paradise is echoed later in the chapter, in the rise of
Bloom as the ruler-prophet of 'the new Bloomusalem' (601–11),
part of a sustained parody of discourses of millennial redemption
or apocalyptic destruction; elsewhere in the passage, a gramophone transforms the hymn 'The Holy City' into 'Whorusalam'
(625).

The soap, which has been purchased from Sweny the druggist, is
an ironic answer to the recurrent references in the episode to
swinish dirt, decay and disease, especially skin disease, of which
the prostitutes are the mediums. Nighttown's 'dirtiness' obviously
represents the underside of bourgeois, Catholic Dublin, unmasking
its sexual repression and hypocrisy in satirical-naturalist mode. But
it also serves as a metonymy for the imperial metropolis as waste-
land. The stage instructions at the beginning of the episode

construct, in almost obsessive detail, a spectacle of urban decay, squalor and stagnation. The inhabitants of Nighttown (ragpickers, drunkards, prostitutes) are associated, in a language redolent of late nineteenth-century evolutionism, with subhuman deformity and degeneracy. They are variously 'stunted', and 'scrofulous', lurking like beasts in 'warrens' and 'lairs', and including among their number a 'deafmute idiot', a 'gnome', a 'pigmy child' and 'a bandy child, asquat' (561ff).[47] The former slum and red-light district, known locally as the 'Monto' (after Montgomery Street, one of its principal thoroughfares), which Joyce calls Nighttown, was closed down in 1922. Dublin's slums, the worst in Europe, were indeed breeding grounds for sickness and disease because of poverty, overcrowding, malnutrition, and lack of sanitation. The urban landscape was characterized by a close proximity of tenement districts and 'respectable' streets, to the extent that the slumlands were seen by the upper classes as a malevolent cancer threatening to engulf the city.[48]

This landscape of degeneration is presided over by the 'Privates', military representatives of an imperilled colonial authority, whose aggression is unleashed on Stephen at the end of the episode, and whose presence in the city was of course instrumental in the spread of venereal disease. Prostitution, syphilis and their effects on the body (including skin disease and paralysis) form a cluster of images linked with the colonial state. Stephen, playing the role of the intoxicated Baudelairean *flâneur*-poet (for example, he makes a speech on the pornographic peepshows of Paris), quotes a line from Villon, 'Dans ce bordel où nous tenons notre état' (664).[49] Joyce's vision is governed less by tropes of catastrophe than by those of comedy (the novel's action is set in 1904, and thus precedes the Great War during which it was written) and he is more sceptical than Benjamin about the possibilities of revolutionary transformation of society, satirizing messianic fantasies like those of the 'New Bloomusalem'. Nonetheless, he too raises the question of the resources of collective fantasy and nostalgia harnessed by capitalism, and of its mutual implication with empire.

For Benjamin, the present self-consciousness of modernity as absolutely new is haunted by the recent past. The apparently ephemeral objects and images of everyday life store a historical knowledge that can be released by a certain kind of vision. For example, the Parisian arcades, which appear to the twentieth century in the guise of the outmoded and the primitive, are emblems of an earlier phase of capitalism. They can be seen as the *ur*-phenomena of modernity, the 'original temples' of commodity capitalism, in which a 'profane glow' bathed the commodity on display.[50] In such outmoded emblems, Benjamin believed, the origins of the present moment could be revealed to his own generation. The instrument of this revelation is the dialectical image, within which the archaic and the modern are dialectically articulated. Benjamin conceives of a particular mode of seeing which, in a flash, seizes the past as an image. This fleeting but pivotal moment of recognition arrests or interrupts linear, progressive narratives of history. It is a configuration of shock which prefigures a messianic cessation of happening and revolutionary possibility.[51] The dialectical image is one of the most elusive and contested notions in Benjamin's writing. Whether it belongs to the level of analytical and historical consciousness – of critique – or whether specific historical objects – such as the arcades, or the prostitute – can be designated as inherently dialectical images is unclear. Moreover, the nature of the dialectical image is bound up with Benjamin's messianism, which is outside the limited scope of this study.[52]

By contrast, the suggestiveness of the phantasmagoria, as I hope to have shown, lies in the broadness of its resonance, which makes it less a concept attributable to any one thinker than the sign of a historic formation of modernity. This formation links urban experience with the development of new optical technologies, but at the same time enacts a return of premodern, animistic or magical modes of thought within modernity. It offers a means of thinking the apparent paradox of the resurgence of the theme of 'the primitive' at the moment when nature is everywhere in the process of being expunged by human praxis. Modernism's attraction towards myth can thus be seen as an outcome of modernity rather than simply its negation. Benjamin belongs, as Margaret Cohen has argued, to a tradition of Gothic Marxism which is 'fascinated with the irrational aspects of society's processes and which takes seriously a culture's ghosts and phantasms as a significant and rich field of social production rather than a mirage to be expelled'.[53] This tradition appropriates Freudian psychoanalysis and uses it to rethink Marxist notions of the subject, of historiography and of critique. The figurative potential of myth is used to enrich the traditional language of Marxism, to make it capable of capturing the concrete presence of history.

The phantasmagoria undermines the boundaries between apparently discrete fields of intellectual endeavour, such as literature, philosophy and history, bequeathing to intellectual inquiry an ambiguous legacy: the privileging of the fragment as the basis of a modernist critique of the linear historical narratives of the Enlightenment. It enables a rethinking of historicity in the light of modernism's claims to a radical epistemological break with the past, and offers new ways of reading the historicity of modernism itself. The continuing relevance of the phantasmagoria in the late twentieth century, which has seen a resurgence of the arcades as emblems of commodity culture, testifies to the impossibility of relegating modernity once and for all to a 'historic' status.

Notes

1. Walter Benjamin, *Gesammelte Schriften*, Vol. V: *Das Passagenwerk*, ed. Rolf Tiedemann and Hermann Schweppenhäuser (Frankfurt am Main: Suhrkamp Verlag, 1972), p. 1256, cited in Susan Buck-Morss, *The Dialectics of Seeing: Walter Benjamin and the Arcades Project* (Cambridge, Mass.: MIT Press, 1989), p. 106.
2. Charles Baudelaire, 'Les Sept Vieillards' in *Baudelaire: The Complete Verse*, ed. Francis Scarfe (London: Anvil Press, 1986), p. 177.
3. Max Weber, 'Science as a Vocation' in *Max Weber's 'Science as a Vocation'*, ed. Peter Lassman and Irving Velody, trans. Michael John (London: Unwin Hyman, 1989), pp. 3–31.
4. Georg Lukács, 'The Ideology of Modernism' in *The Meaning of Contemporary Realism* (London: Merlin Press, 1963), pp. 17–46. See also 'Reification and the Consciousness of the Proletariat' (1922) in *History and Class Consciousness*, trans. Rodney Livingstone (London: Merlin Press, 1971), pp. 83–149.
5. See Jean-Michel Rabaté, *La pénultième est morte: Spectrographies de la modernité* (Paris: Editions Champ Vallon, 1993).
6. Jacques Derrida, *Specters of Marx: The State of the Debt, the Work of Mourning and the New International*, trans. Peggy Kamuf (New York: Routledge, 1994).
7. The so-called *Passagenwerk*, which Benjamin began in 1927 and which he continued working on until his death in 1940, exists only as a mass of fragmentary notes. This essay is indebted to Susan Buck-Morss's authoritative reconstruction and analysis of Benjamin's plan in *Dialectics of Seeing*.
8. Robert Pippin, *Modernism as a Philosophical Problem* (Oxford: Blackwell, 1991), p. 30.
9. Graeme Gilloch, *Myth and Metropolis: Walter Benjamin and the City* (Oxford: Polity Press, 1995), p. 5.

10. For representative instances of these two poles, see Walter Benjamin 'Unpacking My Library' in *Illuminations*, trans. Harry Zohn (London: Fontana, 1992), pp. 60–82 and 'The Author as Producer' in *Reflections*, trans. Edmund Jephcott (NY: Schocken Books, 1986), pp. 220–38.

11. Walter Benjamin, *One-Way Street and Other Writings*, trans. Edmund Jephcott and Kingsley Shorter (London: Verso, 1989), p. 237.

12. Walter Benjamin, *Charles Baudelaire: a Lyric Poet in the Era of High Capitalism*, trans. Harry Zohn (London: Verso, 1983) collects 'The Paris of the Second Empire in Baudelaire' (completed in 1938), 'Some Motifs in Baudelaire' (1939), and Benjamin's draft exposé of the Arcades project, 'Paris – the Capital of the Nineteenth Century' (1935).

13. See Benjamin, 'The Paris of the Second Empire in Baudelaire' (1938) in *Charles Baudelaire*, pp. 67–101. On the impact of technological reproducibility on the cultural status of the artwork, see Benjamin's most influential and frequently cited essay, 'The Work of Art in the Age of Mechanical Reproduction' in *Illuminations* (London: Fontana, 1992), pp. 211–44.

14. See Walter Benjamin 'Central Park', trans. Lloyd Spencer, *New German Critique* 34 (Winter 1985), 32–58. See also Lloyd Spencer, 'Allegory in the World of the Commodity: The Importance of Central Park', *New German Critique* 34 (Winter 1985), 59–77.

15. T. S. Eliot, 'Introduction', *Intimate Journals: Charles Baudelaire*, trans. Christopher Isherwood (London: Blackamore Press, 1930), p. xviii.

16. See Benjamin, 'Some Motifs in Baudelaire', *Charles Baudelaire*, pp. 107–54. On Eliot and Bergson, see, for example, David Moody, *T.S. Eliot, Poet* (Cambridge: Cambridge University Press, 1980), pp. 26–9.

17. On the figure of the prostitute in Benjamin's writings, see Susan Buck-Morss, 'The *Flâneur*, the Sandwichman and the Whore: the Politics of Loitering', *New German Critique* 39 (Fall 1986), 99–140, and Angelika Rauch, 'The *Trauerspiel* of the Prostituted Body, or Woman as Allegory of Modernity', *Cultural Critique* 10 (Fall 1988), 77–88.

18. Benjamin, *Charles Baudelaire*, p. 154.

19. See Margaret Cohen, *Profane Illumination: Walter Benjamin and the Paris of Surrealist Revolution* (Berkeley: University of California Press, 1993).

20. X-rays were discovered by Wilhelm Röntgen in 1895. Eliot was likely to have read an illustrated article on X-ray technology, 'Seeing the Brain', in the *St Louis Daily Globe-Democrat*, 17 January 1897. See Robert Crawford, *The Savage and the City in the Work of T.S. Eliot* (Oxford: Clarendon Press, 1987), p. 8.

21. Terry Castle, 'Phantasmagoria: Spectral Technology and the Metaphorics of Modern Reverie', *Critical Inquiry* 15, 1 (Autumn 1988), 27–61.

22. Castle, 'Phantasmagoria', p. 29.

23. T. S. Eliot, 'Baudelaire', *Selected Essays* (London: Faber & Faber, 1951), pp. 419–30, 427.

24. Karl Marx, *Capital*, Vol. I, trans. Ben Fowkes (Harmondsworth: Penguin, 1976), pp. 163–77.

25.   Marx, *Capital*, p. 128. On Marx's rhetoric of spectrality, see Thomas Keenan, 'The Point is to (Ex)Change It: Reading *Capital*, Rhetorically' in *Fetishism as Cultural Discourse*, ed. Emily S. Apter and William Pietz (Ithaca: Cornell University Press, 1993), pp. 152–85. See also W. J. T. Mitchell, 'The Rhetoric of Iconoclasm: Marxism, Ideology and Fetishism' in *Iconology: Image, Text, Ideology* (Chicago: Chicago University Press, 1986), pp. 160–208.

26.   'The Paris of the Second Empire in Baudelaire' in *Charles Baudelaire*, p. 55.

27.   See William Pietz, 'The Problem of the Fetish I', *Res* 9 (Spring 1985), 5–17. Pietz argues that 'the discourse of fetishism represents the emerging articulation of a theoretical materialism quite incompatible and in conflict with the philosophical tradition' (p. 6).

28.   Jean-Joseph Goux, *Symbolic Economies: After Marx and Freud*, trans. Jennifer Curtis Gage (Ithaca: Cornell University Press, 1990).

29.   Benjamin, *Passagenwerk*, p. 494, cited in Buck-Morss, *Dialectics*, p. 254.

30.   Victor Burgin, 'The City in Pieces', *New Formations* 20 (Summer 1993), 33.

31.   Benjamin, *Reflections*, p. 182.

32.   See Peter Collier, 'Surrealist City Narrative: Breton and Aragon' in *Unreal City: Urban Experience in Modern European Literature and Art*, ed. Edward Timms and David Kelley (Manchester: Manchester University Press, 1985), pp. 214–29.

33.   Louis Aragon, *Paris Peasant*, trans. Simon Watson Taylor (London: Jonathan Cape, 1971), pp. 131–2.

34.   Aragon, *Paris Peasant*, p. 130.

35.   See Haim N. Finkelstein, *Surrealism and the Crisis of the Object* (Ann Arbor: UMI Research Press, 1979).

36.   See James Clifford, 'On Ethnographic Surrealism', *Comparative Studies in Society and History* 23 (October 1981), 542.

37.   Pietz, 'Fetish I', p. 85.

38.   Cited by Gilloch, *Myth and Metropolis*, p. 109.

39.   Benjamin, *Reflections*, pp. 333–6.

40.   Benjamin, 'The Work of Art in the Age of Mechanical Reproduction', in *Illuminations*, pp. 211–14 and 'A Small History of Photography' in *One-Way Street*, pp. 240–57. On the Benjaminian notion of mimesis, see Michael Taussig's claim in his *Mimesis and Alterity: a Particular History of the Senses* (New York: Routledge, 1993), p. 29, that 'precisely in the commodity, more specifically in the fetish of the commodity, Benjamin sees the surreal and revolutionary possibilities provided by the culture of capitalism for its own undoing, its own transcendence'.

41.   Benjamin, *Passagenwerk*, pp. 46–7 (1935 exposé, cited in Buck-Morss, *Dialectics*, p. 114).

42.   Letter, Adorno to Benjamin, in Benjamin, *Passagenwerk*, p. 1128, cited in Buck-Morss, *Dialectics*, pp. 121–2. Adorno also criticizes Benjamin's 'concrete' method of presentation in the essay 'The Paris of the Second Empire', for what he sees as a lack of dialectical mediation between Baudelaire's poetry and the historical treatment of the urban environment.

43. Gilloch, *Myth and Metropolis*, pp. 147–8.

44. Cited by Sydney Bolt, *A Preface to James Joyce* (Harlow: Longman, 1981), pp. 109–46.

45. Richard Ellmann, *James Joyce* (London: Oxford University Press, 1961), p. 311.

46. Declan Kiberd, 'Notes' to James Joyce, *Ulysses*, Annotated Students' Edition (Harmondsworth: Penguin, 1992), pp. 1123–4. All subsequent page references in the text refer to this edition.

47. An ironic contrast to the urban dystopia of Nighttown is furnished by the slides of an idealized rural scene ('the lake of Kinnereth with blurred cattle cropping in silver haze'), projected as (fake) evidence (of Bloom's imagined homestead in Asia Minor, Agendath Netaim) in Bloom's trial (p. 590).

48. See Kevin Kearns, *Dublin Tenement Life: an Oral History* (Dublin: Gill and Macmillan, 1994).

49. On the links between disease imagery and the theme of imperial usurpation of authority in *Ulysses*, see also Christina Britzolakis, 'Speaking Daggers: T. S. Eliot, James Joyce and *Hamlet*' in *New Essays on Hamlet*, ed. Mark Thornton Burnett and John Manning (London: AMS Press, 1995), pp. 227–47.

50. Benjamin, *Charles Baudelaire*, p. 105.

51. See Buck-Morss, *Dialectics*, pp. 66–8.

52. See Anson Rabinobach, 'Between Enlightenment and Apocalypse: Benjamin, Bloch and Modern German Jewish Messianism', *New German Critique* 34 (Winter 1985), 78–124.

53. Cohen, *Profane Illumination*, pp. 2, 12.

4

Spectre and Impurity: History and the Transcendental in Derrida and Adorno

Nigel Mapp

Erkenntnis, die den Inhalt will, will die Utopie.

Theodor Adorno[1]

These remarks are, I suppose, metacritical in a sense. They wish to oppose the dominating falsities and complicities of postmodernist and historicist criticisms and theories. But that engagement will remain pretty much implicit, emerging indirectly through a rather abstract rehearsal of the political and philosophical questions concerning, demanding, and outstripping *abstraction* itself, questions no thinking of difference can bypass without falling into something worse. I will be taking to heart Walter Benjamin's observation that a truly materialist thought can be found only the far side of 'the frozen waste of abstraction'.[2] To name problematical names, this piece is in fact the propaedeutic to another confrontation of dialectics with deconstruction. These are the bodies of writing which promise, in various and countervailing ways, a thinking of non-identity or difference that does not relapse into dogmatic materialism or particularism – idealism's bad inversions, the unthematized abstractions of so much other theory. Now, while this is already to state a convergence of key interests, some kind of jejune synthesis of the writers who are my principal concern – Theodor Adorno and Jacques Derrida – is not being proposed here. Rather, any thinking of difference *as* difference circles round the problems often most acutely revealed in this encounter. And neither of these authorships *simply* falls prey to the radicalizations of the other; comparing them clarifies the force and limitations of both.[3]

This weighing of the negative-dialectical and deconstructionist negotiations of difference above all demands an examination of their respective re-plottings of the transcendental-empirical opposition. This is the knot where Derrida and Adorno bind resistingly together. The problems that according to their critics bedevil each can, it is often said, be traced back to insufficient, incoherent attempts to think through this opposition and its attendant questions.[4] The crucial philosophical armature of each thinker can be explored under this rubric. Both Adorno and Derrida recognize the need to go *through* transcendental questioning to arrive at a thinking which will truly do justice both to its own conditionedness and to its object. For neither philosopher can there be some straightforward disposal of the concept. There is an exigency of abstraction; but this necessity is exposited, and its supersession mooted, in significantly differing ways. And it is in relation to Hegel, and his dealings with Kantian critique, that Adorno's and Derrida's writings most revealingly organize their animadversions to the transcendental-empirical *topos*.

How transcendental questions impact on efforts to think the singular or the other – that which eludes subsumptive conceptual determination – can be illuminated through an argument Derrida ranges against various historicisms and empiricisms, and which can be quickly formalized.[5] To install history, the particular, sense-certainty or whatever ostensibly finite and pre-conceptual component into the position of disruptive condition is precisely to exempt those categories from their own finitizing explanation – they become abstract, universal, unknowable: a conceptual theology of the finite. This kind of sham finitude Derrida dubs 'transcendental contraband [*contre-bande*]'.[6] Neither deconstruction nor dialectics wishes to offer any solace to such unthematized transcendentalism. Derrida shows the collusions, contradictions, and disabling conditions of *any* pure transcendental element, avowed or not; his readings thus disqualify the discarding of transcendental questioning into the brute finitude or particularity that just explains it away, and explanation with it. Those categories – mired in the philosophy they would escape – depend on the discredited purity of the transcendental. Trumpeting finitude and particularity without addressing the passage through the concept which conditions such elements makes the wished-for escape from transcendental thinking all the harder; it ends in a mystified, precisely too theoretical, philosophizing. Such a critique of crypto-idealism (and of more *critical* transcendental thinking) can of course also be read in different terms in Hegel's *Phenomenology of Spirit*, as consciousness moves through its misrecognitions of subject and object to self-consciousness (and on to the sociality of *Geist* and its institutions).[7]

Hegel, Adorno and Derrida concur also, however, on the necessity and desirability of displacing transcendental thought. If, as suggested, abstracting the object from the subject is to collapse them together, to hypostasize both according to the dictates of a subjective reason blind to its determinations, then such a dogmatic operation will be found at the heart of Kant's critical philosophy as well. While Kant isolates and purifies his transcendental conditions, and justifies their critically delimited application to all experience, dialectical thought and deconstruction proceed to characterize the dogmatism that persists, despite his properly non-dogmatic intentions, in both Kant's epistemological analyses and the prohibitions on transcendent metaphysics that they demand.[8] Moreover, despite differences, both Derrida and Adorno disclose the problems in eradicating that dogmatism and the limit it draws (or describes) – problems they both chastise Hegel for liquidating. Anyway, developing the connection of dialectics and deconstruction at first involves a retrieval and analysis of metacritique in this stricter sense: the dialectical radicalization of Kant. Out of the factitious and contradictory detachment, for epistemological purposes, of thinking from what it thinks, concept from intuition, dialectics can expound the compelling force *and* the incoherency of all Kant's radical separations – of knowing and thinking, mechanism and freedom, finite and infinite. More specifically, Kant's critical arguments and criteria are to be enlisted against the categorially inert experience he believes they entail, the false invariance which grounds the critical prohibition on ever experiencing what can now be thought only as transcendent to knowing. This re-mobilization, then, is not a relapse into pre-critical metaphysics (cf. ND, 397–400/405–8).

4.1

Kant's is a critique of metaphysical dogmatism in two solidary forms – associated for him historically with the rationalism of Leibniz and

Wolff and with Hume's empiricism.[9] Crudely put, rationalist dogmatism deduces the real from the ideal structures of consciousness without confronting their possible divergence from that reality.[10] It thus remains in principle prey to the other dogmatism – sceptical empiricism – which, while indicating the problem with rationalism, can find no answer to its own atomization of objective knowledge because it posits the radical divergence of thought and being as an ineliminable possibility.[11] Any cognition that would overcome this possibility must be derived from the very experience whose objectivity is in question. So we land in a quandary as to how knowledge can be possible at all, despite the apparently sense-making possibilities of experience.[12] Both rationalism and sceptical empiricism dogmatically determine the relation of subject and object by reducing knowledge to an unreflected immanence of the subject, one positively, the other negatively.[13] Thus the aporetic terminus of epistemology: the apparently insuperable problem of getting outside the subject–object relationship in order to judge its adequacy.

Kant's answer is to accept that the ground for the objectivity of experience cannot be sought in experience alone or immediately in concepts. His critique of knowledge secures objective cognition at the price of its restriction to the phenomenal realm of possible experience – to the way objects must *appear* in experience. He attempts to detail the transcendental subjective conditions that structure *any* possible experience; it is therefore only within experience that the objectivity of the categories, and the synthetic knowledge built from them, necessarily holds. No knowledge of transcendent objects can be squeezed from pure concepts. Kant thus denies access to the absolute, *knowledge* of things in themselves or of supra-experiential metaphysical entities such as God or an immortal soul (though of course he builds a whole 'rational' faith in the space beyond experience which he is required to *think* by his critical detention of cognition within appearances).[14] So Kant expounds a metaphysics of experience which rescues science from scepticism, but decides in the negative the metaphysical questions in which epistemology lands us. Only in experience do the pure concepts and principles of understanding have objective validity (cf. ND, 374–5/381–2). Beyond appearances the categories cannot help us.[15]

Kant's attempts to show how synthetic knowledge is *a priori* possible, as well as his critical immuring of that knowledge in the finite world of phenomena, rely crucially on his theory of pure intuition.[16] All objective *knowledge* requires both intuition and concept, matter and form, the components of experience (thus the famous dictum: 'Thoughts without content are empty, intuitions without concepts are blind').[17] The founding of synthetic *a priori* cognition limits it to what is presentable in intuition, required to fill out the categories for any experience and cognition of objects to be possible. The ban on transcendent knowledge rests on the intuitive conditions of an inherently cognitive experience. So for Kant's critique to yield truly *synthetic* knowledge, its matter – which constrains thought and prevents its toppling into deductive metaphysics – must be free of the determinations of concepts whose validity it is to guarantee. Yet to deliver *a priori* synthesis, the matter of intuition must necessarily be preformed. Any experience that would be intelligible as such to ourselves must be structured according to the subjective *forms* of space and time. So Kant makes of intuition both a formal principle constraining the objects given in it and an 'immediate relation' constraining concepts.[18] To avoid its deduction from concepts or abstraction from experience, intuition has both to be already mediated appearance and to furnish direct apprehension of experience's contents.[19] This complexity interferes with Kant's attempt to ground in pure intuition the objective, synthetic validity, rather than the subjective indispensability, of the categories.[20] In this argument, all objects in intuition, to be intuited at all, must already conform to the categories they delimit if the latter are to be more than subjective processings of some unknowable given; categorial organization must be found *within* intuition.[21] But then it seems that the whole critical analysis of experience into intuition and concept, matter and form, receptivity and spontaneity, is undermined, along with the synthetic results at which Kant is aiming.[22] Such circular movements in the critical philosophy inspire Hegel, who will read a speculative unity of concept and intuition into Kant's transcendental imagination; it cannot be interpreted, he argues, as just glueing together radically heterogeneous elements.[23] All Kant's operative dualisms supervene later, slicing up this prior unity. This intrusion of concepts into intuition, which is also the self-divestiture of their purity and invariance, changes our conceptions of both; understanding is not the exclusive faculty of conceptual synthesis, which already organizes what is supposedly merely given to thinking. Similarly, givenness is not just liquidated.[24]

Hegel reads Kant's dictum concerning concept–intuition co-operation speculatively; it testifies to the *experience* of intuition and concept's difference, but they cannot for that reason be radically separated.[25] If Kant shows how scepticism ignores the subjective conditions of objective knowledge, Hegel discovers how that demonstration repeats the sceptics' dogmatic fallacy: its own placing of being opposite thought occurs *within* consciousness.[26] So dialectics revisits experience – re-emphasizing its necessity for any cognition of objects – and rethinks its allegedly disjunct components. The separation of concept and intuition in Kant is questioned by insisting on the experiential mediation of all knowledge, including transcendental knowledge. The 'pure' conditions of possibility of experience, intuitive and conceptual, find in that experience their own conditions of possibility. So epistemology has no supra-experiential critical objects in which to ground its purity. Kant's wish to inspect the instrument of knowledge before using it is utterly contradictory since such inspection is already embroiled in knowing: 'to seek to know before we know is as absurd as the wise resolution of Scholasticus, not to venture into the water until he had learned to swim'.[27] The transcendental forms' application to all possible experience and their simultaneous restriction to (and of) such experience rests on this contradiction. Kant's understanding can know neither itself nor its objects.[28] This is a criticism of the epistemological subject itself, its dogmatic opposition to its objects whose aporetic waste-product is the merely intelligible realm over which Kant has always already cognitively legislated. Experience and its conditions mediate each other and are *interdependent*; their relations become thematic for Hegel. The strict division of form and content is rendered a dialectical one of mutable mediation. The possibility emerges of a different *future* experience, a possibility Kant foreclosed in his factitious separation of the subject's necessary, universal spontaneity from the contingent, inert matter of intuition. Experience is historicized.

Hegel is not arbitrarily claiming knowledge of transcendent objects. He prosecutes fully Kant's argument that pure concepts are 'not merely subjective impositions, but determine the nature of objectivity itself in ways that, progressively articulated, eliminate the possibility of skeptical or realist objections'.[29] This will overcome the flat contradiction Hegel diagnoses in limiting genuine knowledge to phenomena.[30] In marking the limit, consciousness is already beyond it, necessitating a re-cognition of both.[31] In the

Science of Logic, the scission of concept and intuition is seen to imply, through the drawing of the limit 'that acknowledges and denies an actuality beyond our apprehension', the 'moral' standpoint, fixed outside experience as the infinite, unrealizable 'ought' (*Sollen*).[32] The infinite thought that contradictorily chains itself to the actual as a mere 'ought' undoes knowledge of both, though it betrays the contradictions of an experience that is *de facto* enslaved.[33] Kant makes human finitude absolute and evacuates of any content and authority the universal reason and the freedom he nevertheless must think. This unconditioned knowledge of essential finitude, its universal changelessness, is itself antinomical, then. And the impossibly absolutist ban on metaphysics is exposed in the contingency of the categories' application to intuition. Kant sees the way the categories can breed contradictions, but his 'tenderness' towards the world allows him to acknowledge them only in thought.[34] Similarly, where Kant glimpses the speculative idea at work, as in his notion of aesthetic judgement, it is trimmed to merely regulative status.[35] All thought and all objects, however, contain contradictions – which are in fact productive. So ordinary and scientific knowledge must be criticized, not just unreflectively invoked. Hegel credits Kant with the insight into the finitude of the categories, their inability to grasp the absolute, but this is his cue to demolish their immutability and essentiality. This finitude is inherent in the concepts themselves, not merely a consequence of their subjective standing, of our having to think them.[36] Knowledge's incarceration in phenomena is not its final term. It needs dialectically to mobilize the concepts by attending to their interrelations and conditioning in experience.

Hegel wants, then, to demonstrate the unsustainability of the organizing dualisms in Kant's thought. Kant's limiting of reason is defined by consciousness itself, a phenomenology of which will expound its contradictions. Infinite and finite are thought together, willy-nilly, which is not the same as the absolute being immediately re-imposable, 'a shot from a pistol' (that is the truth of the antinomies).[37] The object split from consciousness is contradictory, already an in-itself *for* consciousness. The separations of empirical and transcendental, finite and infinite, morality and legality, are part of the experience of consciousness which can be exposited and known, and changed when its determinations change.[38] Kant's 'abstract universality or formal identity' is indeed our finite thinking, but it need not be thought's 'ultimate and invincible mode'.[39]

So the objectivity of consciousness cannot be sought in the anti-nomical immediacy of its inner contents. It is in relation to another self-consciousness that experience can determine itself – and in the social forms of those relations.[40] The experience mediating the conditions of possibility for subjective knowledge is in fact social rather than individual in nature. For Hegel, what is called spirit (*Geist*) is exactly the communal and collective form of that imma-nent relationship-in-tension between an experience with its explicit thoughts and values, and its implied and social norms. This requires a concrete historical account of structures of mutual recog-nition and self-determination. The problems of consciousness lead to the problems of *Geist* which are only accounted for by a phenom-enology of its collective self-transformations. The tensions in the former are to be explained only at that level and according to the very criteria of the positions that are being superseded, or gone behind. The dialectic overcomes the transcendental–empirical distinction by developing it, and showing its determination in social and historical experience.

Gillian Rose argues that Hegel early and late shows the determi-nation of Kant's (and Fichte's) abstractive thought in Roman law's theories of subjectivity and the bourgeois private property relations instantiating them.[41] Kant's antinomical thought is re-cognized in a speculative account of the experience of contradiction between the universal, abstract rights of persons and real unfreedom. Kant thus presupposes and fixes real inequality; his universalizations 'smuggle in' specific social institutions.[42] This exposition develops out of insight into the 'relative identity' hidden within Kant's founding dichotomy of intuition and concept – the domination of one element over the other.[43] Any rigid opposition of infinite and finite, freedom and necessity, means that they can relate only as domination, as mysticism or calculative positivism.[44] Kant's practi-cal reason is a domination of intuition by the concept, the abstract *Sollen*. Both art and religion recognize and misapprehend this expe-rience of loss by raising intuition over the concept, and determining the transcendent realm in the image of social relationships, the finite. Hegel does not lay down a new concept, but describes the misrecognitions involved in such relative identities. These are the contradictions between consciousness's definitions of social institu-tions and its experiences of them. Concept and intuition are to become equal in the mutual recognitions of differences within absolute ethical life (*Sittlichkeit*), which re-substantializes the subjective morality Kant reinforced. So Kant's transcendent realm is exposited as our historical experience of severance from an unknowable freedom.[45] But unfreedom has real determinations that cannot be legislated in perpetuity. An unknowable God is an unknowable world and humanity, and obliterates freedom by rendering it up to the finite it sought to escape.[46] Thus, for Rose, Hegel's speculative reworking of Kant's dictum concerning concept–intuition interaction: it 'represents a real lack of identity'.[47]

Substantial identity re-cognizes their opposition as the negativity of an infinite that includes the finite.[48] The speculative Good Friday is to replace the historical one, and realize God in man by re-cognizing the lack of identity of subject and substance – in which subject does not know itself in the substance it experiences as its sheer determination.[49] In the negativity of the 'absolute standpoint' its finite determinations are known as such, rather than blindly submitted to or dominated.[50] Hegel thus re-cognizes the intuition's unliquidability in the concept, and urges a change in ethical life, not merely in the concepts determined by it.[51]

Dialectical metacritique, which leads beyond any foundationalism or *prima philosophia*, must not be confused, then, with an empiricist, naturalistic, or crudely materialist reduction of Kant. His critique of such dogmatisms cannot just be ignored. To offer social or natural realities as the inert ground of a (thus purely separable) consciousness is to hypostasize and de-historicize both, and it does so as ineluctably as Kant separated out, froze, and universalized his own cognate formalism. The non-identity of intuition and concept is only cognizable according to the speculative re-cognition, in the identity of the concept, of the *experience* of their difference, of the failure of all attempts definitively to separate them. But does Hegel fully acknowledge this experience?

4.2

For Adorno, also, the categorially changeless experience frozen in Kant's universal subject is a totalizing abstraction from our historical experience, where its conditions of emergence obtain.[52] The experience of lack of freedom is our own; Kantian subsumptive conceptuality is the apotheosis of universal exchange-relations (ND, 379–80/389). The social world does confront us as alien, unchangeable. This is the truth hidden in Kant. His untruth is in making experience invariant, in re-legislating this experience universally and for all time. Kant's 'thing in itself', however, keeps the promise alive of the use-value of the commodity, a sense of the objective needs of a realized humanity; but it also sediments an *ineliminable non-identity* which will be the crux in Adorno's retrieval of a Kantian element against Hegel, despite all he owes the latter.[53] He does not agree that Hegel's speculative identifications do full justice to the experience of negativity. Adorno believes that it is in expanding and outstripping the critical questions of Kant that Hegel's greatest merits and his ultimate shortcomings lie.

Adorno echoes – and explicitly endorses – Hegel's critique of Kant. Hegel achieves the self-reflection of epistemology, undoing it by binding it to the content it rejected as contingent. He discovered consciousness intruding into what it delimits by the very act of filleting experience of its static forms (HTS, 65–6). Similarly, this mediacy is mediated by the immediate, and Hegel pursues the 'self-divestiture' of immediate consciousness, not the internalization of all exteriority (HTS, 50). The exertions of the absolute subject are what do justice to this objectivity, an understanding of objects from the 'inside out' (HTS, 6, 68). Hegel can show real difference in the negative mediation of idea and what is true by appealing to the experience of consciousness (HTS, 32, 53–4). Dialectics works against idealism and its misidentifications by 'overextending' the idealist claim (HTS, 37, 68–9). Identity thus allows the non-identical it depends upon to be discovered. It reveals what cannot be reduced to the subject precisely by not relegating it to unknowability (HTS, 39). The concept must develop according to the demands of its object, as 'the ever-present consciousness of both the identity of and inevitable difference between the concept and what it is supposed to express' (HTS, 71). Adorno extrapolates these elements in Hegel in order to disqualify the Hegelian totalization of thought and being in the concept; concepts are concepts-of, and they emerge from, and inexpungibly refer to, the negativity of experience (cf. HTS, 147). Thus one stated aim in the opening pages of *Negative Dialectics*: 'To use the strength of the subject to break through the fallacy of consti-tutive subjectivity' (ND, 10/xx). The non-identical that scuttles the purity and primacy of the concept is to be revealed only in the nega-tive mediacy of concepts. Adorno wants to show that dialectics implies the 'preponderance' of the object, not an absolute subject; an immediacy mediating mediation which cannot intelligibly be absorbed, without remainder, into it (ND, 184ff./183ff.).

In his metacritique of Kant, Adorno detects a disabling contradiction in the description of pure intuitions as pure *forms* of intuition: to keep the apriorism, Kant wants forms; to ensure the synthesis, he needs intuitions.[54] A cognate incoherency is pointed up in the very idea of synthetic *a priori* judgement (HTS, 66). The purity of neither concept nor intuition can be established for the kind of analysis that Kant essays.[55] Epistemology cannot be purged of an ontological component, or cleanly disengage its deductions of validity from the genesis of the ideas in the social experience. So Kant runs aground on the brute inexplicable fact that there just *are* these categories, despite his attempt to deduce their validity, because he cannot confront the fact that he has assumed the very experience in question. 'What in the Kantian deduction of the categories remains ultimately "given" and, by Kant's own admission, accidental – that reason can have these and no other basic concepts at its disposal – is attributed to what the categories, according to Kant, have yet to establish' (ND, 173/171).[56] Thus an historical experience gets stencilled with a bogus absoluteness. The forms of experience cannot uncontradictorily be stipulated for all future experience, and so the block on transcendence is not indestructibly absolute, but *historical*: 'If the material element lies in the forms themselves, the block is shown to have been made by the very subject it inhibits. The subject is both exalted and debased if the line is drawn inside it, in its transcendental logical organization' (ND, 379/386).

It is this enslaved absoluteness that Hegel will release from contradiction and prosecute, ultimately, into the false mythology of the concept vetoed by Kant (ND, 381/389). If Kant's limit was fashioned only by transgressing it, Hegel's transgression stays within the immanence defined by Kant. Hegel fabricates a logical metaphysics: 'it is precisely by its denial of objectively valid cognition of the absolute that the critique of reason makes an absolute judgment. This is what idealism stressed. Still, its consistency bends its motif into its opposite and into untruth. [...] A thought that is purely consistent will irresistibly turn into an absolute for itself' (ND, 375/382). Hegel does not escape Kant's immanent course of the concept, but extends it *over* Kant's block, squeezing true transcendence out of the picture (ND, 379/386). Adorno's materialism will demand a genuinely metaphysical moment to outstrip this logicized context of immanence, which enthrones the concept only by re-enslaving the subjects from whom it abstracts.

Hegel's transcendence is immanent to the indigent experience it wants to slough off (ND, 385/393). Ultimately, it airbrushes out this experience's factual contingency and its own metalogical reference. The difficulties of crossing Kant's limit necessitate a fuller acknowledgement, or speculative re-cognition, of the historical experience sedimented in it.

Adorno detects a contradiction, from which its conditions can be deciphered, in the speculative thinking which attempts to effect logical coherency at the level of the concept in this way. This contradiction, when recognized from the object's side as much as the subject's, points in the dialectic of experience beyond absolute idealism to the antagonistic totality or irrationality of society. Kant returns to haunt Hegel because reality has not achieved a rational form. The preconceived identity of identity and non-identity in the form of the immanent concept is to be criticized as a false totalization of dialectical negativity that itself has social determinations: 'the idea of a positivity that can master everything that opposes it through the superior power of a comprehending spirit is the mirror image of the experience of the superior coercive force inherent in everything that exists by virtue of its consolidation under domination' (HTS, 87). Hegel ends in a 'deification of the quintessence of what is', passing domination off as freedom (HTS, 26, 81). Like Kant, Hegel speaks the truth of the social experience of the total system, an absolutized principle of domination; but the whole is *untrue* (HTS, 86–7).[57] If the whole is dialectical contradiction, it is not to be totalized in absolute spirit: 'The dialectic could be consistent only in sacrificing consistency by following its own logic to the end' (HTS, 148);[58] whereas the consistent unfolding of the thesis of absolute identity condemns dialectics to paving over real contradictions. Hegel cannot clamber out of the world as it is, for identity is only absolute as already realized in misrecognition. This inconsistent consistency lands Hegel in untruth; but Adorno has to blame the world as much as Hegel for that (HTS, 30–1).

Unliquidable non-identity is revealed in spirit's necessary metalogical connection with the subject, and thus with human beings. Hegel wants that reference 'melted down' into identity (HTS, 14–17). But the grim reality of social labour – which lay congealed in Kant's separation of pure activity from inert material (ND, 379–80/387) – is now readable in Hegel's identification of all material, all contents, with the supernal concept (HTS, 18). The totality of the in- and for-itself expresses the truth of a labour always for something else, exchangeable with other things, of a production that forgets its human ends (HTS, 19). Hegel's truth is that social labour is a closed system, scrubbing out what lies beyond its extorted universality (HTS, 26, 68). The absoluteness of spirit is a totality of disunity. Society is the falsely coadunated concept, abstract but real, mediating the isolated moments of empirical reality whose negativity it would eliminate (cf. HTS, 20). Spirit underwrites the ascendancy of abstract equivalences of exchange which hide and perpetuate real inequalities. If all transcendental syntheses are derived from labour, from which they cannot be intelligibly separated, idealism elevates it into universality, invariant, eternal and right (HTS, 21–3). Yet this reality is only realized through individuals. And labour is always labour-upon, constellated with a mediating non-identical natural moment, though spirit wants to expunge that fact. This non-identity punctures the metaphysical super-principle that endorsed labour's absolutization. Hegel's philosophy presses the non-identity of the totality into an absolute; and by crumbling into absolute negativity, it at last derisively fulfils its pledge to coincide with its 'ensnared subject matter' (HTS, 32). Hegel's metaphysics of the reconciled whole depends on a totalized antagonistic society, and its dialectic cannot be stopped just to shore up the logical integrity of philosophy (HTS, 78–80). Thus Adorno deciphers from Hegel society's totalization by the contradictions of domination.

If thought requires identification, identification itself relies upon a moment of irreducible difference or non-identity (HTS, 40). And while the contradiction of the ban on metaphysics cannot but be recapitulated in any effort to iron it out by sheer intellection, pondering the possible *reconciliation* of the concept with its (ineliminably different) objects already thinks beyond these contradictions of concept and intuition, immanence and transcendence. Reason's hopes of realizing itself rest on its acknowledging itself as the 'reason of existence itself', as mediated by things whose preponderant non-identity makes reason the 'pivot point' for dislodging the 'burden of mere existence' (HTS, 46–7). Reason understands the existing as more than merely existing and so acquires the standpoint of emancipation (HTS, 44–5). Adorno's demand, unlike Hegel's, is to think metaphysically for the sake of a materialism, the only way to acknowledge the historical force of the ban on metaphysics. Adorno's materialism relies upon a *metaphysics* of this double-bind.

Kant's discontinuities, then, also encrypt a non-identity that conditions Hegel's understanding of identity; the social experience they witness and unfortunately ratify still prevails (HTS, 11). The need to legislate what is, supposedly, a natural limitation of the (natural) propensity of reason to burst through its limits, testifies to a metaphysical experience, not just a metaphysical thinking.[59] So Kant's postulate of immortality indexes the intolerability of extant things: 'The secret of his philosophy is the unthinkability of despair' (ND, 378/385). Adorno records the untruth, stipulated by social labour, of the separation of body and soul, and recognizes the metaphysical moment as an ineliminable hope of redemption of human suffering – 'what hope clings to, as in Mignon's song, is the transfigured body' (ND, 393/400) – rather than its obliteration by a production untethered to human ends. While transcendence only feeds on the experiences we have in immanence, it is not to be crushed by it (ND, 390–2/398–400). The non-identical emerges only in the constelled negative mediation of objects and concepts. It cannot be quarried out and made a new positive.

Kant's prohibitions on the use of transcendental principles to yield knowledge of transcendent objects witness the conditioned-ness – and hence conditionality – of consciousness and what is not identical with it:

> To be spirit at all, spirit must know that it does not exhaust itself by what it touches upon, by the finitude it is like. Thus spirit thinks what would be beyond it. Such metaphysical experience [*Erfahrung*] inspires Kant's philosophy, once that philosophy is drawn out of the armour of its method. The question whether metaphysics is still possible at all must reflect the negation of the finite demanded by finitude. Its riddle-image animates the word 'intelligible'. The conception of that word is not wholly unmotivated, thanks to that moment of independence which the mind forfeited in its absolutization, and which – as itself not identical with entities – it obtains as soon as non-identity is insisted upon, as soon as all there is does not evaporate into spirit. Spirit, with all its mediations, shares in existence, which substitutes for its alleged transcendental purity. In its moment of transcendent objectivity, if it is not split off and ontologized, metaphysics' possibility has its unobtrusive site. (ND, 385/392-3)[60]

These are the difficult thoughts of Adorno's materialism. He elaborates a metaphysical moment as a condition of thinking which cannot be cleansed from thought *as* thought.[61] Thinking has to experience its non-identity with its objects. The transcendence of thought is its freedom to think the conditions it suffers and propagates, whereas the absolutization of its freedom will destroy it. Adorno states that freedom requires its own non-identical, heteronomous moment (ND, 262/265, for example). Freedom depends on acknowledging our mediation by things, including the moment of non-identical naturality that undoes the totalizing abstractions of society and the unifying concept. Impurity is the condition of *all* intelligibility, and dialectics comes into its own as the thought of implicatedness whose only resource is its experience of the negativity of its necessarily identifying behaviour. Non-identity is not a sheer given, any more than spirit produces it. Thus real antagonisms are expressed; their wished-for logical elimination issues only in further aporias. Such aporias allow *natural*-historical experience to be traced out. Adorno's speculative moment is the proleptic thought of a possible real reconciliation in non-identity. Concerning speculation, Adorno writes:

> what will not have its law prescribed for it by given facts transcends them even in the closest contact with the objects, and in the refusal of a sacrosanct transcendence. That wherein thought is beyond that to which it binds itself [*sich binden*] in resistance, is its freedom. Freedom follows the subject's urge to expression. The need to let suffering speak is the condition of all truth. For suffering is objectivity that weighs down the subject; what it experiences as its most subjective concern, its expression, is objectively mediated. (ND, 29/17–18; translation modified)

Speculation holds itself to the painful experience of difference it transcends in wishing things were different (cf. ND, 399/407). It in no way ratifies the world by extruding a theodicy from it, but preserves the promise of a different future out of the experience of 'resistant' binding to the world. This reconciliation with non-identity as such cannot yet be experienced, but the need for it is ineliminable from thought, if there is to be thought. Reconciliation requires escape from contradiction itself, which is why negative dialectics is also 'the ontology of the wrong state of things' (ND, 22/11). Thought cannot be purged of its conditioning by memory and love, and by hope. Thus it transcends what exists without betrayal, by thinking the world's indigence, its conditionality.[62] This reason is restricted to experience, but experience outstrips cognition, as it never does in Kant and Hegel. Adorno's materialism depends on the irreducibility from thought of the possibility of an experience of transcendence. The aporia of the empirical–transcendental opposition is not liquidable into identity, which is just another transcendentality. The condition of thinking its displacement, and the overcoming of the social labour it canonizes, is the metaphysics that lives off it.

Adorno links such speculation with aesthetic illusion (*Schein*) (most fully in *Aesthetic Theory*).[63] Kant's transcendent world is illusion, but it is a *necessary* one, given by non-illusion; and aesthetics unwraps this promise of transcendence in art:

> What marks aesthetic comportment as irrational according to the criteria of dominant rationality is that art denounces the particular essence of a *ratio* that pursues means rather than ends. Art reminds us of the latter and of an objectivity freed from the categorial structure. This is the source of art's rationality, its character as knowledge. Aesthetic comportment is the capacity to perceive more in things than they are; it is the gaze under which the given is transformed into an image.[64]

A precise absorption of reality is the condition of this illusion or semblance, which can comprehend possibility from the point of view of its realization, as 'something reality is putting out feelers to' (HTS, 83–4). For Adorno, art's semblance of being an in-itself, more than a thing, which is given in its fetishization, has truth as a possibility of reconciled non-identity. It alludes to the experience of misidentification of persons and things in commodity exchange by illusorily exempting itself from it, and preserves the thought of their mediating non-identity. Art's semblance reflects the *light* of transcendence; its eye 'does not want the colours of the world to fade' and thereby it expresses a wish indelible from the resistance to the bleaching of the world by exchange. 'No light falls on men and things', Adorno says, 'without reflecting [*widerscheinen*] transcendence' (ND, 396–7/404–5).

4.3

Derrida's relationship with transcendental thinking, Kantian and other, is complex. If Adorno's metacritique of transcendental thinking and its speculative sublation eschews sociology, so too Derrida's contamination of the transcendental requires that the empirical be re-thought in turn.[65] His thinking is no longer dominated by that opposition, though deconstruction must think through it.[66] Kant's (re)productive imagination is the site of an inexpungible remembrance to Adorno.[67] For Derrida it is the locus of *différance*, a constitutive dislocation of the present – any intuition or concept – that makes its purity impossible.[68] Derrida even associates its processes with haunting.[69]

Derrida's thinking uncovers non-conceptual conditions of possibility *and* impossibility that Rodolphe Gasché has called 'infrastructures', but to which Derrida gives various nicknames – trace, supplement, re-mark, parergon, *différance*, and so on – drawn from the texts or philosophical corpora he is analysing, but whose functioning cannot be strictly limited to that context.[70] They are shown to be both the terms whose exclusion such a structure's purity and self-command depend upon, *and* the enabling condition for such a constitution – upon which they therefore inflict a certain rupture. The necessary possibility that a performative act might be fictive or infelicitous is a condition of any performative at all – for a celebrated example – and hence sullies the purity of any performative.[71] No context can finally anchor the purity *or* impurity of such an act, which depends on an iterability – repetition in different contexts – to achieve any effect of presence or ideality; but this force of transcendence is thus also constrained, and no present perception, experience or concept can escape the finitizing effects of context. Derrida's most encompassing rubric for what he is thus delimiting is indeed the *metaphysics of presence*. There is always, necessarily, the possibility of regrafting. Derrida's *quasi*transcendentals, the iterable terms whose transcendentality is weighed down by the necessity of contextual sediments, name strategically this necessary double possibility of attachment and detachment (G, 151–62).[72] 'Context', for instance, abyssally reflects the ungrounding of ground entailed by the aporia of context.

Derrida also poaches 'writing' to figure such necessary contextuality, the supplementary matrix where necessarily excluded terms constitute and hence de-constitute the meanings and conceptual articulations wrought out of them.[73] As the signifier of the phonic signifier, writing is doubly displaced from its origin in the signified, and thus its name is *reinscribed* to capture the sense that *all* signs are secondary because their signifieds – determined as meaning, experience, perception – are always already positioned as signifiers, always regraftable, recontextualizable.[74] Reflection here is unable in principle to totalize the resulting differential field. This deconstruction implies that there are no pure signifiers *or* signifieds, no simply secondary writing (that is, writing within earshot of a determined meaning or presence).[75] The logic of writing's subordination to speech is deconstructed precisely by retaining just those predicates of writing which secondarize it and generalizing them to cover everything that was an instance of presence opposed to writing – speech, thought, world. The new term ('arche-writing') no longer simply opposes speech, nor does it reduce everything to text.[76] Derrida identifies the dislocating force of an originary secondarity, a *repetition* constitutively supplementing the 'origin' of all 'effects' of presence, absence, originality and secondarity.[77] The reinscribed terms reflect the aporetic conditions of reflection, and detotalize themselves with it. All effects of presence have the *idiomatic* status of signatures, whose condition is their iterability and necessary forgeability – they require the contexts which recognize and determine them in the similarly delimited form of counter-signature.[78] Signature is always called for and promised again because of the undecidability of context. A pure event, a sheer idiom, is unintelligible; that which comes to presence requires the ideality that iterability simultaneously promises and corrupts.

Such repetition and the difference it entails haunt all presence, its condition of possibility and impossibility. And haunting is no accidental figure here: repetition beyond the signatory's death, and beyond the death of any addressee, is the impossible condition of ideality, of any presence, with which it cannot be reconciled.[79] Derrida: 'this absence is not a continuous modification of presence; it is a break in presence, "death", or the possibility of the "death" of the addressee, inscribed in the structure of the mark (it is at this point, I note the fact in passing, that the value or the effect of transcendentality is linked necessarily to the possibility of writing and of "death" analyzed in this way)'.[80] Iterability is the possibility of repetition beyond death, beyond a certain absolutizing of absence, and is the *condition of (im)possibility* of the transcendental effort to demote the death of the subject to contingency.[81] While iterability transcends death, it also therefore transcends life. All presence is haunted. Everything lives an afterlife, a *sur-vie*, by which Derrida wants to indicate a more differentiated field of impurity, not some flat homogeneity (SM, xx, 147, 186–8).

Derrida associates a thinking of affirmation with the aporia of context, which he wants to give a quasitranscendental status in regard to real strategies and decisions:

> I have on several occasions spoken of 'unconditional' affirmation or of 'unconditional' appeal. [...] Now, the very least that can be said of 'unconditionality' (a word that I use not by accident to recall the character of the categorical imperative in its Kantian form) is that it is independent of every determinate context, even of the determination of context in general. It announces itself as such only in the *opening* of context. Not that it is simply present (existent) elsewhere, outside of all context; rather, it intervenes in the determination of a context from its very inception, and from an injunction, a law, a responsibility that transcends this or that determination of a given context. Following this, what remains is to articulate this unconditionality with the determinate (Kant would say, hypothetical) conditions of this or that context; and this is the moment of strategies, of rhetorics, of ethics, and of politics. The structure thus described supposes both that there are only contexts, that nothing *exists* outside context, as I have often said, but also that the limit of the frame or the border of the context always entails a clause of non-closure. The outside penetrates and determines the inside. This is what I have analyzed so often, and so long, under the words 'supplement', 'parergon' [...] This unconditionality also defines the injunction that prescribes deconstruction.[82]

The contextual moments always have to be thought in their determination by the unconditional opening to otherness, but the radically exterior injunction 'announces itself', it signs itself in this opening. It is from the first a promise of its own repetition, owing to its imbrication in what it transcends; it 'opens a future in which one will again say "yes"'.[83] The affirmation is an opening to the future that dislocates the present. It finitizes itself *and* its future countersignatures since, as signature, it is already doubled up, a simulacrum.[84] All thought, by answering the affirmation with its own insufficient 'yes' – or 'no' – mourns for the loss, from the start, of the first time. Transcendental thinking is similarly afflicted by a mourning that only haunts it as *promise*.[85]

The aporia of context and the archi-affirmation that speaks in it cast all judgement into a domain of undecidability, while requiring that judgement be made. Indeed, an experience of its ultimate impossibility is judgement's motivating condition and the space of its possibility (SM, 169). Any law-giving obeys this aporetic law of the law, and must institute itself with unavoidable violence and risk.[86] Judgement's opening to the future – or the future's opening of judgement – to ratification, simulation or negation, is, for Derrida, its inherent democratization. It affirms, however indirectly, its finitude, promises to avow the violence of judgement, if not to minimize it. Such 'democracy to come' cannot ever arrive in the present – it is not even a regulative idea – because it is the event of disruption of presence the future works in all experience (SM, 64–5).[87] The reference to justice is ineliminable – or 'undeconstructible' – but it is not to be experienced as such at present or in a future present. 'What remains as irreducible to any deconstruction as the very possibility of deconstruction is perhaps a certain emancipatory promise' (SM, 59). A 'messianic' moment, without messianism, is announced in the transcendent 'structure of experience', in the aporia of time (SM, 167).

This nexus of issues seems to bring Derrida into the purview, or sights, of dialectics. Derrida's writings suggest a general affinity with Adorno's in their unearthing of an irreducible non-identity, the displacing of transcendentality and foundationalism, the reflections on an inextirpable (reinscribed) metaphoricity or simulation,[88] and the constitutive opening to a past and a future. But Derrida's ideas concerning originary affirmation – and the concatenated motifs of justice beyond legislation and the gift before exchange – allow the differences between deconstruction and dialectics to be profiled. (And it is here only a question of silhouetting.) Simply: should Derrida be criticized as Hegel criticized Kant, as the blind legislator of an unknowable law, a high-handed deposer of the concept?[89]

For his dialectical critics, Derrida provides too little analysis of the natural-historical antagonisms his aporetic thought feeds on.[90] It has been claimed that although Derrida wants to undermine any transcendental thinking by appealing to the necessity of context *and* its openness, with the latter move he in fact shuts himself up in an endless exploration of the (*de facto* transcendental) aporia of the concept 'context' itself.[91] Despite his disclaimers, in this irreducible historicizing of our experience (which history cannot think), what is lost to Derrida is any sociohistorical account, and he has accordingly been indicted of reproducing and fixing this history when he should be recognizing its changeable determinations. For example: Derrida stands accused, despite all his subtle reworkings of the empirical-transcendental opposition, of installing a justice aporetically opposed to law for all time, a justice utterly formal, too, which in fact re-legislates, blindly, the aporia of judgement for all future experience.[92] The plausibility of an affirmation prior to reflection and questioning is not so much at issue as its alleged transcendental role. Its priority is indestructible and invariant, and so Derrida empties his thinking of any *possibility* of thinking its determinations:

> even if [...] affirmation is in some sense conditional for undertaking certain or all activities, that we make this affirmation concrete only as a result of specific entanglements, that actual affirmations are empirical, defeasible and a *result*, deprives the idea of pre-originary affirmation of any force – or rather its meaning and force is so utterly dependent on what comes of actual affirmations or their opposite that the pre-originary disappears as an identifiable kind of relation. To believe otherwise would be to separate the event of affirmation from its effects, its meaning from its reception. And while believing in this radical separation may simplify our ethical lives, it also radically falsifies it. This, of course, is just the Hegelian challenge to the transcendental/empirical distinction.[93]

So if Derrida calls for strategies and politics – they are indeed unerasable for him – he has in principle to neuter them in advance, to cut down the scope of decision that he wishes to maximize. Derrida re-legislates Kant's primacy of practical reason. The conditions and effects of affirmation can only be thought beyond deconstruction, which can offer no guidance in itself for actual judgements and actions, and indeed lets their content slip out of view by permanent self-detention in a 'quasitranscendental' analysis of their conditions. Derrida on this view never in fact levers himself out of the transcendental position.[94]

A sense of these problems has motivated the various efforts to glue some kind of ethics or politics on top of Derrida's work, as a stimulus to hegemonization according to the lesser violence, or to exposit the opening to the other in Levinasian terms as an already *ethical* relation.[95] Whatever the merits of such endeavours, it is the claim to think the historicity of experience as well as the (non-absolute) institutions of the trace (in contexts) which calls for further analysis.[96] Perhaps Derrida reveals thinking's relations with what is not identical with it, and holds off on the kind of analyses demanded of him because they would betray the historicity of thinking – its constitutive experience of the aporia of time – and, like Adorno's Hegel, install a crypto-transcendentalism of their own that disavows this experience.

In *Glas*, Derrida explores under the name 'stricture' the singular eventhood of a quasitranscendental binding-unbinding which conditions transcendentality and its speculative intensification. Derrida argues that striction is not yet dialectical opposition, bound as it is to an anteriority that cannot be reduced to the 'not yet' of dialectics (G, 244a). All attempts to avoid transcendentality are constrained by this stricture, which re-positions them as the transcendental they hoped worsted. This helps clarify deconstruction's dealings with the desideratum of metaphysics, a point of non-substitutivity that remains unliquidable through what befalls it.[97] Stricture is the transcendental's quasitranscendental, its controlling excluded term.

One point where Derrida unfolds the account of the gift, which grants all dialectics, is in his reading of the sections on natural religion in Hegel's *Phenomenology* (G, 236aff.).[98] The key paragraphs are those concerning God as a *light* of sheer donation.[99] Derrida analyses this passage as an indirect means of interpreting '*le Sa*' (*savoir absolu*) and its sublation of religious *representation.* The shapeless light-essence (*Lichtwesen*) anticipates the figurelessness of the absolute.[100] This essential light is God's pure manifestation, and its blaze consumes everything, including itself. It leaves no mark or sign of passage, says Derrida (G, 238a). Subjectless 'pure being' destroys all structured form.[101] Derrida compares this to Heidegger's thinking of being prior to its determination in respect of beings (G, 242a).[102] So how does this in-itself dialectically entwine itself in the mediacy of the for-itself? Hegel says this 'reeling' life *must* determine itself by giving 'its vanishing "shapes" an enduring subsistence'.[103] Dialectics requires that the light-essence must, in order to be such a pure outlay, retain its loss, become its own *keeping* – its opposite. It must bind itself to be itself – and is therefore no longer pure expense and loss. The dialectic of history rolls itself out of this negativity:

> In order to be what it is, purity of play, of difference, of consuming destruction, the all-burning must pass into its contrary: guard itself, guard its own movement of loss, appear as what it is in its very disappearance. As soon as it appears, as soon as the fire shows itself, it remains, it keeps hold of itself, it loses itself as fire. Pure difference, different from (it)self, ceases to be what it is in order to remain what it is. That is the origin of history, the beginning of the going down, the setting of the sun, the passage to occidental subjectivity. Fire becomes for-(it)self and is lost. (G, 240a).

The all-consuming fire must burn itself, in a sacrifice or holocaust to the for-itself, so that the singular may take its subsistence from its substance (G, 241aff.). This sacrifice ensures its keeping as loss, *binds* it to itself, allowing it to coincide with itself. By burning burning, it begins to be what it is (G, 242a). Thus it goes out, in a sacrifice that 'belongs, as its negative, to the *logic* of the all-burning. If you want to burn all, you must also consume the blaze, avoid keeping [*garder*] it alive as a precious presence. You must therefore extinguish it, keep it in order to lose it (truly), or lose it to keep it (truly). Both processes are inseparable' (G, 241a). Undecidability, now: to think dialectically the gift of fire that precedes beings involves holding it so that it can be lost, but just that smuggles into being and the for-itself what simultaneously is argued to overflow it.

Derrida sees the gift having to (Hegel says: *muss*) exchange itself for philosophy, whose indebtedness dissolves the gift into its simulacrum. Stricture for Derrida is this binding-itself of pure gift, which thus binds itself to being and issues in exchange and reappropriation. It therefore grants the possibility of ontology and subjectivity, and exceeds them: 'Before, if one could count here with time, before everything, before every determinable being [*étant*], there is, there was, there will have been the irruptive event of the gift [*don*]. An event that no more has any relation with what is currently designated under this word' (G, 242a).[104] Stricture thinks, then, the quasitranscendental giving of effects of transcendentality in terms of an *unconsumable* outside of beings which immediately binds itself within them.

Derrida thinks a moment of transcendence that is embroiled with existence, not one falsified by being picked out and ontologized – what Adorno upbraids in Heidegger (ND, 116/110). What is indestructibly given is the indebted finitude of thought, and the relation between affirmation, or the gift that folds into its simulacrum, and what becomes of them thus unavoidably perdures. The light of transcendence illuminates people and things, but its negativity cannot be *simply* negated in the dialectics of subject and object, since it gives negation and exchange, too (cf. ND, 178/176). (Hegel and Heidegger think of the disclosive nature of light as life, the differentiated unity of the same that resists identity.)[105] This necessary quasitranscendental moment must be thought through the differentiations of the philosophical experiences that condition it, for sure. But such differentiation is betrayed if the historicity of the access to the historical is not addressed in terms of this aporia of the transcendental and empirical, origin and repetition, law and instance. In terms of the aporia of time.

Perhaps what should be stressed, with Adorno, is not the disruption of any attempt to excavate natural-historical conditions in terms of their dialectical negativity (in themselves and in their relation to consciousness), nor an opacity that can only ever be thought rather than known, but rather the implicitly avowed need for deconstruction to learn from empirical enquiry – even natural science – and to explore the *concrete* ways it has to jump into knowing, however finite, anyway.[106] The gift, which displaces concepts without abstractly eliminating their content, cannot be thought outside the mechanisms of social and intellectual exchange to which it is irreducible.

4.4

In a comment on the phantasmagorization of the commodity, Derrida begins by quoting Marx (SM, 157):

> If commodities could speak, they would say this: our use-value may interest men, but it does not belong to us as objects. What does belong to us as objects, however, is our value. Our own intercourse as commodities proves it. We relate to each other merely as exchange-values.[107]

This is the ghostliness Marx wants to run to ground. But Derrida goes on:

This rhetorical artifice is abyssal. Marx is going to claim right away that the economist naively reflects or reproduces this fictive or spectral speech of the commodity and lets himself be in some way ventriloquized by it: he speaks from the depths of the soul of commodities. But in saying 'if commodities could speak', Marx implies that they cannot speak. He makes them speak (like the economist he is accusing) but in order to make them say, paradoxically, that inasmuch as they are exchange-values, they speak, and that they speak or maintain a commerce among themselves only insofar as they speak. That to them, in any case, one can at least lend speech. To speak, to adopt or borrow speech, and to be exchange-value is here the same thing. It is use-values that do not speak and that, for this reason, are not concerned with and do not interest commodities – judging by what they seem to say. With this movement of a fiction of speech, but of speech that sells itself by saying, 'Me, the commodity, I am speaking', Marx wants to give a lesson to econ-omists who believe (but is he not doing the same thing?) that it suffices for a commodity to say 'Me, I am speaking' for it to be true and for it to have a soul, a profound soul, and one which is proper to it. We are touching here on that place where, between speaking and saying 'I am speaking', the difference of the simu-lacrum is no longer operative. (SM, 157–8).

Double bind: Marx's critique depends on the fiction it recognizes as such – anthropomorphism – because, in noting the fiction, appeal is made to the propriety of its speech. The originality of spectrality – 'autonomization and automaticization of ideality as finite-infinite processes of *différance*' (SM, 170) – is revealed *within* critical reflection. Similarly, the critique of commodity exchange will exceed critique by finding iteration already in its anchor-point: use-value (SM, 159–63). So Derrida does not totalize reflection, nor eliminate it. Such phantasmagorization does not signal the triumph of commodification, but the ineliminable promise of its being over-come. We are summoned to respect other differences, and fashion new concepts adequate to such a paradoxical retrieval of the commodity's fictive claim to speak for itself (SM, 162–3). Thus Derrida outlines what is at stake in making history talk.

Yet it must speak, in its borrowed body: 'If a work of art can become a commodity, and if this process seems fated to occur, it is also because the commodity began by putting to work, in one way or another, the principle of an art' (SM, 162). Art, as simulacrum, erects a semblance of autonomy by co-opting the predicates of personhood, and thus reveals the reification of persons in the intensification of its own fetish character. This fictive cognition, because it cannot be absolutized as fiction, is also the cognition of fiction. For both Adorno and Derrida such an impure thinking holds open a place for transcendence. We are also touching in Derrida, then, upon the place where the necessarily aporetic nature of (self-)reflection enters into contact with its expropriative history.[108]

Notes

1. 'Cognition, which wants content, wants a utopia.' Theodor W. Adorno, *Negative Dialektik*, in *Gesammelte Schriften* (Frankfurt: Suhrkamp, 1973), vol. 6, p. 66; *Negative Dialectics*, trans. E. B. Ashton (London: Routledge & Kegan Paul, 1973), p. 56; translation modified. (Hereafter ND in the text.)
2. Benjamin was commenting in 1937 on the final chapter of Adorno's *Zur Metakritik der Erkenntnistheorie*; see ND, 9/xix.
3. Both Derrida and Adorno are suspicious of the value of *radicality* itself: cf., for examples, ND, 158/155; Jacques Derrida, *Specters of Marx: the State of the Debt, the Work of Mourning, and the New International*, trans. Peggy Kamuf (New York and London: Routledge, 1994), pp. 88, 92, 184n. (Hereafter SM.)
4. Adorno never discussed Derrida, to my knowledge; Derrida hardly ever mentions Adorno. Criticism of Derrida normally fixes on his perceived Heideggereanism. Few Derrideans have discussed Adorno at any length. But see Rodolphe Gasché, 'Yes Absolutely', *Inventions of Difference: On Jacques Derrida* (Cambridge, MA and London: Harvard University Press, 1994), pp. 199–226; Christoph Menke, *Die Souveränität der Kunst: Ästhetische Erfahrung nach Adorno und Derrida* (Frankfurt: Suhrkamp, 1991); Michael Ryan, *Marxism and Deconstruction* (Baltimore: Johns Hopkins University Press, 1982), pp. 73–81; and on Heidegger, Alexander García Düttmann, *Das Gedächtnis des Denkens: Versuch über Adorno und Heidegger* (Frankfurt: Suhrkamp, 1991). Derrida's reflections on dialectics concern Hegel above all (see below). Some significant critics of Derrida attack Adorno too over his misprised debts to Hegel: Gillian Rose, 'From Speculative to Dialectical Thinking – Hegel and Adorno', in *Judaism and Modernity: Philosophical Essays* (Oxford: Blackwell, 1993), pp. 53–63; cf. Andrew Bowie, '"Non-Identity": the German Romantics, Schelling, and Adorno', in Tilottama Rajan and David L. Clark (eds), *Intersections: Nineteenth-Century Philosophy and Contemporary Theory* (Albany: State University of New York Press, 1995), pp. 243–60.

5. See Derrida, 'Cogito and the History of Madness', in *Writing and Difference*, trans. Alan Bass (London: Routledge & Kegan Paul, 1978), pp. 31–63.

6. Jacques Derrida, *Glas*, trans. John P. Leavey, Jr and Richard Rand (Lincoln and London: University of Nebraska Press, 1986), p. 244a (G hereafter).

7. G. W. F. Hegel, *Phenomenology of Spirit*, trans. A. V. Miller (Oxford: Oxford University Press, 1977). See, for example, the discussion of the German and French Enlightenments in §578, pp. 351–2.

8. Immanuel Kant, *Critique of Pure Reason*, trans. Norman Kemp Smith, 2nd edn (London: Macmillan, 1933); on dogmatism, see, for example, B xxxv–vii; Kant's criticisms of transcendent metaphysics are pursued in the Transcendental Dialectic (A 293–704/B 349–732). Derrida's fullest readings of Kant centre on the third *Critique*: see *The Truth in Painting*, trans. Geoff Bennington and Ian McLeod (Chicago and London: University of Chicago Press, 1987); 'Economimesis', trans. Richard Klein, *Diacritics* 11:2 (1981), 3–25. See also 'On a Newly Arisen Apocalyptic Tone in Philosophy', trans. John Leavey, Jr, in Peter Fenves (ed.), *Raising the Tone of Philosophy: Late Essays by Immanuel Kant, Transformative Critique by Jacques Derrida* (Baltimore and London: Johns Hopkins University Press, 1993), pp. 117–71; and Chapter 2 of Richard Beardsworth, *Derrida and the Political* (London and New York: Routledge, 1996), pp. 46–97.

9. Kant, *Critique of Pure Reason*, B xxxvi–vii; A 760–9/B 788–97, for example.

10. Kant, *Critique of Pure Reason*, B xxxv: 'This critique is not opposed to the *dogmatic procedure* of reason in its pure knowledge, as science, for that must always be dogmatic, that is, yield strict proof from sure principles *a priori*. It is opposed only to *dogmatism*, that is, to the presumption that it is possible to make progress with pure knowledge, according to principles, from concepts alone [...] and that it is possible to do this without having first investigated in what way and by what right reason has come into possession of these concepts. Dogmatism is thus the dogmatic procedure of pure reason, *without previous criticism of its own powers*.' The problem Hegel will raise concerns the 'previousness' of the critique, not the critical passage through the concept. Cf. B xxx, 23.

11. Kant, *Critique of Pure Reason*, B 127.

12. Indeed, Kant will be chastised by Hegel and Adorno for taking the compelling descriptions of experience in systematic and universal natural science as a *given*, a necessity Kant merely tries to explain – circularly – rather than to establish; cf. *Critique of Pure Reason*, B 20–1.

13. In fact, Kant and Hegel distinguish Humean empiricism from Greek scepticism (for example, Hegel, *Logic* [Part I of the *Encyclopedia of the Philosophical Sciences*], trans. William Wallace, 3rd edn [Oxford: Clarendon Press, 1975], §39, pp. 64–5). Hume does not query the certainty of sense-impressions, only the necessity of any knowledge inducing upon them.

14. Kant, *Critique of Pure Reason*, B xxx; Kant re-establishes 'rational faith'

in the postulates of pure practical reason, *Critique of Practical Reason*, trans. Lewis White Beck (New York: Macmillan, 1956), Book II.

15. A result already apparent from Kant's Transcendental Deduction (*Critique of Pure Reason*, B 148, 166) and prosecuted fully in the Antinomies (A 405–571/B 432–599).

16. Kant, *Critique of Pure Reason*, B 73. Cf. Hegel, *Faith and Knowledge*, trans. Walter Cerf and H. S. Harris (Albany: State University of New York Press, 1977), pp. 76–8.

17. Kant, *Critique of Pure Reason*, A 51/B 75.

18. Kant, *Critique of Pure Reason*, A 20/B 34.

19. Kant, *Critique of Pure Reason*, A 42/B 59.

20. In the second part of the second edition's Transcendental Deduction, B 129–69. For the instructive account that informs my comments here, see Robert B. Pippin, *Hegel's Idealism: the Satisfactions of Self-Consciousness* (Cambridge: Cambridge University Press, 1989), pp. 24–41.

21. Kant, *Critique of Pure Reason*, B 138, 145, 160; and A 158/B 197: '[T]he conditions of the *possibility of experience* in general are likewise conditions of the *possibility of the objects of experience*, and [...] for this reason they have objective validity in a synthetic a *priori* judgment.'

22. Pippin, *Hegel's Idealism*, p. 31.

23. Hegel, *Faith and Knowledge*, pp. 69ff. Two of Kant's other genuinely speculative notions are transcendental apperception (see especially Hegel, *Difference between the Systems of Fichte and Schelling*, trans. H. S. Harris and Walter Cerf [Albany: State University of New York Press, 1976]); and the intuitive intellect (this last – Kant, *Critique of Judgment*, trans. Werner S. Pluhar [Indianapolis: Hackett Publishing Co., 1987], §§76–7, pp. 283–94 – is discussed by Hegel, who releases it from its regulative status, in *Faith and Knowledge*, pp. 88ff.).

24. Pippin, *Hegel's Idealism*, pp. 31, 37. On the deduction, see also Dieter Henrich, 'The Proof-Structure of Kant's Transcendental Deduction', *Review of Metaphysics* 22 (1968–9), pp. 640–59; and cf. Henry E. Allison, 'Reflections on the B-Deduction', in *Idealism and Freedom: Essays on Kant's Theoretical and Practical Philosophy* (Cambridge: Cambridge University Press, 1996), pp. 27–40.

25. Gillian Rose, *Hegel Contra Sociology* (London and Atlantic Highlands, NJ: Athlone Press, 1981), pp. 102–3.

26. Hegel, *Phenomenology*, §§78, 85, pp. 49–50, 54-5.

27. Hegel, *Logic*, §10, p. 14.

28. Rose, *Hegel Contra Sociology*, p. 44.

29. Pippin, *Hegel's Idealism*, p. 40.

30. Hegel, *Faith and Knowledge*, pp. 69–70; *Logic*, §60, p. 91.

31. Hegel, *Logic*, §§43-4 and addition, pp. 71–2.

32. Hegel, *Science of Logic*, trans. A. V. Miller (London: Allen & Unwin, 1969), pp. 131–7. See Rose, *Hegel Contra Sociology*, pp. 188ff.

33. Cf. Rose, *Hegel Contra Sociology*, pp. 191–2.

34. Hegel, *Logic*, §48, p. 77.

35. Hegel, *Logic*, §§55-9, pp. 88–90.

36. Hegel, *Logic*, §60 addition, pp. 93–4.

37. Hegel, *Phenomenology*, §27, p. 16.

38. Rose, *Hegel Contra Sociology*, pp. 44-7.

39. Hegel, *Logic*, §61, p. 95.

40. On the determinations of the movement from consciousness to self-consciousness to sociality, epistemology to politics, see, for example, Robert B. Pippin, 'You Can't Get There from Here: Transition Problems in Hegel's *Phenomenology of Spirit*', in Frederick C. Beiser (ed.), *The Cambridge Companion to Hegel* (Cambridge: Cambridge University Press, 1993), pp. 52–85.

41. Rose, *Hegel Contra Sociology*, pp. 56, 68, 86–7, 118, etc. I am following Rose's readings of the early works in this passage.

42. See Hegel's early (1802–3) essay, *Natural Law. The Scientific Ways of Treating Natural Law, Its Place in Moral Philosophy, and Its Relation to the Positive Sciences of Law*, trans. T. M. Knox (Philadelphia: University of Pennsylvania Press, 1975), p. 79. On how subjective (Kantian) morality emerges out of private property relations for the 'mature' Hegel, cf. Part Two of *Elements of the Philosophy of Right*, trans. H. B. Nisbet (Cambridge: Cambridge University Press, 1991), pp. 133–86.

43. Rose, *Hegel Contra Sociology*, p. 185.

44. Rose, *Hegel Contra Sociology*, p. 98.

45. Rose, *Hegel Contra Sociology*, p. 94.

46. Hegel, *Faith and Knowledge*, pp. 57–8.

47. Rose, *Hegel Contra Sociology*, p. 99.

48. Rose, *Hegel Contra Sociology*, p. 103.

49. Hegel, *Faith and Knowledge*, p. 191; *Phenomenology*, §§17ff., pp. 9ff.

50. Rose, *Hegel Contra Sociology*, p. 106.

51. Rose, *Hegel Contra Sociology*, p. 187.

52. See Georg Lukács's account of Kant's transcendental subject as the internalized fetish character of social commodity relations: abstract, universalized relations between exchange-values that pass themselves off as relations between human beings. See 'Reification and the Consciousness of the Proletariat', in *History and Class Consciousness: Studies in Marxist Dialectics*, trans. Rodney Livingstone (London: Merlin Press, 1971), pp. 83–222 (pp. 110ff.).

53. This debt is most clearly to be read in *Hegel: Three Studies*, trans. Shierry Weber Nicholsen (Cambridge, MA and London: MIT Press, 1993). (Hereafter HTS.) But cf. also ND, pp. 295–353/300–60.

54. On the paradoxical concept of a 'pure' intuition in Kant, see Adorno, *Against Epistemology: a Metacritique. Studies in Husserl and the Phenomenological Antinomies*, trans. Willis Domingo (Oxford: Blackwell, 1982), pp. 145–7.

55. ND, 23/12: 'Dissatisfaction with their own conceptuality is part of their meaning, although the inclusion of nonconceptuality in their meaning makes it tendentially their equal and thus keeps them trapped within themselves. The substance of concepts is to them both immanent, as far as the mind is concerned, and transcendent as far as being is concerned. To be aware of this is to be able to get rid of concept fetishism.' Cf., on pure concepts, ND 53, 139ff./62, 135ff. And on all these issues, see Simon Jarvis, *Adorno: a Critical*

Introduction (London: Polity, 1998), an important book to which my essay's sketchy exposition is heavily indebted.

56. Kant: 'This peculiarity of our understanding, that it can produce *a priori* unity of apperception solely by means of the categories, and only by such and so many, is as little capable of further explanation as why we have just these and no other functions of judgment, or why space and time are the only forms of our possible intuition' (B 146–7). This interferes with Kant's attempt to decoct an account of the categories' legitimacy (question of right, *quaestio quid juris*) rather than of their '*de facto* mode of origination' (question of fact, *quid facti*): A 84–5/B 116–17. Cf. Paul Guyer, 'Thought and Being: Hegel's Critique of Kant's Theoretical Philosophy', in Beiser (ed.), *Cambridge Companion*, pp. 171–210 (pp. 186–7).

57. Cf. Hegel, *Phenomenology*, §20, p. 11.

58. Cf. ND, 149/145–6; Adorno, *Minima Moralia: Reflections from Damaged Life*, trans. E. F. N. Jephcott (London: New Left Books, 1974), p. 152; and the comments on immanent and transcendent critique in Adorno, 'Cultural Criticism and Society', *Prisms*, trans. Samuel Weber and Shierry Weber (Cambridge, MA: MIT Press, 1981), pp. 17–34.

59. For example, Kant, *Critique of Pure Reason*, A 298/B 354–5: 'There exists, then, a natural and unavoidable dialectic of pure reason [...] inseparable from human reason, and which, even after its deceptiveness has been exposed, will not cease to play tricks with reason and continually entrap it into momentary aberrations ever and again calling for correction.'

60. Translation modified. On how the transcendence in thinking gets pinned down and eliminated, cf. Adorno, *Minima Moralia*, pp. 68–9.

61. I am following the illuminating conclusion of Jarvis, *Adorno* (no page numbers available).

62. Cf. Adorno, *Minima Moralia*, p. 247.

63. Adorno, *Aesthetic Theory*, trans. Robert Hullot-Kentor (London: Athlone, 1997).

64. Adorno, *Aesthetic Theory*, p. 330.

65. See Geoffrey Bennington, 'Derridabase', in Derrida and Bennington, *Jacques Derrida*, trans. Geoffrey Bennington (Chicago and London: University of Chicago Press, 1993), pp. 278–9.

66. Derrida, *Of Grammatology*, trans. Gayatri Chakravorty Spivak (Baltimore: Johns Hopkins University Press, 1976), pp. 60–2.

67. Adorno, *Minima Moralia*, pp. 122–3. See, for instance, Kant, *Critique of Pure Reason*, A 78/B 103.

68. Cf. Derrida, 'The Pit and the Pyramid: Introduction to Hegel's Semiology', *Margins of Philosophy*, trans. Alan Bass (Chicago: University of Chicago Press, 1982), pp. 69–108 (pp. 78–81); 'Ousia and Grammè: Note on a Note from *Being and Time*', *Margins of Philosophy*, pp. 29–67 (pp. 48ff.). See also Geoffrey Bennington, 'Deconstruction and the Philosophers (The Very Idea)', in *Legislations: the Politics of Deconstruction* (London and New York: Verso, 1994), pp. 11–60 (especially pp. 30–44).

69. See Derrida, *Mémoires: for Paul de Man*, trans. Cecile Lindsay *et al.*, 2nd edn (New York: Columbia University Press, 1989), p. 64.

70. Rodolphe Gasché, *The Tain of the Mirror: Derrida and the Philosophy of Reflection* (Cambridge, MA.: Harvard University Press, 1986).

71. Derrida, 'Signature Event Context', *Margins of Philosophy*, pp. 307–30.

72. Translated in *Glas* as 'almost transcendental'.

73. See Derrida, *Limited Inc*, trans. Samuel Weber (Evanston, IL: Northwestern University Press), p. 136, for this identification.

74. Derrida, *Of Grammatology*, pp. 6–7.

75. Cf. the arguments concerning uncompletable reflection in, for instance, Dieter Henrich, 'Fichtes ursprüngliche Einsicht', in Henrich and Hans Wagner, *Subjektivität und Metaphysik* (Frankfurt am Main: Klostermann, 1966), pp. 188–232.

76. Derrida, *Of Grammatology*, pp. 158, 163.

77. For the classic account of supplementarity, see *Of Grammatology*, pp. 141–64.

78. Derrida, 'Signature Event Context', pp. 327–30.

79. See Derrida's account of Husserl in *Speech and Phenomena: and Other Essays on Husserl's Theory of Signs*, trans. David B. Allison (Evanston: Northwestern University Press, 1973).

80. Derrida, 'Signature Event Context', p. 316.

81. Derrida, 'Signature Event Context', pp. 315–16; *Speech and Phenomena*, p. 54n.

82. Derrida, *Limited Inc*, pp. 148–9.

83. Bennington, 'Derridabase', p. 199. Cf. Friedrich Nietzsche, *The Genealogy of Morals*, in *The Birth of Tragedy and The Genealogy of Morals*, trans. Francis Golffing (New York: Doubleday, 1956), pp. 189–90.

84. See Derrida, 'Ulysses Gramophone: Hear Say Yes in Joyce', in *Acts of Literature*, ed. Derek Attridge (New York and London: Routledge, 1992), pp. 253–309 (for instance, pp. 279, 296–300); Bennington, 'Derridabase', pp. 202–3.

85. Cf. Derrida, *Of Spirit: Heidegger and the Question*, trans. Geoffrey Bennington and Rachel Bowlby (Chicago and London: University of Chicago Press, 1989), pp. 94, 129–36n.

86. Cf. Walter Benjamin, 'Critique of Violence', in *One-Way Street and Other Writings*, trans. Edmund Jephcott and Kingsley Shorter (London: New Left Books, 1979), pp. 132–54; Derrida, 'Force of Law: "The Mystical Foundation of Authority"', trans. Mary Quaintance, in Drucilla Cornell, Michel Rosenfeld, David Gray Carlson (eds), *Deconstruction and the Possibility of Justice* (New York and London: Routledge, 1992), pp. 3–67.

87. Cf. Simon Critchley, 'On Derrida's *Specters of Marx*', *Philosophy and Social Criticism* 21:3 (1995), 1–30.

88. See Derrida, 'White Mythology: Metaphor in the Text of Philosophy', *Margins of Philosophy*, pp. 207–71; 'The *Retrait* of Metaphor', trans. Frieda Gasdner *et al.*, *Enclitic* 2:2 (1978), 5–33.

89. For Kant as Judaic thinker, see: G 34a, 213a; cf. Bennington, 'Derridabase', pp. 292–302; 'Mosaic Fragment: If Derrida Were an Egyptian ...', *Legislations*, pp. 207-26.

90. See Gillian Rose, *Dialectic of Nihilism: Post-structuralism and the Law* (Oxford: Blackwell, 1984), pp. 131–70; *Judaism and Modernity*, pp. 65–88; and Peter Dews, *The Limits of Disenchantment: Essays on Contemporary European Philosophy* (London and New York: Verso, 1995), pp. 31–3.

91. Compare and contrast with Derrida's context and *différance* Adorno's reflections on constellation and parataxis: ND, 164-6/162–3; 'Parataxis: On Hölderlin's Late Poetry', *Notes to Literature*, vol. 2, trans. Shierry Weber Nicholsen (New York: Columbia University Press, 1992), pp. 109–49.

92. Cf. Gillian Rose, *Mourning Becomes the Law: Philosophy and Representation* (Cambridge: Cambridge University Press, 1996), pp. 65–76.

93. J. M. Bernstein, *The Fate of Art: Aesthetic Alienation from Kant to Derrida and Adorno* (Cambridge: Polity, 1992), p. 284n.

94. Dews, *Limits of Disenchantment*, p. 82.

95. For examples, see Ernesto Laclau, '"The Time is Out of Joint"', in *Emancipation(s)* (London and New York: Verso, 1996), pp. 66-83; Beardsworth, *Derrida & the Political*; Simon Critchley, *The Ethics of Deconstruction: Derrida and Levinas* (Oxford and Cambridge, MA: Blackwell, 1992).

96. On institutions, see, for example, Derrida, 'Languages and Institutions of Philosophy', trans. Sylvia Söderlind *et al.*, *Recherches Sémiotiques/Semiotic Inquiry* 4:2 (June 1984), 91–154; 'Mochlos; or, The Conflict of the Faculties', trans. Richard Rand and Amy Wygant, in Richard Rand (ed.), *Logomachia: the Conflict of the Faculties* (Lincoln and London: University of Nebraska Press, 1992), pp. 1–34. And on absolute (or dialecticizable) difference, cf. Dews, *Limits of Disenchantment*, p. 85.

97. On desire and its condition in *différance*, see Derrida, *Of Grammatology*, p. 143.

98. My reading of these pages is indebted to Simon Critchley, 'A Commentary upon Derrida's Reading of Hegel in Glas', *Bulletin of the Hegel Society of Great Britain* 18 (Autumn/Winter 1988), pp. 6–32; and Bennington, 'Derridabase', pp. 299–302.

99. Hegel, *Phenomenology*, esp. §§685–8, pp. 418–20; Derrida, *Glas*, pp. 237aff.

100. Hegel, *Phenomenology*, §686, p. 419.

101. Hegel, *Phenomenology*, §§686–7, p. 419.

102. This topic is unpacked in Critchley's 'Commentary', pp. 24–5.

103. Hegel, *Phenomenology*, §688, p. 420.

104. On these topics, cf. Derrida, *Given Time: I. Counterfeit Money*, trans. Peggy Kamuf (Chicago and London: University of Chicago Press, 1992).

105. Jacques Taminiaux, *Dialectic and Difference: Modern Thought and the Sense of Human Limits*, ed. Robert Crease and James T. Decker, pbk edn (Atlantic Highlands, NJ: Humanities Press International, 1990), pp. 55–77 (p. 70). Taminiaux reads these parallels out of Hegel's and Heidegger's privileging of Kantian productive imagination, the

abyssal root of finite transcendence. Cf. Taminiaux, 'From One Fundamental Ontology to the Other: the Double Reading of Hegel', in *Heidegger and the Project of Fundamental Ontology*, trans. Michael Gendre (Albany: State University of New York Press, 1991), pp. 145–59.

106. Jarvis, *Adorno*, conclusion, n.p. Cf. Beardsworth, whose *Derrida and the Political* appeared too late for me to take its arguments fully into account, pp. 95–7, 145–57.

107. Karl Marx, *Capital: a Critique of Political Economy*, vol. 1, trans. Ben Fowkes (London: Penguin, 1976), pp. 176–7.

108. I would here like to thank Julie Bishop, Simon Jarvis, and Andrew Stott for inspiration and their patient help during the writing of this paper and beyond.

Part II
Uncanny Fictions

5

Anachrony and Anatopia: Spectres of Marx, Derrida and Gothic Fiction

Ruth Parkin-Gounelas

5.1

When Derrida finally came to write at length about Marxism, it was to be in terms not of a recent engagement, but of hauntings from the past.[1] Derrida's text is haunted by Marx, just as Marx's texts, especially *The German Ideology*, are haunted by Max Stirner, whose own texts, Derrida tells us, are haunted by Hegel's, especially *The Phenomenology of Spirit*.[2] The ancestral spectres go back, we may assume, *ad infinitum*.

But *Specters of Marx* is as much, at least, about ends as about debts or origins. 'Hantologie' in the Derridean sense is to a certain extent a playful challenge to a Marxist 'ontologie' of presence (or materialist philosophy). But his point about spectres and spectrality does represent a serious attempt at what Simon Critchley calls 'a politicization or, better, a repoliticization' of deconstruction via Marxism.[3] In an age when Fukuyama is proclaiming the 'end of history' in the perpetual present of the postmodern market economy, there is an urgent need for deconstruction to account for beginnings and ends, the past and the future, in new and radical ways. Rather than the 'end of history', we need to find ways of figuring new eschatologies (and Derrida suggests a Benjaminian 'messianic', which he sees as the outcome of the '*ineffaceable* mark ... of Marx's legacy'.)[4]

Derrida confronts the challenge of assessing Marxism's heritage in a post-Soviet era by invoking concepts of spectrality which encourage what Spivak calls 'a learning to live at the seam of the past and the present'.[5] The spectrality effect, in fact, works to disturb all boundaries, seeping out to contaminate distinctions ranging from the classic Marxist distinction between exchange value and use value, to those between ends and beginnings, life and death. *Specters of Marx* returns to and repeats, with the obsession of a repetition compulsion, the central idea that, in the final analysis, *everything* is a ghost: 'everything [the Holy Spirit, truth, law, the "good cause"] comes back to haunt everything, everything is in everything, that is, "in the class of specters"' (146). Marx's 'ten ghosts' in *The German Ideology*, which start with 'God' and move, in descending onto-theological order, to 'Everything' (143–6), are the immediate source of Derrida's list. But his revision of Marx's list, as we might expect, has a specifically anti-ontological, deconstruction-ist focus – on the 'paradoxical incorporation' of the 'non-present present' of the spectre, its defiance of 'semantics as much as ontol-ogy, psychoanalysis as much as philosophy' (6). Like Hamlet's father, perhaps the most vivid spectral presence in Derrida's pages, the spectre has to do with the disturbance or impossibility of origins, the 'pre-originary and properly spectral *anteriority*' of every crime, tragedy or action (21, emphasis added). Non-present pres-ence, pre-originary anteriority: in the spectre's defiance of space and time, Derrida finds the embodiment of his most consistent project, the deconstruction of the metaphysical desire for presence and origin.

The difficulty (or attraction) of ghosts has always been their chal-lenge to the fixity of space and time. Stirner–Marx–Derrida problematise the *spatial* aspect by using the German phrase 'es spukt', that indeterminate verbal form which appears as 'it spooks' in the English translation of Derrida's French translation of Marx's German. To refuse the noun is to refuse the spatial identification (a ghost 'is' somewhere). '*It is a matter*', writes Derrida,

> in the neutrality of this altogether impersonal verbal form, of something or someone, neither someone nor something, of a 'one', that does not act.... but where? In the head?... And what if the head ... were defined ... by the very thing that it can neither contain, nor delimit, by the indefiniteness of the 'es spukt'? (172)

Here, in the shady *atopia* of the 'neither in the head nor outside the head' (172), is the site of the meeting of psychoanalysis and language. Many of Derrida's views on this problematic encounter were published in the 1970s – in his engagement with the work of Lacan and of Nicolas Abraham and Maria Torok.[6] Rejecting the Lacanian phallus as transcendental signifier, Derrida found in the work of Abraham and Torok the 'antisemantic[ist]' approach he needed from psychoanalysis.[7] Abraham had taken as his pretext Freud's reference to the Unconscious as 'the Kernel of Being', and called (in his essay 'The Shell and the Kernel') for an 'anasemia', a 'radical semantic change' to be brought about in psychoanalysis. Pleasure, Discharge, the Unconscious, capitalized in Freudian metapsychology, 'do not', in Abraham's words, 'strictly speaking signify anything, except the founding silence of *any act of significa-tion'*.[8] Psychoanalysis, then, needs not Laplanche and Pontalis's *Language of Psychoanalysis*, a dictionary of equivalences, but an 'anasemic' discourse capable of registering 'the untouched nucleus [kernel] of non-presence'.[9] The spectre, then, for Derrida, functions importantly as

> an an-identity that ... invisibly occupies places belonging finally neither to us nor to it ... *this* that comes with so much difficulty to language, *this* that seems not to mean anything, *this* that puts to rout our meaning-to-say.[10]

But it is the *temporal* indeterminacy of the spectrality effect which will concern us here above all. Going back in time, over and over, we 'return'; Marx's definition of 'revolution' meaning return or recurrence, as Jeffrey Mehlman suggests, contains within it the seeds of Freud's definition of the repetition compulsion in terms of the Uncanny and the death instinct.[11] (The same could be said, we might add, for the ghost, as one French word for it, 'revenant', suggests.) The important point for Derrida is that both of these (the Uncanny and the death instinct) demand that we come to terms, at the outset, with the problem of what he calls 'repetition *and* first time'.[12] One of the many paradoxes of the ghost is that it represents both the first originating 'time' (the 'first paternal character?', Derrida wonders [13]), as well as its endless repetition. Freud has been interpreted as suggesting, in *Beyond the Pleasure Principle*, that there is an initial impulse which sets the repetition compulsion in motion.[13] This is a question that has occupied Derrida since at least 'Freud and the Scene of Writing' in *Writing and Difference*. Here he wrote:

[In *Beyond the Pleasure Principle*] [i]s it not already death at the origin of a life which can defend itself against death only through an *economy* of death, through deferment, repetition, reserve? For repetition does not *happen to* an initial impression; its possibility is already there, in the resistance offered *the first time* by the psychical neurones. Resistance itself is possible only if the opposition of forces lasts and is repeated at the beginning. It is the very idea of a *first time* which becomes enigmatic.... No doubt life protects itself by repetition, trace, *différance* (deferral).... He [Freud] complies with a dual necessity: that of recognizing *différance* at the origin, and at the same time that of crossing out the concept of *primariness*.... To say that *différance* is originary is simultaneously to erase the myth of a present origin.... The irreducibility of the 'effect of deferral' – such, no doubt, is Freud's discovery.[14]

And thus, no doubt, is the Derridean project haunted by the Freudian.

It is thus, also, within these terms that we need to read what Derrida calls 'this radical untimeliness or this *anachrony* on the basis of which we are trying ... to think the ghost'.[15] Ghosts are untimely/ anachronous (with the Greek prefix 'ana' carrying the idea of repetition) in their disturbance of the distinction between beginnings and returns as well as between death and life. *Hamlet*, read in this way, represents for Derrida a series of originary repetitions – as he shows in his choice of quotations from the play:

> (*Marcellus:* 'What has this thing appear'd again tonight?' Then: *Enter the Ghost, Exit the Ghost, Enter the Ghost, as before*). A question of repetition: a specter is always a *revenant*. One cannot control its comings and goings because it *begins by coming back*. (11)

To return, now, to the related concept of spatial (as opposed to temporal) repetition. I have already used the word 'atopia' – also used, notably, by Barthes, to designate the language that constitutes the writer, that which is 'always outside-of-place ... by the simple effect of polysemy'.[16] Freud's (and Derrida's) range of reference, however, seems to accord more with the concept of *ana*topia, at least as it occurs in Freud's 'The "Uncanny"' ('Das Unheimliche'), written almost contemporaneously with *Beyond the Pleasure Principle*. The key to an understanding of Freud's controversial definition of the uncanny is his insistence on the mutual dependence and replacement of the two terms *heimlich* and *unheimlich*. As Freud put it in a much-quoted passage: '*heimlich* is a word the meaning of which develops in the direction of ambivalence until it finally coincides with its opposite, *unheimlich*'.[17] One of the many meanings he gives of *heimlich* is 'belonging to the house' (222). What is originally homely, a place with which we are familiar, becomes unhomely through the process of repression. This place may be the red-light district to which Freud found himself uncomfortably returning one hot summer afternoon in Italy. Or, more commonly, it is a haunted house.

Places return, repeatedly. And the type of all places is, as Derrida suggests, and Gothic fiction has always known, 'ein unheimliches Haus' – or, in 'spectral' terms, 'ein Haus, in dem es spukt'. This is hardly surprising, because Freud considers haunting to be 'perhaps the most striking of all [examples] ... of something uncanny' (241) – as 'a kind of prototype' as Derrida puts it in his gloss upon Freud (n.37, 195). 'We might indeed have *begun* our investigation with this example [of the haunted house]' (241, emphasis added), Freud adds, in anxious acknowledgement of the tangle of beginnings and returns. But is it really just an example, Derrida wonders: 'what if it were the Thing itself, the cause of the very thing one is seeking and that makes one seek?' (173).

5.2

For Gothic fiction the house has always been 'the Thing itself'. If the genre had any 'beginning', it was surely a particular house, that 'prototype' constructed in both fact and fantasy by Horace Walpole in the forms of his pseudo-Gothic castle Strawberry Hill, as well as his self-styled 'Gothic story', *The Castle of Otranto*.[18] Since then, the genre has remained fixated on anatopias, the repetition of other forms of this house, as well as of its contents: its villains, incestuous relationships, disembodied parts, and above all, the buried secrets of its origins.

If social realism in fiction is the genre of presence, the gothic has long been recognised as that which elides the distinction between presence and non-presence – or rather the genre of disappearances and re-appearances. In *Otranto*, the body of Alfonso the Good (in armour) re-appears, generations later, in fragments – first the gigantic helmet, then the foot and leg, the sword, the hand, and so on. These parts are closely linked with the parts of the larger enclosing body of the castle: the helmet and sword, symbols of civic responsibility, appear in the public space of the castle, the court-yard, the foot and leg in the gallery-chamber, the hand on the uppermost banister of the great stairs.

As the site of the appearing-disappearing phantom, the castle presents that moment when all that is associated with the home or house (the *heimlich*) becomes the *unheimlich*, the crucial moment of defamiliarization to which all Gothic returns. The uncanny, to quote Freud's famous definition again, is 'that class of the frighten-ing which leads back to what is known of old and long familiar', that which 'ought to have remained secret and hidden but has come to light'.[19] As to what this ancient knowledge comprises, Freud's essay does no more than hold out a range of possibilities: from the mother's genitals to that which 'belong[s] to the prehis-tory of the individual and of the race' (245). The suggestiveness of these possibilities provides one of the most tantalizing challenges to analysts of Gothic fiction.

Holland and Sherman are surely right to refuse what they call the 'easy isomorphism' of the one-to-one equation – castle symbol-ises body[20] – in spite of their subsequent elaborations on the 'possibilities' of the equation. For all this, the castle does act, like the maternal body at least, as a point of ultimate return, the source of birth and sexuality.[21] Equally importantly, it serves as an emblem of material status, of ownership – undoubtedly one of the reasons for the genre's prominence in a rising bourgeois economy. If we examine the stories chosen for inclusion in the 1991 Oxford anthol-ogy of *Victorian Ghost Stories* (and I'm going to focus, as a sample, on the first two of these), we notice that a large number of them centre on the family dynasty, of which the castle is the material emblem. The ghost is invariably the agent, either as protector or claimant, of property under threat. In other words its function is to explore dynastic histories, or, more accurately, mysteries (which are nothing but buried histories). In early Gothic, the house was always a castle. As Holland and Sherman point out, 'Inherited riches mean [that Gothic] characters never work, never, that is, construct distinctive identities for themselves apart from parental inheritance' (286). The genre thus began by offering exclusive insight into inheritance as concurrently economic and psychic determinant. It is in this sense, we might add, that Derrida's

Specters, with its insistence on the 'unheimliches Haus' as proto-type, represents the conjunction of the spectres of Freud and Marx, the psychoanalytic and the economic.

Like most Gothic stories, the first one in the Oxford anthology, Elizabeth Gaskell's 'The Old Nurse's Story', does not give the impression of having much to do with inheritance of any kind. Much of the tale is taken up by the foregrounded and very homely presence of the nurse-narrator Hester, whose role, like that of Nellie in *Wuthering Heights* of five years earlier, is to register the Gothic tremors and restore the common light of day. Her story concerns the Furnivall family of Northumberland and the spectral return of the former lord and his outcast daughter and grand-daughter, the latter, as the 'Phantom-Child' wailing at the window, like Cathy Earnshaw, luring the living out to their death in the storm. Furnivall Manor House is at the centre of the story. But 87 years after *Otranto*, and the move from Romantic archetypes to Victorian realism, no explicit mention is made of any concern over the inheritance. Instead, there is an elaborate preoccupation with the house's features: from its overall mass (compared to a 'wilderness')[22] to its obsessively repeated details – the great oak, the gnarled holly tree, the portrait gallery, the organ, the chandelier and above all the safe, familiar west wing as opposed to the unfamiliar east one.

And yet the opening words of the tale hint at a different, buried preoccupation: 'You know, my dears, that your mother was an orphan and an only child' (1). Dynastic concerns are the absent presence; the family tree looms invisibly,[23] eliciting anxiety over the safety of its branches and fruit. The orphan and only child of the opening sentence, Rosamond, does manage to make it through the hauntings to bear children. The line is secured. But this is only after the story has worked to show its fragility by two means: firstly by elaborating on the non-issue of the various other family members, and secondly by focusing on the threat by the phantom (a rival claimant, for all her garb of childhood innocence) to the one remaining heir (Rosamond) to Furnivall Manor.

The recipients of Hester's narrative are Rosamond's children, the last of five generations of Furnivalls to appear in the story. Like all Gothic readers, at least on the surface, they 'don't care so much' for an elaboration of the past (1). Their interest is in 'what [they] think is to come' (1), illustrating what Peter Brooks calls 'the contradictory desire of narrative, driving toward the end which would be both its destruction and its meaning'.[24] But in defiance of her listeners'

conscious wishes, Hester's narrative loops and turns back to beginnings repeatedly in its drive to the end, rotating upon an
anachronic axis of repetition *and* first time. For the long-awaited
ghosts, in the end, lead the narrative as much to the origin of its
mystery as to its deferral. The line of descent will remain threatened. 'At bottom', Derrida says, 'the specter is the future, it is
always to come.'[25] The Phantom-Child, it is assumed, will return to
Furnivall Manor, in spite of its avoidance by the present generation.
Rosamond narrowly escapes its clutches through the homely atten-
tions of her nurse. But there will always be the agent of
defamiliarization, in this case the 'dark foreigner' (14) who comes to
seduce the heiress and release the phantoms. The narrator says that
this foreigner 'could easily ... hide himself in foreign countries' (14).
He is the living embodiment of that which 'ought to have remained
secret and hidden'; his concealment, like that of the phantom itself,
is only a deferral of his re-appearance.

Continuity, the life force, is the contested site of Gothic. From
Walpole to today, its enemy, illegitimacy, plots to threaten (or
threatens the plot of) this deeply patriarchal genre. In The *Castle of
Otranto* (1765) the plot is centred on the threat of the possible
mixing of the blood of the true heir (Theodore) with that of the
usurper (Matilda). The form taken by the threat to continuity/legit-
imacy has varied at different historical moments, as we might
expect. In *Otranto* it was incest, suggested in the subtle swapping of
daughters by Manfred and Frederic, which is prevented at the last
moment. Much the same is true for the Gothic romances published
in the following decades. Ann Radcliffe's villains, who only just
miss raping the heroine, invariably turn out to be blood relations.
With the approach of the Victorian period, as the revisions to
Frankenstein show, this possibility had to be suppressed. In the first
(1818) edition of Mary Shelley's text, as is often remarked, Elizabeth
is Frankenstein's cousin; the third edition of 1831 changes her to an
adopted (foundling) sister.

If it was not incest, what was it that threatened legitimacy in
Victorian Gothic? In Gaskell's story, even illegitimacy itself is
veiled: the foreign musician and Maud Furnivall are said to have
married, though in secrecy and defiance of paternal authority, so
that their daughter's 'illegitimacy' is moral rather than legal. The
uncanny repetition of the family name (and Manor House) seems
to suggest that the ultimate crime is the 'evil' of 'fornication' (the
Latin *fornix-icis* means both a vault or arch and a brothel, aptly

conflating the architectural and the erotic). Or, equally possible, is it the presence of the spinster-companion Miss Stark, whose devotion to the other Furnivall daughter/heiress, Grace, prevents *her* from marrying and bearing children? Miss Stark is a familiar type in Victorian fiction; it was the Gothic rather than the realistic genre of the period which enhanced her disruptive rather than her nurturing status through its obsession with the continuity of the family line.

5.3

The second tale in the Oxford anthology, Sheridan LeFanu's 'Account of Some Strange Disturbances in Aungier Street', was published only a year later (in 1853) but has a much more modern feel about it. Firstly, like many later Victorian ghost tales, it draws frequent attention to the problem of authentication in the perception of ghosts. 'Was this singular apparition ... the creature of my fancy, or the invention of my poor stomach? Was it, in short, *subjective* (to borrow the technical slang of the day) ...?',[26] the narrator wonders. Secondly, it sets the hauntings not in a feudal manor or castle but in the bourgeois Dublin of 'Aungier Street',[27] in a once semi-fashionable but now rather dissolute part of town inhabited by students and drunkards. In this modern setting, property no longer remains in the same family for generations, keeping its mysteries intact and ingrowing, but instead changes hands at the whim of market forces, as the opening paragraphs detail. The family romance, then, must be split, its traumas dispersed among a wider community.

It is the community, the street (Aungier Street) which carries the burden of the secrets. Without the portrait gallery, which served in Gaskell's tale and earlier Gothic to keep past generations in the consciousness of the living, the modern house rarely ventures back further than one generation of the same family. The house remains at the centre, however. As the narrator Dick puts it: 'what the flesh, blood, and bone hero of romance proper is to the regular compounder of fiction, this old house of brick, wood, and mortar is to the humble recorder of this true tale' (36). The return, as it were, is of the house itself – anatopia, the site of haunting over time – anachrony. Like Furnivall Manor with its west and east wings, it embodies both the homely (the 'cosy' front bedroom [20]) and the unhomely which disrupts it: the back bedroom, which embodies a 'latent discord – a certain mysterious and indescribable relation, which jarred indistinctly upon some secret sense of the fitting and the safe' (21). Here Tom and Dick, the types of modern democratic ordinariness, as their names suggest, are subjected to the violence and vengeance of their luridly named patrician predecessors in the house, Sir Thomas Hacket, Lord Mayor of Dublin in James II's time, and Judge Horrocks, 'who ha[d] earned the reputation of a particularly "hanging judge"' (20). The word 'Aungier' itself suggests haunting, revenge and hanging. The crime, it seems, is not so much Judge Horrocks' professional sadism as his final turning of this sadism upon himself. In hanging himself from the banisters with the skipping-rope of his unacknowledged illegitimate daughter, born of his housekeeper, he projects on to future occupants of the house the burden of his concealment.

According to Nicolas Abraham in 'Notes on the Phantom', the phantom which returns to haunt not just Gothic fiction but all human subjects is 'not the content of repression Freud called a *familiar stranger*', but rather a *'bizarre foreign body'* within us.[28] This alien within results from 'the gap produced in us by the concealment of some part of a love object's life' (171), 'not the dead, but the gaps left within us by the secrets of others' (171), invariably those of parents or grandparents. The illegitimate or taboo past of ancestors, whether direct ancestors as in Gaskell's tale or merely those who shared the same house/topos (anatopia) and history (anachrony) and are responsible for their violence, as in LeFanu's, figure in Gothic as this foreign body which cannot be expelled.

Derrida's 'Foreword' to Abraham and Torok's *The Wolf Man's Magic Word*, published some 17 years before his *Specters of Marx*, elaborates on this theory of the phantom as a figuring of the relation between self and other in a way that throws light on Gothic's concern with gaps and concealments. With Freud's 'Mourning and Melancholia' as a base,[29] Abraham and Torok build their argument for the 'possession' of the ego by the object, observing that the Freudian return of the repressed, in clinical experience, does *not* occur in transference in numerous cases of neurosis, including those of the Wolf Man, Little Hans and indeed of Hamlet.[30] Their addition to Freud's theory depends on a distinction between the concepts of introjection and incorporation. Refusing the healthy option of mourning or introjection whereby we 'reclaim ... as our own the part of ourselves that we placed in what we lost',[31] the subject often resorts to incorporation, the process whereby 'the prohibited object is *settled in the ego* in order to compensate for the lost pleasure and the failed introjection'.[32] Incorporation involves keeping the object alive *as other*, in a crypt, 'a sealed-off psychic space ... in the ego'.[33] It is not until the crypt's contents have been revealed to the subject that the healing process of introjection and transference can begin.

What does it mean to keep the object alive *as other*? Here, I think, we have the question underlying Derrida's – and Gothic fiction's – preoccupation with the phantom. Freud's model of the uncanny as the return of the repressed, helpful as it is for a recognition of symbols and symptoms, proves inadequate in face of encrypted objects.[34] Keeping the ghost alive as other entails, for Derrida, a redefinition of the self: 'the paradox of a foreign body preserved as foreign but by the same token excluded from a self that henceforth deals not with the other, but only with itself'.[35] Whence, with all its enigmatic suggestiveness, his (via Abraham and Torok's) image of the Self as 'cemetery guard':

> The crypt is enclosed within the self, but as a foreign place, prohibited, excluded. The self is not the proprietor of what he is guarding. He makes the rounds like a proprietor, but only the rounds ... and in particular he uses all his knowledge of the grounds to turn visitors away.[36]

We, as visitors to the cemeteries of Gothic texts, are no doubt repeatedly 'turned away' from their real secrets, the secrets of their incorporated objects. It is only in the interstices of these texts (these 'mutilated texts') that we may glimpse evidence of their 'riddles with no key'.[37] I am not suggesting, for it would hardly be possible or even interesting, that we set about writing 'Sixth Acts' to all the tales in the Oxford anthology, like Abraham's to *Hamlet*, to reveal the specific contents of their crypts. What is interesting, however, is to re-think Gothic's figuration of the other in relation to its obsession with ancestral phantoms and with the 'living dead'. Rosemary Jackson, in her influential book on fantasy, argues that fictional ghosts reveal the drive to 'aid human affairs by restoring justice and moral order' or 'to be unified with th[e] "other"'.[38] In opposition to this I would argue that the ghost embodies the disruption and alienation of that other which resists assimilation (introjection), the other of which the self as cemetery guard is not the proprietor.

Its non-present presence makes it inaccessible to symbolization. Its haunting 'untimeliness'/anachrony, to use Derrida's words again, puts to rout our meaning-to-say.

Gothic is rarely about exorcism; ghosts, as I have said, are not laid to rest to enable the restorative process of mourning – as the unresolved endings of most of the tales in the Oxford anthology show. Embedded like a small *mise en abyme* in LeFanu's tale is a scene with Dick lying in bed in the unhomely back bedroom waiting for another ghostly visitation. From here, far off in the street, he hears a drunkard singing of 'Murphy Delany', another drunkard who, as the song goes, falls into a river and is pronounced 'dead as a doornail, so there was an end', only to return to life and prove his 'endlessness' by engaging in pitched battle with the coroner (30–1). The paradox of phantoms is that they are the dead kept alive in us – '*da capo*' (31) – from the beginning and all over again, like the song of Murphy Delany repeated in Dick's head. Is the suicide of Judge Horrocks or of the many other suicide ghosts in the anthology (or indeed the pseudo-suicide of the unfortunate Delany) an attempt, however futile, to put an end, once and for all ('dead as a doornail'),[39] to the line of descent, the line which must go on being haunted? If Gothic is preoccupied with continuity and legitimacy, it is more insistently drawn to their negation.

Another conjunction of Derrida's and Gothic fiction's phantoms occurs to me here. Derrida subtitled his *Specters of Marx* 'The State of the Debt, The Work of Mourning, and the New International'. Leaving aside the first and last of these three, it could be argued that 'the work of mourning', Derrida's (af)filiative invocation of Marx,[40] is his text's most unfulfilled promise. Not only has the spectre of Marx *not* been laid to rest. It has also, according to contemporary commentators on Derrida's text, not been completely persuasively called up.[41] It is as if Derrida, as guard but not proprietor of Marx's cemetery, has released his ghost merely to observe its disruptive presence/ non-presence, to parade its non-assimilation into late-capitalist society. In this respect, a comment by Fredric Jameson, perhaps the most perceptive reader of *Specters* to date, is relevant. Talking about class, another conspicuous non-presence in Derrida's text, Jameson writes:

> each of the opposing classes [and he has written, earlier, that 'there are only two fundamental classes in every mode of production'] necessarily carries the other around in its head and

is internally torn and conflicted by a foreign body it cannot exorcize.[42]

The messianic, eschatological promise that Derrida holds out for late capitalism is thus little more than this 'tearing', conflictual body incapable of expulsion. The most that can be said for spectrality, as Jameson puts it, is very little:

> Spectrality does not involve the conviction that ghosts exist or that the past (and maybe even the future they offer to prophesy) is still very much alive and at work, within the living present: all it says, if it can be thought to speak, is that that living present is scarcely as self-sufficient as it claims to be; that we would do well not to count on its density and solidity, which might under exceptional circumstances betray us. (86)

Spectrality, he writes, is 'what makes the present waver' (85).

I began this chapter by pointing to the impossibility of origins and have ended by invoking the interminability of ends. Between these two (non-) limits flits the phantom, definable (or elusive of definition), as Abraham puts it, as 'this hiatus,... this non-presence of the self to itself ... [which is the] ultimate reason behind all discourse'.[43] Gothic fiction, as an attempt to figure this hiatus, goes perhaps some way towards solving the problem facing psychoanalysis: 'how to include in a discourse – in any one whatever – the very thing which, being the precondition of discourse, fundamentally escapes it'.[44] Given this, his point would seem to be that it is *not* possible, as Derrida speculates that it might be, after Marx's ten ghosts, to 'stop the counting. And the recounting. And the story, and the fable, and the gothic novel.'[45]

Notes

1. In 'Positions', an interview given in 1971, Derrida responded to the charge that his references to Marxism and dialectical materialism had been 'marginal' and 'lacunary' by saying that his lacunae 'are explicitly calculated to mark the sites of a theoretical elaboration which remains, *for me*, at least, *still to come*. And they are indeed lacunae, not objections'. *Positions*, trans. Alan Bass (London: The Athlone Press, 1987), pp. 37–96, p. 62. Further on in the interview, he elaborates on his reservations about the signifier 'matter' as 'an ultimate referent' (65).

2.   Jacques Derrida, *Specters of Marx: the State of the Debt, the Work of Mourning, and the New International,* trans. Peggy Kamuf (New York: Routledge, 1994), p. 121.

3.   Simon Critchley, 'On Derrida's *Specters of Marx*', *Philosophy and Social Criticism* 21:3 (May 1995), 1-30, p. 6.

4.   Derrida, *Specters of Marx*, p. 28.

5.   Gayatri Chakravorty Spivak, 'Ghostwriting', *Diacritics* 25:2 (Summer 1995), 65–84, p. 78.

6.   For Derrida on Lacan, see in particular 'Le Facteur de la Vérité', *The Post Card: from Socrates to Freud and Beyond,* trans. Alan Bass (Chicago: Chicago University Press, 1987), pp. 411–96; for Derrida on Abraham and Torok, see his 'Foreword: *Fors*: The Anglish Words of Nicholas Abraham and Maria Torok', trans. Barbara Johnson in *The Wolf Man's Magic Word: a Cryptonymy,* trans. Nicholas Rand (Minneapolis: University of Minnesota Press, 1986), pp. xi–xlviii, and 'Me – Psychoanalysis: an Introduction to the Translation of "The Shell and the Kernel" by Nicolas Abraham', *Diacritics* 9:1 (March 1979), 4–12.

7.   Derrida, 'Me – Psychoanalysis', p. 5.

8.   Nicolas Abraham, 'The Shell and the Kernel: the Scope and Originality of Freudian Psychoanalysis' in Nicolas Abraham and Maria Torok, *The Shell and the Kernel: Renewals of Psychoanalysis,* trans. Nicholas T. Rand (Chicago: University of Chicago Press, 1994), pp. 79–98, 84.

9.   Derrida, 'Me – Psychoanalysis', p. 10.

10.   Derrida, *Specters of Marx*, p. 172.

11.   Jeffrey Mehlman, *Revolution and Repetition: Marx/Hugo/Balzac* (Berkeley: University of California Press, 1977), pp. 2–4.

12.   Derrida, *Specters of Marx*, p. 10.

13.   By Terence Hawkes, in a lecture entitled 'The Heimlich Manoeuvre: Arnold, Eliot and the Function of English Literary Criticism' (ESSE/ 2 Conference, Bordeaux, 7 Sept., 1993). This would possibly be comparable to the way 'the attributes of life were at some time evoked in inanimate matter by the action of a force of whose nature we can form no conception'. Sigmund Freud, *Beyond the Pleasure Principle, On Metapsychology: the Theory of Psychoanalysis,* Vol. 11, *Pelican Freud Library* (Harmondsworth, Middlesex: Penguin, 1984), pp. 269–338, 311. But as Jean Laplanche argues, the multiple patterns of seemingly antithetical constructs in Freud's work (here that of life and death) in fact all dissolve, in the final analysis, into unity or inter-penetration. The death drive (or 'principle of energy-entropy'), which is enacted by the compulsion to repeat, is not in opposition to but rather on a continuum with the constancy principle, just as it is with Eros or the libidinal circulation. Jean Laplanche, *Life and Death in Psychoanalysis,* trans. Jeffrey Mehlman (Baltimore: Johns Hopkins University Press, 1976), pp. 108–24.

14.   Jacques Derrida, *Writing and Difference,* trans. Alan Bass (London: Routledge, 1978), pp. 202–3.

15.   Derrida, *Specters of Marx*, p. 25, emphasis added.

16.   Roland Barthes, *The Pleasure of the Text,* trans. Richard Miller (Oxford:

Basil Blackwell, 1994), pp. 34–5.

17. Sigmund Freud, 'The "Uncanny"' *The Standard Edition of the Complete Psychological Works of Sigmund Freud*, Vol. 17, trans. and ed. James Strachey (London: Hogarth Press, 1955), pp. 219–52, 226.

18. See the famous letter Walpole wrote in March 1766 describing the origin of his 'Gothic story', an extract from which is cited by Mario Praz, 'Introductory Essay', *Three Gothic Novels*, ed. Peter Fairclough (Harmondsworth, Middlesex: Penguin, 1987), pp. 7–34, 17.

19. Freud, 'The "Uncanny"', pp. 220 and 225.

20. Norman Holland and Leona F. Sherman, 'Gothic Possibilities', *New Literary History* 8:2 (Winter 1977), 279–94, p. 281.

21. Holland and Sherman, 'Gothic Possibilities', p. 286.

22. Elizabeth Gaskell, 'The Old Nurse's Story', *Victorian Ghost Stories: an Oxford Anthology*, ed. Michael Cox and R.A. Gilbert (Oxford: Oxford University Press, 1992), pp. 1–18, 4.

23. Its reconstruction looks something like this:

LORD FURNIVALL ('The Old Lord')

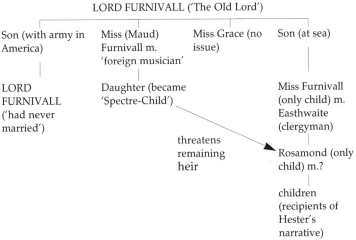

24. Peter Brooks, *Reading for the Plot: Design and Intention in Narrative* (Oxford: Clarendon, 1984), p. 58.

25. Derrida, *Specters of Marx*, p. 39.

26. J. S. LeFanu, 'An Account of Some Strange Disturbances in Aungier Street', *Victorian Ghost Stories: an Oxford Anthology*, ed. Michael Cox and R. A. Gilbert (Oxford: Oxford University Press, 1992), pp. 19–36, 22.

27. David Punter has discussed 'LeFanu's insistence on not Irish but anglicised Gothic settings', relating them both to those of Collins and the Brontës, and to Le Fanu's own obsessional dreams about 'vast and direly foreboding old mansions … in a state of ruin and threatening imminently to fall upon and crush the dreamer rooted to the spot'. David Punter, *The Literature of Terror: a History of Gothic Fictions from 1765 to the Present Day* (London: Longman, 1980), p. 236.

28.   Nicolas Abraham, 'Notes on the Phantom: a Complement to Freud's Metapsychology' *The Shell and the Kernel*, pp. 171–6, 175.

29.   For Abraham's summary of the aspects of Freud's article which provided the starting point of their theory, see Abraham, 'The Shell and the Kernel', especially p. 93.

30.   The Wolf Man is of course Abraham and Torok's most famous case. For their discussion of Little Hans, see Maria Torok, 'Story of Fear: the Symptoms of Phobia – the Return of the Repressed or the Return of the Phantom', *The Shell and the Kernel*, 177–86; for Hamlet, see Nicolas Abraham, 'The Phantom of Hamlet *or* The Sixth Act *preceded by* The Intermission of "Truth"'*, The Shell and the Kernel*, pp. 187–205.

31.   Nicolas Abraham and Maria Torok, 'Mourning *or* Melancholia: Introjection versus Incorporation', *The Shell and the Kernel*, pp. 125–38, 127.

32.   Maria Torok, 'The Illness of Mourning and the Fantasy of the Exquisite Corpse', *The Shell and the Kernel*, pp. 107–24, 113, emphasis added.

33.   Nicolas Abraham and Maria Torok, '"The Lost Object – Me": Notes on Endocryptic Identification', *The Shell and the Kernel*, pp. 139–56, 141.

34.   For Abraham and Torok's distinction between '*constitutive* [i.e. dynamic] *repression*' apparent in hysterics, and the '*preservative repression*' specific to cryptophores, see 'The Topography of Reality: Sketching a Metapsychology of Secrets', *The Shell and the Kernel*, pp. 157–61, 159.

35.   Derrida, 'Foreword', p. xvii.

36.   Derrida, 'Foreword', p. xxxv. In this section of (and indeed throughout) the 'Foreword', Derrida is heavily indebted to Abraham and Torok's 'The Topography of Reality' (1971), reprinted in *The Shell and the Kernel*. For Abraham and Torok's discussion of the 'cemetery guard', see p. 159.

37.   Abraham and Torok, 'The Lost Object', p. 139.

38.   Rosemary Jackson, *Fantasy: the Literature of Subversion* (London: Methuen, 1981), pp. 97 and 100.

39.   Later in the story, one of the many other victims of Judge Horrocks's visitations is pronounced 'dead as a mackerel' (35).

40.   Aijaz Ahmad writes that *Specters* is 'A text that offers not analysis but performance: a ritual performance of burial and recouping, hence the motifs of oath and spectrality and promise – a mourning for the dead, as well as the oath and the promise that the promises of the dead shall be kept; in short, a text of affiliation, and more than affiliation, a text of filiation, the invoking of the ancestral in a register of the spectral.' Aijaz Ahmad, 'Reconciling Derrida: "Spectres of Marx" and Deconstructive Politics', *New Left Review* 208 (Nov./Dec. 1994), pp. 88–106, 91.

41.   Simon Critchley asks: 'What force does Marxism retain if [like Derrida] we set to one side its materialist account of life, production, praxis and history?' 'On *Specters*', p. 5. For Aijaz Ahmad, it is not 'at all clear … how – beyond his very salutary affiliation with what he

calls "a certain spirit of Marxism", and beyond the metaphorical language of "inheritance" and "promise of Marxism" – the politics he recommends is fundamentally different from the more sophisticated, less cruel kinds of liberalism'. 'Reconciling Derrida', p. 98. He complains, in conclusion, that '[Derrida's] gesture of affiliation with Marx includes the acceptance neither of the principal categories of political Marxism nor of the slightest responsibility for any part of its history' (p. 106).

42. Fredric Jameson, 'Marx's Purloined Letter', *New Left Review* 209 (Jan./Feb. 1995), 75–109, pp. 94-5.
43. Nicolas Abraham, 'The Shell and the Kernel', quoted in Derrida's 'Foreword', p. xxxii.
44. Nicolas Abraham, 'The Shell and the Kernel', p. 84.
45. Derrida, *Specters*, p. 146.

6

Theft, Terror and Family Values: the Mysteries and Domesticities of *Udolpho*

Natalka Freeland

Of all the romances in the world, this is perhaps the most romantic.

T. Talfourd

From the perspective of the realist and sentimental novelists who followed her, Ann Radcliffe's gothic terrors were both too frightening and not frightening enough. This dual response is encapsulated, most famously, by Jane Austen's *Northanger Abbey*, which in its first volume ironically deflates the exaggerated terrors invoked by gothic novels, and in its second volume rewrites these fantastic dangers as real threats to the safety and happiness of a modern, middle-class heroine. Catherine Morland, Austen's unremarkable protagonist, learns that she need not fear murder, ghosts or incarceration, only to be threatened instead by slurs to her reputation, romantic mishaps and distressing machinations concerning the property which she is erroneously believed to possess. Yet by domesticating as well as demystifying novels such as *The Mysteries of Udolpho*, *Northanger Abbey* does not simply satirize them, but rather calls attention to the interplay between sentimental and supernatural plotting which structures Radcliffe's novel.[1] What is at stake here is not simply the ambivalent self-parody which characterizes the gothic from its genesis in Walpole's *The Castle of Otranto*, and which, in Udolpho, is reflected in the protagonist's own contradictory responses to 'superstitious terror': 'though she sometimes felt its influence herself, she could smile at it, when apparent in other persons' (247). Rather, it is the unexpected *means* by which Radcliffe, incompletely and seldom satisfactorily, exorcizes the supernatural from her text, which merit closer attention.

While many critics have noted, and most deplored, the eleventh-hour 'explanations' which realistically account for *Udolpho*'s fantastic terrors, they have generally ignored the content of these rationalizations, and have thereby discounted what Radcliffe describes as the real source of the novel's threats and dangers. In effect, the standard response to gothic novels – exemplified by Varma's insistence that 'they are characterized by an awestruck apprehension of Divine immanence penetrating diurnal reality' – can only proceed by completely disregarding the endings of Radcliffe's novels.[2] As a result, it comes as some surprise when we realize that *The Mysteries of Udolpho*, apparently a tangential aside to the materialist literary history whose trajectory runs from *Moll Flanders* to *Oliver Twist*, is yet another novel primarily concerned with property, whose central action, consequently, is theft. Most spectacularly, the apparitions and the unaccountable disappearance of Ludovico at Chateau-le-Blanc leave even the most cynical of Radcliffe's characters suspecting some kind of supernatural agency. Yet the end of the novel leaves no doubt that the apparently haunted chateau is really just the haunt of a band of pirates, who pragmatically chose the abandoned Villefort estate as a safe place to hide their stolen goods. This information comes to light when Ludovico, who was abducted by the pirates, escapes from the bandits with whom they left him. At the unexpected return of the bandits' captive, Emily's servant Annette reinforces the links between theft and spectrality by declaring that 'she has seen his ghost' (629), and behaving as though 'he had arisen from the grave' (630). Emily's response is somewhat more perceptive: she is surprised, above all, at the thieves' cautious and domesticated habits, and wonders why they chose to secure their property in a castle instead of leaving it in a cave (633).

Emily's comment underscores the proximity between the wealthy inhabitants of the castle and the thieves who threaten them. As we shall see, fortified domestic spaces and the dangers which they are meant to shut out are never easily distinguishable in *The Mysteries of Udolpho*. Of course, Emily has already discovered that the threat to domestic safety can come from within the home, since, in Montoni's case, the potential slippage between thieves and proprietors emerges as a *de facto* identity. Consequently, foreshadowing the events at Chateau-le-Blanc, the supernatural

dangers of Udolpho turn out to involve simple, and wholly material – if not entirely legal – property transactions. The narrative's
repeated implications that Montoni is nearly demonic in his
villainy fall flat when we find that this Italian gentleman in reduced
circumstances is guilty of no more serious crime than theft.[3] Even
this characterization is withheld for most of the text, in long digres-
sions which split semantic hairs to explain that Montoni is 'not
precisely what Emily apprehended him to be – a captain of banditti'
nor are his men 'common robbers' although they 'had not only
pillaged, whenever opportunities offered, the helpless traveler, but
had attacked, and plundered the villas of several persons' (397–8).
This distinction without a difference is not abandoned until the
'defeat and signal humiliation' of the Udolpho 'banditti,' as they
are finally designated, by the Venetian Senate (522).

Yet if all of the apparent sources of otherworldly menace in *The
Mysteries of Udolpho* thus pose no more serious threat than robbery,
the result is that theft itself begins to appear truly terrifying.[4] The
novel's professional thieves, the Spanish smugglers, best recognize
that property crimes are never far removed from more frightening
acts of violence: they know that 'if they are taken, they must
expiate the breach of the law by the most cruel death' (605) and are
therefore willing 'to commit murder ... [as] a hopeful way of escap-
ing the gallows' (612). Similarly, Montoni is morally if not legally
responsible for his wife's death, which stems directly from his
(mostly verbal) attempts to convince her to relinquish her property
to him.

That anxieties about the security of property so easily slip into
forebodings of personal danger helps to explain Emily's hyperbolic
response to Montoni's threats. In point of fact, the worst Emily has
to fear is the surprisingly banal possibility of being married to the
wrong man, or married for the wrong reasons. Nonetheless, when
the secret door about which she has had typically gothic forebodings of ghosts and apparitions opens to admit Count Morano, she
is disproportionately terrified by this blatant anti-climax. The melodramatic heroine even goes so far as to refer to the 'evils more
certain and not less terrible' than the 'misery and oppression' of
Udolpho (263) which the prospect of marrying Morano conjures.
Surely the fear inspired by Morano is misplaced; we can safely
assume that it would not actually be a fate worse than Udolpho to
be married to a man whose only faults are sending gondoliers to
serenade Emily, and having met her after Valancourt had done so.

The descriptions of Emily's response to Morano reflect her undeniable ambivalence:

> Emily, when she looked on Count Morano, remembered Valancourt, and a sigh sometimes followed the recollection.... His manner, figure and accomplishments, which were generally admired, Emily would, perhaps, have admired also, had her heart been disengaged from Valancourt, and had the Count forborne to persecute her with officious attentions (189).

Emily's complicated response to Morano is simplified, however, by her discovery that the real threat he poses involves, once again, a potential violation of property rights. First, Emily inadvertently agrees to marry him when reluctantly signing a letter giving permission – because of her desperate financial straits – for her estate to be let. Later, in a famous exchange with the Count as he tries to abduct her from Udolpho, Emily pronounces Montoni's attempt to sell her to Morano, and Morano's willingness to purchase her, equally villainous, and gives this as her reason for refusing to marry him (262). As Emily recognizes, in these exchanges conducted between men about but not with her, whether she is married for her estate or purchased at the cost of it, she can only lose by the transaction.[5]

Evidently, what is most frightening, in Udolpho as at Chateau-le-Blanc, is that the thieves do not attack from outside the castle, but are themselves in it: neither Montoni nor Morano, but the domestic realm itself is experienced by Emily as a threat to her autonomy and property. As a result, she refuses, with much more vehemence and far less reason than the typically modest heroine of a courtship novel, even the proposals of Valancourt and Du Pont, although both are thoroughly unobjectionable suitors, and one is the man she professes to love. Innumerable critics have discussed Emily's apparent sexual frigidity, her masochistic leanings toward Montoni and the homoerotic implications of her desire to enter a convent rather than marry.[6] This emphasis on psycho-sexual motivation ignores the straightforward explanation that Emily appears to perceive her heroic suitors, like the Italian villains, as threats to her property.[7] In fact, Emily's attention to preserving her property is explicitly juxtaposed with the short-circuit of a possible love plot involving Du Pont, the first of the novel's many thieves: within the space of only a few paragraphs, Emily meets him, rejects him as a suitor, and coldly forbids him to keep the miniature of her which he stole, since, as she explains, 'that would be doing myself an injustice' (448).

Meanwhile, it is initially up to Emily's aunt Madame Cheron, who consistently serves as an appropriately gothic double for her niece, to stand in the way of another threat to Emily's property. She begins by openly calling Emily's other suitor, Valancourt, 'a young adventurer ... who is out looking for a good fortune' (125). The course of the novel seems to validate her suspicion – Valancourt manages to reconcile with and marry Emily only after she has become the heiress to several estates, and even his own legacy comes to him because his brother is so pleased with her. The task of identifying Valancourt as a threat to Emily's property does not devolve on Madame Cheron alone, though: he is taken, or mistaken, for a thief on four separate occasions in the novel. In fact, his first appearance is in this inauspicious role, when Emily's father, hearing gunshots in the woods, draws out his own pistol to defend himself and his daughter against the presumed bandit (31). This understandable fear that Valancourt is a thief is quickly dispelled by no more compelling evidence than the 'hunter's dress' (31) in which he is attired. As Valancourt acknowledges, though, this unthreatening costume is a deception or at least a disguise: 'I am only a wanderer here', he admits, 'This [hunter's] dress ... gives me an ostensible business, and procures for me that respect from the people, which would, perhaps, be refused to a lonely stranger, who had no visible motive for coming among them' (32). Together with Valancourt's prepossessing countenance, his confession of his own dishonesty is unaccountably enough to secure the trust of St Aubert and the affections of his daughter; yet the reader can hardly fail to notice the parallel between Valancourt and the outright bandits who inhabit the same mountains, who also pretend to be hunters to lull their victims into complacency (609). At any rate, being taken for a thief is a decidedly mixed blessing for Valancourt. He is shot on two separate occasions, first by Emily's father protecting her person, and then by her gardener protecting her property – but since both of these incidents inspire Emily's pity, appearing to be a thief actually furthers Valancourt's romantic designs.

Of course, Valancourt never quite earns the gunshot wounds which he receives at the hands of Emily's protectors. Or does he? In fact, he does steal from Emily, although she is both too naive and too polite to use this term. When the hero leaves the heroine and her father in the bandit-infested woods, Emily discovers a threat to her property from an entirely unexpected quarter:

> On searching for [a] book, she could find it no where, but in its stead perceived a volume of Petrarch's poems, that had belonged to Valancourt, whose name was written in it, and from which he had frequently read passages to her, with all the pathetic expression, that characterized the feelings of the author. She hesitated in believing, what would have been sufficiently apparent to almost any other person, that he had purposely left this book, instead of the one she had *lost*, and that love had prompted the *exchange* (emphasis added, 58).

The terms of this 'exchange', which is suspiciously described as Emily's loss, are painfully clear: like a good heroine, Emily should sacrifice control over her possessions for sentimental or erotic fulfilment. The subsequent events in the narrative suggest, however, that this displacement, which relegates Emily to the passive and objectified position of Petrarch's Laura, is not entirely satisfactory: as we have seen, Emily's agents continue to shoot at her lover for his supposed thefts; later, when she believes that Valancourt may be Montoni's prisoner, Emily finds the thought comforting (438); and, until the last pages of the novel, she refuses to marry him because she believes that he has stolen, cheated or otherwise unscrupulously acquired his property.

Emily's apprehensions about Valancourt are merely one instance of the novel's generalized portrayal of the dangers of erotic union. From the outset, the marriage of Monsieur and Madame St Aubert, centred around their whole-hearted pursuit of 'domestic virtues' (1), is described as a financial loss – a sacrifice of wealth to sentiment. This inverse relation between love and property becomes more troubling when Emily, noticing that her mother's bracelet has been stolen, immediately assumes that love is behind the larceny. By taking for granted this connection between theft and romance, Emily is able to correctly deduce that the culprit must be the anonymous stranger (later introduced as Du Pont) who has been trespassing on her father's fishing-house to play love-songs on her lute and write her bad love-poetry. In a remarkable exegesis of a poem that merely blazons her beauty, Emily thus concludes that 'from the purport of these lines it was not unreasonable to believe, that the poet, the musician, and the thief were the same person'

(10). While succinctly expressing the gothic novel's equation between its love and property plots, here Emily also begins to explain why a novel such as *The Mysteries of Udolpho* imbues its portrait of marriage with so much terror. If the most frightening moments in the text all revolve around theft and property crimes, and love and marriage are inextricably linked with the threat to property, it stands to reason that the normal domestic relations in the novel are in the end result at least as frightening as any of the overt dangers of mountain banditti or Emily's incarceration at Udolpho. Notably, the only significant corpse in the novel is that of the Marchioness de Villeroi, who is murdered by her husband, both because of his own extra-marital attachments and because of his fear that she has violated her marriage vows. The regulation of domestic relations thus takes precedence over human life – on the one hand, the Marquis would rather commit murder than allow his wife to commit adultery, and on the other, he is encouraged to carry out this horrible crime in order to legally marry his mistress. Significantly, though, even after murdering for her sake, the Marquis decides not to marry his immoral mistress, Signora Laurentini. Instead, he insists that she enter a convent to atone for her 'unresisted passion' – and apparently for his too, since his only penance is 'to lose the sense of his crime amidst the tumult of war, or the dissipations of a capital' (659). Immured within a convent at the Marquis' order until she loses her identity and finally her sanity, Laurentini (now Sister Agnes) is hardly better off than the Marquis' victimized wife, and certainly no freer than Emily was at Udolpho.

Meanwhile, even the good husbands in the text have their unmistakably despotic traits.[8] In particular, the Count de Villefort sounds almost as severe as Montoni when 'he forb[ids] any person ... on pain of punishment' (538) to voice their opinion that the North wing of the castle is haunted. Neither Emily nor the other members of his household are surprised by this apparent over-reaction to what the Count calls a 'serious evil'; evidently, this menacing and melodramatic response to servants' gossip is justified by the goal of keeping the household running smoothly. In this light, Montoni's own commands and threats appear as simply an extension of the ways in which good husbands and fathers keep their wives, daughters, and servants in line. Ultimately, it can be difficult to distinguish between Montoni's villainous confinement of his wife, niece and dependants and, for instance, Ludovico's chivalrous protection of Annette. The conscientious and responsible behaviour by which Ludovico wins Annette's hand and Emily's approbation (434) consists, after all, of locking Annette into various rooms in Montoni's castle. The echoes of Montoni's sinister paternalism are clear to the reader, if not to Annette, when she relates how he 'locked me up to keep me out of harm, as he said.... and he took away the key with him' (322).[9]

Ludovico's equation of domestic security with confinement simply confirms that not only the threat to property, but the domestic realm itself, even or especially when it is secure, can be dangerous. In this context, we should recall that the most frightening of Udolpho's mysteries, the notorious black-veiled figure, is just a peculiar family heirloom, whose preservation is a condition for inheriting the estate. Emily, who believes that this macabre waxwork is a decomposing corpse and suspects that Montoni murdered Udolpho's former owner, could therefore not be farther from the truth, since this gruesome figure is involved in the legal transmission, rather than the usurpation, of the estate. This wax replica of a corpse, designed to remind the inhabitants of the castle of mortal decay (662), thus serves more as a sign of the endurance of property than of the transience of life. If Udolpho comes with a ghost, in other words, it has more to do with what Jeff Nunokawa has called the 'afterlife of property' than with foul play and the spirit world; if anything in this castle is possessed, it is only its possessions.[10]

Moreover, while this horrifying condition attached to inheritance is reassuringly projected onto the remote and orientalized theatre of an isolated Italian fortress, it remains evident that the manner in which past sins and punishments constitute the haunting legacy of Udolpho is more of a reification or clarification than a foil to the transmission of property on the apparently unthreatening soil of France. Emily herself acquires a stock of terrible secrets along with her paternal estate, and both the deathbed promise to which her father binds her, and the hidden compartment in which the mementos of his murdered sister are kept, are suspiciously reminiscent of Udolpho's Italian mysteries. The frightening connotations of inheritance are further amplified by Emily's dual inheritance of her unknown aunt's appearance along with the blood-money meant to compensate for her murder. Emily resembles the late Marchioness so closely that she is not simply haunted, but possessed by her – the young heroine, who appears to be the ghost of her own murdered aunt, has to play out a history which is not her own, by moving Laurentini to remorse, before inheriting her considerable fortune.

Therefore, if threats to property are frequently mistaken for supernatural and frightening events, wealth itself is much more ineluctably haunted. Even at the end of the novel, when most of its mysteries have been unveiled, Annette's description of the lavish adornments at Emily's wedding call attention to the supernatural and unreal connotations of wealth: 'she almost fancied herself in an enchanted palace, and declared, that she had not met with any place, which charmed her so much, since she read the fairy tales; nay, that the fairies themselves, at their nightly revels in this old hall, could display nothing finer' (671). Moreover, this characterization of Emily's wedding directly echoes Annette's similar description of Udolpho, as a place where she is likely to see both ghosts and 'fairies ... hopping about in the great old hall' (231) – and this disconcerting resemblance forces us to question the novel's apparent happy ending. If her marriage subjects her to supernatural forces very much like the ones she feared at Udolpho, what has Emily gained?

In an attempt to explain the popularity of the gothic among female readers and writers, critics such as Claire Kahan have suggested that, for all their trials and terrors, gothic novels finally empower their heroines, by having them emerge victorious in the end, with their honour and especially their property intact, no thanks to the novels' progressively emasculated and victimized heroes (a description which certainly fits Valancourt).[11] Yet if *The Mysteries of Udolpho* is a novel about female empowerment, this is not simply because Emily acquires such an overabundance of property that she spends the last paragraphs of the novel confusedly trying to give it away. Much more important than the size of Emily's bank balance is the process by which this conclusion, about which even the heroine appears embarrassed, is reached. Despite her apparent powerlessness, Emily demonstrates that she is capable of countering any overt threats against her property on their own terms: for while, as we have seen, she fears that Montoni, like Valancourt and Du Pont, may be a thief who is after her property, in fact he never successfully steals from her. Instead, shockingly, she steals from him. In a stereotypical exercise of poetic justice, the victimized heroine thus turns the villain's own wealth against him: when fleeing Udolpho, she helps herself to two of his horses, and when she finds gold beneath one of their saddles, she does not hesitate to spend it to aid her escape.

But this blatant action is extremely uncharacteristic of Radcliffe's heroine; much more telling are the indirect steps she takes to recover the estate which she signed over to Montoni. Almost as soon as she returns to France, we find Emily consulting a lawyer, who assures her that the law will uphold her right against Montoni's might. It is therefore not hard to understand why Emily so often invokes the law, and why it is of such paramount importance for her. Like most gothic novels, despite its ghosts, murders and apparitions, *The Mysteries of Udolpho* finds nothing so frightening as transgressions of the law. None of Montoni's actions are as terrifying as his attitude: it is his basic disregard for limitations other than his own strength and inclination, which (even as an abstract concept) leaves Emily trembling 'at the power of Montoni, which seemed unlimited as his will, for she saw, that he would not scruple to transgress any law, if, by so doing, he could accomplish his project' (219). It is similarly, if counter-intuitively, more frightening to imagine that Montoni will not relinquish control of her when legally obliged to do so, at her majority, than that he has that control while he is her legal guardian: Valancourt's biggest worry is hence that Montoni may be a force 'whose dominion over [Emily] would not cease with [his] rights' (147).

The problem with Valancourt's description of Montoni is that it is completely inaccurate. Although Montoni likes to threaten his wife and niece, the section of the novel set at Udolpho is remarkable, above all, for the absence of any exercise or display of force against these female dependants. The ruses which both Morano and Montoni devise underscore the fact that they do not – although they could – physically compel Emily to do what they wish: consequently, Morano's complicated schemes to lure her out of the castle backfire, and Montoni's early attempt to trick her into signing away her property fails. Emily eventually gives in to Montoni, not because he threatens her with violence, but simply because he may otherwise withdraw her from his 'protection' (436). Similarly, after hinting that Madame Montoni may have been killed by her husband, the novel is careful to clarify that she died less sensationally, of an illness. Emily herself, when worrying that her aunt has met a premature death, repeatedly tries to diminish the violence involved, as when she comes upon 'instruments of torture' and can only imagine that they were used to abandon 'some poor wretch ...

[to] starv[e] to death' (348). In general, Emily's attempt to redefine the terms of her conflict with Montoni from his position of might to her insistence on right is thus surprisingly successful: she is even able to appeal to his 'pangs of conscience', until 'the divinity of pity, beaming in Emily's eyes, seemed to touch his heart. He turned away, ashamed of his better feelings.... but finally consented' (366).

The arena of the novel's action is accordingly shifted from an actual to a sentimental one. This shift from an emphasis on force to an adherence to moral codes and social mores is even clearer in Emily's relationship with Valancourt. Acting as her lover's moral preceptor, Emily subjects Valancourt to a strictly monitored sentimental education, in which he learns to give up the stereotypically masculine pleasures of his Parisian life, which include gambling, soirées with women of uncertain virtue and the profligacy which he copies from his fellows in the army. In return he secures the protection of Emily's superior virtue, which wins him the approval and assistance of the various figures of authority in the text, notably his brother and the Count De Villefort. Valancourt's transformation is not, however, as drastic as it may first appear, since the army in which he serves is already modelled on the domestic or feminine virtues of propriety, law and obedience. In fact, Valancourt joins the army for reasons that have more to do with propriety and reputation than with ambition or valour. As he explains, he chooses the military as his profession because it is 'the only one in which a gentleman could engage without incurring a stain on his name' (117). His place in the army then prevents him from filling the role of the novel's hero: he is unable or unwilling to protect Emily from Montoni for no better reason than that he is '*confined* by his profession to a distant kingdom' (emphasis added, 202). By the end of the novel, even the Italian army has adopted Emily's feminine desire to avoid unnecessary violence: when Montoni is finally captured, the commander insists that it should be by contrivance and stealth rather than force (522).

Therefore, if we recall Emily's own violation of the law, when she steals from Montoni, we will not be surprised to find that what motivates it is a consideration for a more minute and detailed set of laws, those which govern the details of feminine propriety: while fleeing Udolpho, and still subject to recapture, Emily pauses to worry about not having a hat, and she spends the bandit's gold to purchase one. Moreover, Emily's obsessive interest in propriety is not limited to the outside of Udolpho: even when in Montoni's captivity, and fearing that she may never be allowed to leave it, she has one of her most impassioned outbursts upon discovering that her aunt had spoken of her indelicately back in France:

> 'Good God!' exclaimed Emily, blushing deeply, 'it is surely impossible my aunt could have thus represented me!... Is this, the reward of my ingenuousness?... the treatment I am to receive from a relation – an aunt – who ought to have been the guardian, not the slanderer of my reputation – who, as a woman, ought to have respected the delicacy of female honour, and, as a relation, should have protected mine! But to utter falsehoods on so nice a subject – to repay the openness, and, I may say with honest pride, the propriety of my conduct, with slanders – required a depravity of heart, such as I could scarcely have believed existed, such as I weep to find in a relation'(286).

In case Emily's manifest distress at her aunt's irrelevant gossip were not enough to establish her extreme delicacy, the narrative specifies that she withheld this outburst until she was alone so that even her servant would not see her behaving inappropriately. She even chides Annette for having reported the slander to her: '"However that may be, Annette," interrupted Emily, recovering her composure, "it does not become you to speak of the faults of my aunt to me. I know you meant well, but – say no more – I have quite dined"' (286).

Yet if most of *The Mysteries of Udolpho* reveals an exaggerated fear of transgression in an increasingly regulated society, the concomitant sentimental fantasy in which behaviour is governed by moral considerations and concern for propriety is in many regards the mirror-image of Montoni's villainous excesses. If, as Foucauldian critics have argued, social regulation operates most effectively when it is internalized – when incarceration becomes self-suppression and a moral code replaces physical force – it is crucial to recognize that Emily's regulation of her own behaviour is at least as strict as that practised by Montoni. By the time Montoni takes Emily to Italy, for example, this forced relocation is manifestly superfluous, since Emily has already repeatedly refused to marry her lover out of a concern for 'duty ... [combined with] her repugnance for a clandestine marriage, [and] her fear of emerging on the world with embarrassments' (155). Later, the same 'prudence and dignity' (518) compel her to refuse the connection she ardently desires simply because it appears that Valancourt may have 'ruined circumstances and ... corrupted habits' (518). Even her confinement in Udolpho is in large measure of her own choosing. While Montoni locks her in the castle, Emily locks herself in her room, and even barricades herself within it, to escape the undifferentiated 'danger, or impertinence' (329) to which she fears Montoni's men will subject her. She then fails, several times, to solicit information which might allow her to escape because 'an unwillingness to tamper with the integrity of a servant, had checked her enquiries on this subject' (234), or again, because she 'disdained to tempt [an] innocent girl to a conduct so mean, as that of betraying the private conversation of her parents' (418), although those parents are Emily's jailers. And it goes without saying that she 'forebore ... to take advantage of her situation, by listening to a private discourse ' (258); even in the midst of confronting Montoni with her suspicion that he killed her aunt, she stops to resent his implication that she has been eavesdropping (326).

Yet the most important way in which Emily confines herself, more thoroughly than Montoni could dream of doing, is in the control which she exercises over her emotions.[12] Emily's incarceration is therefore a type of what Nina Auerbach has called 'romantic imprisonment', in which 'social prisons adore what they arrest'.[13] From the first pages of the text, she is inculcated in a moral regimen so severe that it forbids her to lose control even at the deaths of her parents: she is instructed in 'our duties ... what we owe to ourselves as well as to others' to learn to 'command' her feelings, to 'let reason ... restrain sorrow' and to limit even the indulgence of virtue to a healthy moderation (20). The effect of this training is two-fold, as it at once defines the interior or emotional realm as the most important one and reveals that social regulation has a role to play within it as well.[14] Law or convention thus becomes so completely internalized that it is indistinguishable from personal and private morality: Du Pont, for example, is relieved to find himself free to return to France 'without reproach to his conscience, or apprehension of displeasure from his commander' (462). The only variation to this pattern confirms the social order, since in the serving class it is greed, rather than duty, which cannot be dissociated from morality, as Du Pont finds when describing the 'pity, or the avarice' (457) of the guard who allowed him occasionally to leave his prison.

Thus, the terrors and confinements of *The Mysteries of Udolpho* are not, as they may at first appear, relegated to the textual and geographical margins of the story, but are rather totalized and diffused throughout the narrative until they are all but transparent. As a result this self-defined 'Romance', along with romance in general, begins to acquire a new meaning: no longer about the masculine values of adventure and heroism, it comes to represent the sentimental, feminine, mannered domestic sphere. Emily makes this shift explicit: after Montoni describes her daring refusal to sign over her property to him as heroic (381), she gives up her claim to this title by giving in and signing the documents – and later recovering her estate through the legal process. This emerging insistence on the rule of law is even evident in Radcliffe's hybrid form, which both indulges in the presence of supernatural terrors and finally makes them conform to the laws of nature, civilized society – and, of course, realist fiction.[15] Moreover, as Nancy Armstrong has suggested, this emerging ideology, 'the insistence [on] a form of authority whose wellsprings were the passions of the human heart', could just as well be called middle-class as feminine.[16] Moral rather than hereditary considerations dictate the final distribution of property in the novel, when Laurentini of Udolpho leaves her wealth to her victim's heirs. Yet Emily refuses this apparently haunted legacy. Evidently, the property system being created – and not just described – by texts such as *The Mysteries of Udolpho* was still the occasion of a certain anxiety. Despite the attempt to naturalize this ideology and the social structure which it authorizes by anachronistically projecting the novel's late-eighteenth-century concerns into a distant past, property in *The Mysteries of Udolpho* remains frightening and dangerous, conjuring fears of ghosts rather than circulating freely and without history as in the bourgeois ideal. From this perspective, *Northanger Abbey*'s uncomfortably crude response to *Udolpho* becomes somewhat more explicable. Austen, championing middle-class values, takes for granted the ideology which Radcliffe describes with equal measures of terror and longing. If Austen cannot understand the claustrophobic fear of incarceration by the moral codes as well as in the homes of the middle class, though, it is only because this incarceration – which is also an infiltration – has been so successful. Which is to say that Austen cannot understand Udolpho's ghosts because she herself is, inescapably, haunted by Radcliffe's legacy.

Notes

1. All references to *The Mysteries of Udolpho* are from the Oxford edition,
    ed. Bonamy Dobrée (Oxford: Oxford University Press, 1980); page
    numbers appear in the text. I am indebted to Judith Wilt's detailed
    discussion of *Northanger Abbey* as an imitation, rather than a parody,
    of Radcliffe's gothic precedent in *Ghosts of the Gothic: Austen, Eliot,
    and Lawrence* (Princeton: Princeton University Press, 1980), esp.
    pp.126–64. Wilt observes that 'Radcliffe's Gothic set machines ...
    always deliver less than they promise: the "something" that enters
    Emily's bedroom is only someone she knows; the "spectacle in the
    portal chamber" was only the body of a stranger; the "black veil"
    itself discloses not a murdered woman but a wax simulacrum'
    (p.136); but unfortunately fails to discuss the real dangers lurking
    behind these disappointing disclosures.
2. Devendra Varma, *The Gothic Flame: Being a History of the Gothic Novel
    in England, Its Origins, Efflorescence, Disintegration, and Residuary
    Influences* (London: Arthur Barker, 1957), p. 211, see also pp. 106–8.
    Critics such as J. M. S. Tompkins have in fact extrapolated from the
    fact that Radcliffe's novels contain no supernatural threats to assume
    that they contain no threats at all, and that their plots are purely
    psychological: Radcliffe's 'theme is not the dreadful happening –
    very often nothing dreadful happens – but the interval during which
    the menace takes shape and the mind of the victim is reluctantly
    shaken by its impedance'. For Tompkins, Radcliffe is therefore
    notable primarily for her 'analysis of fear' (J. M. S. Tompkins, *The
    Popular Novel in England, 1770–1800* (Lincoln: University of Nebraska
    Press, 1961), p. 258). Similarly, referring to works as disparate as
    Nelson Smith's 'Sense, Sensibility and Ann Radcliffe' (*Studies in
    English Literature, 1500–1900* 12, 3 [1973]: 557–70), D. L. MacDonald's
    'Bathos and Repetition: The Uncanny in Radcliffe' (*Journal of
    Narrative Technique* 19, 2 [1989]: 197–204), and William Patrick Day's
    In the Circles of Fear and Desire: a Study of Gothic Fantasy (Chicago:
    University of Chicago Press, 1985), all of which focus on the 'non-
    events' of *The Mysteries of Udolpho*, Steven Bruhm has recently
    concluded that since 'supernatural events are all exposed as having
    natural causes, and perceived dangers are mostly constructions of
    Emily's frenzied imagination', 'it has become a critical commonplace
    that one of Udolpho's most outstanding characteristics is that
    nothing happens in it' (Steven Bruhm, *Gothic Bodies: the Politics of
    Pain in Romantic Fiction* (Philadelphia: University of Pennsylvania
    Press, 1994), p. 153, n. 3).
3. As Birgitta Berglund comments, this 'explanation' plays an impor-
    tant role in constructing the generic identity of the novel: Montoni 'is
    not, in other words, an extravagant stage villain or a fairy-tale ogre
    without any bearing on real life. On the contrary, he is a sordidly
    well-known phenomenon: a man who uses his legal power over
    women to exploit them economically – which can be bad enough',
    Women's Whole Existence: the House as an Image in the Novels of Ann

Radcliffe, Mary Wollstonecraft and Jane Austen (Sweden: Lund University Press, 1994), p. 69.

4. Even critics such as S. L. Varnado, whose emphasis is on the 'numinous' in gothic fiction, and who therefore claim that 'the ghost story, by its very nature, maintains only the weakest connections with the central themes of mainstream literature: romantic love, conflict between man and man, greed, ambition, political questions, and the like' (*Haunted Presence: the Numinous in Gothic Fiction* [Tuscaloosa: University of Alabama Press, 1987] p. 2), have run up against a contradiction when addressing the incidence of theft in Radcliffe's novels. On the one hand, Varnado insists on the purely immaterial nature of the threats in these novels: '*Ghosts rarely steal anything of value*, seldom use bad language, kill less often than one might suppose, and are almost universally chaste' (emphasis added, p. 3). On the other hand, though, he strangely includes theft in a catalogue of the 'seemingly occult incidents' in *Udolpho*: 'a series of "terrific" incidents – including threats from banditti (ever present in the Gothic tradition), mysterious music heard at night, a haunted villa, and other indications of the occult – are combined with descriptions of sublime mountain scenery'(p. 29).

5. Kari Winter's comparisons of gothic novels, early feminist theory and slave narratives are very thought-provoking in this context. She notes, for example, that all of the structures of power and property in the text are founded on the suppression of women's rights: 'As Radcliffe presents it ... Montoni's power is inherently illegitimate because it is founded on his appropriation of a female cousin's estates. If this cousin (Laurentini) were to appear, he would lose all claim to Udolpho. He is safe only because she is buried alive in a convent', *Subjects of Slavery, Agents of Change: Women and Power in Gothic Novels and Slave Narratives* (London: University of Georgia Press, 1992), p. 128.

6. See, for example, Cynthia Griffin Wolff, 'The Radcliffean Gothic Model: a Form of Feminine Sexuality', in *The Female Gothic*, ed. Julian Fleenor (London: Eden Press, 1983), pp. 207–23, Kenneth Graham, 'Emily's Demon-Lover: the Gothic Revolution and *The Mysteries of Udolpho*', in *Gothic Fictions: Prohibition/Transgression*, ed. Kenneth Graham (New York: AMS Press, 1989), pp. 163–71, and Leona Sherman's attention to Emily's alternating 'moral and sexual masochism' (*Ann Radcliffe and the Gothic Romance: a Psychoanalytic Approach* [New York: Arno, 1980], p. 128). Notably, although Sherman recognizes that Emily's final seclusion at La Vallée is simply another form of self-denial, her emphasis on emotional, moral and sexual power to the exclusion of material considerations, makes her unable to perceive the difference in Emily's position at the end of the novel.

7. Mary Poovey is one of the few critics who has recognized that Emily's decisions have at least as much to do with finances as with sexual or even spiritual considerations ('Ideology and *The Mysteries of Udolpho*', *Criticism* XXI:4 [Fall, 1979], pp. 307–30, esp. 323–4); Janet

Todd makes a similar observation in *The Sign of Angellica: Women, Writing and Fiction, 1660–1800* (London: Virago, 1989), pp. 262–3.

8. As Nina Auerbach observes, this slippage between the characterizations of the good and bad patriarchs resurfaces in *Northanger Abbey*'s General Tilney, 'who simultaneously is and is not a Montoni', *Romantic Imprisonment: Women and Other Glorified Outcasts* (New York: Columbia University Press, 1985), p. 16.

9. Berglund has discussed Radcliffe's use of the domestic space as both a 'prison and a refuge', concluding, 'thus confined and exposed, protected and exploited; at the same time longing for shelter and liberty.... It is this aspect of Radcliffe's novels that makes them work as metaphors for women's lives in general. With practically no legal rights and no economic independence, most eighteenth-century women's lives would seem to us either very much confined and oppressed or no less terribly insecure and exposed, and in some cases both', *Women's Whole Existence*, p. 75.

10. See Jeff Nunokawa, *The Afterlife of Property: Domestic Security and the Victorian Novel* (Princeton: Princeton University Press, 1994). Of course, Radcliffe's novel, set in France, was written in the midst of a revolution which had everything to do with how the inherited distribution of property constitutes a kind of material haunting. Following Marx's comments on another French revolution, Jacques Derrida has theorized this ghostliness which constitutes 'the condition of *inheritance*. Appropriation in general, we would say, is *in the condition of the other* and of the *dead* other', *Specters of Marx: the State of the Debt, the Work of Mourning, and the New International*, trans. Peggy Kamuf (London: Routledge, 1994), p. 108. Roland Paulson has also written perceptively about the historical situation of the gothic: 'the popularity of gothic fiction in the 1790s and well into the nineteenth century was due in part to the widespread anxieties and fears in Europe aroused by the turmoil in France finding a kind of sublimation or catharsis in tales of darkness, confusion, blood, and horror', *Representations of Revolution (1789–1820)* (New Haven: Yale University Press, 1983) pp. 220–1. Studies like Paulson's are, however, limited, since they sidestep the novels' property-plots to focus only on how they encode the psychic turmoil of the French revolution.

11. Claire Kahan, 'The Gothic Mirror', in *The (M)Other Tongue: Essays in Feminist Psychoanalytic Criticism*, ed. Shirley Nelson Garner, Claire Kahan and Madelon Sprengnether (Ithaca, NY: Cornell University Press, 1985), pp. 334–51. Similarly, Bette Roberts argues, in *The Gothic Romance: Its Appeal to Women Writers and Readers in Late Eighteenth-Century England* (New York: Arno, 1980), that 'by the end of the eighteenth century, the writer of gothic novels could assume both the premium placed upon female propriety and the female legal and financial dependence upon men, within a social context characterized by the emergence of the tenets and practices of economic and social individualism. Unlike the domestic novel, which allowed for the parallel reinforcement and idealization of the female status quo

in the domestic sphere, the gothic novel provided an outlet for the literary expression of repressed female wishes and fears' (p. 225). Also see Patricia Meyer Spacks, *Desire and Truth: Functions of Plot in Eighteenth-Century English Novels* (Chicago: Chicago University Press, 1989), pp. 147–74, and Katherine Ferguson Ellis, *The Contested Castle: Gothic Novels and the Subversion of Domestic Ideology* (Urbana: University of Illinois Press, 1989), pp. 121–4.

12.   In other words, as Claudia Johnson has convincingly argued, in *Udolpho* 'the civilized practices of sentimentality conceal rather than alleviate the wrongs of women', *Equivocal Beings: Politics, Gender, and Sentimentality in the 1790s: Wollstonecraft, Radcliffe, Burney, Austen* (Chicago: University of Chicago Press, 1995), p. 116. Johnson traces a pattern in which men are rewarded for their sentimentality, while 'the many stories about dying, murdered, abandoned, and otherwise wronged women which Emily hears, imagines and exemplifies – are presented finally not as cumulative evidence of male oppression, but as misrecognitions borne of excess of the wrong, pathological, female sort, and accordingly are demoted to "superstitious" tales (the adjective is always a pejorative in Radcliffe) believed only by credulous servants, paranoid maidens, and (for a time) spell-bound readers' (p. 97). While I agree with Johnson that *The Mysteries of Udolpho* suspiciously incriminates women for all of men's sufferings, she dismisses the corollary of this argument – that Radcliffe thereby empowers her female agents – somewhat too quickly (p. 115). While, to borrow Foucault's terms, Emily is compelled by the codes of sentimentality to practise strict self-discipline, the novel's shift from Montoni's anti-sentimental perspective to Emily's moral code ultimately punishes his more overt transgressions. After all, Emily ends up in control, not only of herself, but also of the lion's share of the novel's power and property. Thus, while I agree with Anne Williams' provocative suggestion that 'Gothic romance is family romance', this is not, as she suggests, because 'a new assertion of power by the family (and by a state operating according to the implicit rules of patriarchy) in conflict with a new impulse toward "self-fashioning" is precisely the materials of which eighteenth-century Gothic is made', since this assertion of power by the family and the state relies on precisely this impulse towards individual self-fashioning (see Anne Williams, *Art of Darkness: a Poetics of Gothic* (Chicago: University of Chicago Press, 1995), p. 32).

13.   Auerbach, *Romantic Imprisonment*, p. xi.

14.   Coral Ann Howells has noted that 'with Gothic novels the stability of the external world breaks down ... it has become interiorized, translated into the private world of imagination and neurotic sensibility', *Love, Mystery, and Misery: Feeling in Gothic Fiction* (London: Athlone, 1978), p. 26. Although recognizing the consequent importance of emotion in the gothic – 'we are talking about a fictive world whose topography is shaped by and is the shape given to emotional responses of uncertainty and threat' (p. 27) – and the power of gothic heroines – 'the gothic heroine is.... so delicately elusive that she

deprives aggression of its reality' (p. 9) – Howells pays almost no attention to the ways in which, in addition to internalizing the action of the novel, these heroines also internalize a whole system of controls and regulations by which they keep both internal and external dangers in check.

15. George Haggerty's well-known claim that 'the great challenge to the Gothic writer was the paradox between the subjective world of dreamlike private experience and the public objective world of the novel.... Radcliffe's insistence on "explanation"... is a measure of her refusal to take the formal implications of her material seriously' (*Gothic Fiction/Gothic Form* (University Park: Pennsylvania State University Press, 1989), pp. 20–2) inexplicably ignores this straightforward convergence of Radcliffe's method and moral.

16. Nancy Armstrong, *Desire and Domestic Fiction: a Political History of the Novel* (Oxford: Oxford University Press, 1987), p. 14.

7

The Medium of Exchange
Mandy Merck

Man has often made man himself, under the form of slaves, serve as the primitive material of money.

Karl Marx, *Capital*

The subject of this essay was the sleeper success of the 1990 film season, the year's number-one box-office draw in the United States, and a similar hit in Britain, winning Oscars for its screenwriter and supporting actress, and bringing its theme song, the Righteous Brothers' 1965 'Unchained Melody' back into the charts. Like its supernatural successor, *Bram Stoker's Dracula,* with its slogan 'Love Never Dies', this film was marketed as a 'date movie' – a 'date movie', we should note, in which the hero is posthumously penetrated, the heroine exhibits an enormous phallus, and the two of them engage in a climactic act of inter-racial troilism with Whoopi Goldberg. Furthermore, this is a film whose theme of untimely death was sometimes read as an AIDS allegory, and one which subsequently attracted the attention of lesbian critics for what Terry Castle has described as its 'peculiarly homoerotic effect'.[1] I am, of course, referring to the yuppie elegy, *Ghost* (written by Bruce Joel Rubin, directed by Jerry Zucker).

Judith Mayne's account of the film in *Cinema and Spectatorship* offers this synopsis:

Ghost tells the tale of a young couple, Sam and Molly, and the seemingly random mugging that kills Sam. As a spirit visible to the spectator but invisible to the rest of the characters in the film, Sam discovers that his best friend and co-worker Carl was responsible for his death, and he tries to warn Molly that her life may be in danger. When Sam discovers his murderer, Willie Lopez, who was hired by his co-worker, he follows him to the

Brooklyn neighborhood where he lives and by chance encounters Oda Mae Brown, a phony psychic who turns out to be genuine, since she is the only human being able to hear (although not to see) Sam and communicate with him. He convinces her to visit Molly, and after a series of complications involving embezzlement, fraud and disbelief, Molly not only believes that Oda Mae is in touch with Sam, she engages, through her, in one last embrace with him. At the conclusion of the film, the evil friend is dead and so is Sam, but each has gone his separate way, while Molly and Oda Mae are left in the land of the living.[2]

Unlike similar films of the ghost cycle of the period – notably *Always* and *Truly, Madly, Deeply* – *Ghost* offers no male substitute for the deceased loved one. This in itself tells us nothing about the film's attitude to heterosexuality – indeed, it may attest to the couple's undying devotion, or at least to the film's refreshing disregard for the familiar thematics of working through grief, learning to love again, etc. There are, however, significant other ways in which *Ghost* could be seen to suggest that heterosexual relations may be in crisis, or spent (a term whose ramifications I will pursue below), or in some sense *fantasmic*. Take, for example, the characterization of the two leads. Not only is Demi Moore's Molly – as an artist, intrepid interior decorator (her last name, Jensen, echoes that of the Danish Modern design group) and an apparent Shakespeare enthusiast – Sam's educational and class superior, she also spends a good deal of the film in the dark tailoring and gelled hairstyle of the metropolitan designer dyke. As for Patrick Swayze's Sam, he is both hunk and hayseed (his last name is Wheat), whose ducktail and tight trousers trail reminiscences of the actor's role in *Dirty Dancing* (and a masculinity so overstated as to be suspect) into the Wall Street precincts of the bank where he works.

There Sam seems, both in class and professional terms, somewhat out of his depth, anxiously attempting to deal with Japanese clients while desperately crunching numbers in a vain effort to identify the source of the vast sums which have mysteriously appeared in the bank's computerized accounts. Meanwhile, Molly rises from the couple's bed for a nocturnal session at her potter's wheel which is so frankly masturbatory and so unmistakably phallic that Sam must collapse the clay column which she straddles in order to initiate the film's only sex scene. ('I hope it wasn't a masterpiece', he laughs ruefully, acknowledging that it was *precisely* that.) Is it surprising then that this waning principle of masculine eminence should be extinguished altogether at the moment Molly (sporting a leather jacket and a quiff) protests that he never says 'I love you' and proposes marriage, and that this should occur after the couple attend a performance of *Macbeth*? But if this romance is 'unmann'd' (to quote that play) almost from its outset, how did it achieve its remarkable success? How did it manage to sell what its British critics easily recognized as its refusal of 'the robust assertiveness of the traditional male lead' (*The Sunday Times*)[3] and its transformation of the heroine into 'a ravishing boy' (*The Scotsman Weekend*)?[4]

The first answer to this question, the one which originally prompted its lesbian re-reading, is race. In her brief remarks on *Ghost* in *Feminism Without Women*, Tania Modleski proposes Whoopi Goldberg's Oda Mae as the film's most expressly liminal figure. The medium is the mediator in this movie because her racial difference, Modleski argues, can be read as sexual difference.[5] As she notes, Goldberg (who made her screen debut as a lesbian in *The Color Purple* and played one again in the 1995 *Boys on the Side*) has consistently functioned as the sexual other for her films' white characters, whether that otherness is represented as maternal (the literal 'mammy' role in *Clara's Heart* and *Corrina, Corrina*) or as masculine (Goldberg as the only logical father for Drew Barrymore's mysteriously black baby at the end of *Boys on the Side*). In part, this masculinity can be conveyed by Goldberg's sturdy build, contralto voice and broad face (whose ethnic connotations were registered with the cheerful racism of the British press in the *Daily Mirror*'s phrase, 'a smile as wide as a frying pan').[6] In *Ghost*, this impression of expansiveness and solidity is directly counterposed to Swayze's ethereal pallor and pixie features, as well as to the delighted narcissism with which Sam dons the colourful suspenders of the Wall Street financier. (There is less distance between Sam and Vida Boheme, Swayze's subsequent drag queen character in *To Wong Foo, Thanks for Everything! Julie Newmar*, than one might suppose.) Where the murdered Sam discovers his spectral state when a hospital trolley is driven right through him, Oda Mae's characterization is wholly within the traditional representation of the black subject as embodiment, physicality, even – despite her initial resistance to legitimate work – 'the human body as labour', labour which will be invisibly transmuted into money.[7]

Finally, in *Ghost*, as in the earlier *Jumping Jack Flash*, an impression of masculinity is conveyed by presenting Goldberg's character as a total travesty in feminine clothing (an effect elaborated in the later *Sister Act* films when she is forced to masquerade in the cumbersome robes and veil of a nun).

The central comic scene in *Ghost* has Oda Mae impersonate a wealthy client of Sam's bank in order to withdraw four million dollars which Carl has been laundering for a drugs ring – 'laundering', in the sense of 'whitening' and therefore legitimating, money being a densely impacted issue in this film. On the one hand, the drugs trade is visibly represented by a man of colour, Willie Lopez, and the black Brooklyn neighbourhood where both he and Oda Mae live. On the other, the ghostly Sam's effective appropriation of Oda Mae's physical capacities to warn Molly and thwart Carl calls to mind the embodied black labour on which white wealth is founded, 'slave labour' as Sam himself can joke when referring to his white friend's willingness to move furniture into his new loft. Fittingly, it is the black woman who foils Carl's efforts to cleanse the ill-gotten money of its criminal origins by claiming it herself.

The joke of the bank scene resides in the inadequacy of Oda Mae's performance as the holder of the account. Compelled by Sam to speak lines identifying herself with the appropriate name, account number and social background, she veers between erroneous repetition and wild improvisation in what is virtually a textbook demonstration of colonial mimicry.[8] To be sure, Oda Mae's ludicrous efforts to impersonate a wealthy (and therefore 'whiter') woman is itself an expert performance of a poor performance by a skilful comedienne. Yet, as with the British comic Lenny Henry's 1980s impressions of familiar black characters, Goldberg's rendition of a slum-dweller's awkward impersonation of a bourgeoise opens her to charges of minstrelsy, with the black actress herself adopting blackface. Goldberg's film roles have frequently been slated for such stereotyping. Witness bell hooks' complaints about Goldberg's 'sexist, racist' casting 'as mammy or ho'[9] or Michael Atkinson's censure in *The Guardian* newspaper's *Guide*:

> She's black and sexless like Hattie McDaniel used to be black and sexless, and it's no accident that Whoopi has played domestic maids several times, something I doubt you'll ever find Halle Berry or Whitney Houston doing.... Whoopi is the nineties

version of a lovable minstrel performer: eager to please, inoffensive and thoroughly objectified.[10]

Even Goldberg's stage name has been indicted by Michael Rogin in his study of black representation in American cinema, which notes its allusion to 'Making Whoopee', the title song of Eddie Cantor's 1930 Jewish blackface western, as well as her participation in a literal act of blackface, when she collaborated with her corked-up companion and co-star (of *Made in America*) Ted Danson, in a much-criticised attempt to parody racial stereotypes at New York's Friars Club.[11]

Whether or not we bring these indictments to the bank scene, its comic effect depends upon another trademark schtick of Goldberg's, her characters' discomfort in feminine clothing. Asked by Sam to wear 'a nice dress', Oda Mae abandons her comfortably flowing (and vaguely African) garb for a tight skirt, pink jacket and matching hat with high-heeled shoes. Her attempt to pass is thus also marked as one of gender, a masquerade which is predictably (cue awkward walk in heels) unsuccessful. Moreover, the name under which the bogus account is registered is Rita Miller, which in combination with Oda Mae Brown gives us Rita Mae Brown, the lesbian novelist whose best-known character, the autobiographical heroine of *Rubyfruit Jungle*, is called 'Molly'.

So, the black woman can, by means of a racial difference historically connoted as the negation of feminine sexuality, 'stand in' – Modleski argues – 'for the body of the white male'.[12] This substitution is made explicit when Oda Mae appears with the spectral Sam at the door of the couple's loft to warn Molly that she's in danger. Having ventriloquized Sam's lines and provided him with his props, Oda Mae is finally allowed to enter the immense apartment. As the two women wait for the police to arrive, Sam and Molly express their desire to touch each other once more – a touch which Oda Mae reluctantly offers to facilitate. 'You can use my body', she declares to a bewildered Sam, who eventually draws near and is dissolved into her. When Oda Mae opens her eyes and looks at Molly, a cut reveals a pair of white hands which are then clasped and stroked by a larger pair of black ones, adorned with vivid red nail polish. (The ambiguity of the shot contrasts the conventional handholding of the séance with the erotic implications of the gesture.) In a continuation of the same take, the camera cranes up Molly's bare arm past her bosom to track around until her face is revealed in profile, with eyes closed and lips parted expectantly. Then a white hand reaches out to caress her cheek....

Where, in a previous scene, Oda Mae remained in vision during spirit possession, now (after the moment of homoerotic anticipation implied by the continuous take) she is safely replaced by Sam. So different is her difference (in a film where white and black egregiously signify heaven and hell) that she cannot compete for a leading role in the romance, but instead functions – as Judith Mayne points out – 'to enable the fantasy of the white participants'.[13] (Never was a Supporting Actress Oscar so well earned.) At the crucial moment of contact, it is Oda Mae who is disembodied, who becomes the ghost, 'a living subaltern ghost', or, in her own racier vocabulary, a 'spook'.[14]

Here it should be noted that the ghost motif is virtually as old as cinema itself. There is now, of course, an entire library of spectral studies of the cinema, from Lotte Eisner's *The Haunted Screen*[15] to Geoffrey O'Brien's recent commentary on the cultural delirium created by what he calls *The Phantom Empire*.[16] But Gorky said it first, and most eloquently, after he saw the Lumière programme at the Nizhni-Novgorod fair in 1896:

> Last night I was in the Kingdom of Shadows.... Everything there – the earth, the trees, the people, the water and the air – is dipped in monotonous grey.... It is not life but its shadow, it is not motion but its soundless spectre.[17]

As if in recognition of its own peculiar 'hauntology'[18] as the medium of exchange which transforms the pro-filmic event into an apparition, the early cinema produced scores of 'phantom rides', in which cameras were mounted on gondolas, cars, balloons, funiculars, and especially trains, to provide the first eerily moving shots of the landscape; and it soon specialized in ghostly characters created by double exposure and superimposition. An entire comic genre was created to deploy these effects, the 'trick film', whose extensive numbers include Meliès' 1897 *Enchanted Hotel* (in which the bewildered lodger finds his clothes disappearing, his boots walking away without him, his furniture collapsing); the British director G. A. Smith's 1898 *Photographing a Ghost* (itself now a 'ghost film' remembered only in a catalogue synopsis); and a ten-minute 1901 version of *The Christmas Carol* entitled *Scrooge, or Morley's Ghost*.

And if the ghost motif dates back to the origins of cinema, the theme of racial substitution is nearly as ancient. Where the early cinema screened spectral rides by fastening cameras to moving trains, it also developed a much-repeated tunnel joke, in which a male railway passenger steals a kiss under the cover of darkness.[19] The joke begins with two white characters in the carriage, but by 1903 the transgressive theme is intensified, and the darkness of the tunnel duplicated, in the skin of the person kissed. The director of that year's *What Happened in the Tunnel*, the Edison pioneer Edwin S. Porter, is better known in the annals of racial representation for *Uncle Tom's Cabin*, in 1902 the longest American film and the first to use intertitles. Michael Rogin locates this film as the earliest of four major 'race movies' in the American cinema. (His other choices are *The Birth of a Nation*, *The Jazz Singer* and *Gone with the Wind*: an 'entire cycle', he argues, 'played out under white supremacy'.)[20] Despite previous experiments with multiple perspectives in Porter's semi-documentary *The Life of an American Fireman*, *Uncle Tom's Cabin* (whose slave characters are performed by whites in blackface) has only one 'point of view, and it is not an abolitionist one'.[21] As Rogin observes, the film's emphasis is on the interracial harmony of the plantation (literalized in shots of dancing slaves) where Tom and Little Eva are paired in a primitive prefiguration of Shirley Temple and Bojangles Robinson.

Months later, Porter's *What Happened in the Tunnel* restages this interracial eroticism without the camouflage of childhood. The generic kiss is given a new twist by the race of its recipient, the black servant of its intended target. (The characteristic fade to black covers their exchange of seats.) When the indignant suitor discovers that he has kissed the maid rather than the mistress, both women laugh in shared amusement, but their reversal of his masculine presumption is emphatically racist.[22] (The level of insult might be measured by an earlier version of the joke, the 1901 *An Idyll in the Tunnel*, in which the destination of the kiss is revealed to be a baby's bottom.) Eighty-seven years later, *Ghost* reworks this cinematic chestnut to affirm another cross-racial female alliance, even potentially to eroticize it, only to make the last-minute colour adjustment which whites-out Oda Mae.

This dematerialization of the perverse possibility, its 'apparitional' ontology, has been widely remarked in queer studies. The homosexual phantom offers heterosexual culture the advantage of its plausible deniability. Indeed, it could be said to enter eighteenth-century representation (specifically, a Gothic representation already disavowed by modernity) on condition of its incredibility.[23] But if the temporary 'ghosting' of Oda Mae renders any union between her and Molly equally incredible – no more than the erotic 'fantasy' which Modleski confesses to – neither can it save Sam. Having at last pronounced the loving declaration which he has avoided throughout the film with the term 'ditto', he bids Molly a final 'see you' and ascends into the white radiance of eternity. How should we read a romance whose titular ghost is the heterosexual hero and whose presiding spirit that of New Age credulity?

To answer this question, it is not necessary to forgo our consideration of either race or sexuality, but to situate it within the film's governing metaphors of commerce and communication. We should, as the anthropologist Jean-Joseph Goux advises, 'put ourselves therefore resolutely under the patronage of Hermes', better known to us under his Roman name, Mercury, the divinity of exchange.[24] In his essay on 'Numismatics', Goux develops Freud's observations on the unconscious association of the phallus with money (an association which the latter placed in the anal stage, and the infant's equation of the penis with the faeces and the faeces with the gift). Taking up Marx's argument that only those commodities whose value exceeds mere utility, which are not the object of immediate need (historically, gold metal), can achieve 'the form of general direct exchangeability'[25] or money, Goux compares the medium of exchange with the privilege of the phallus, a privilege achieved, as Lacan famously argues, at the expense of any immediacy whatsoever ('the phallus can only play its role as veiled, that is, as in itself the sign of the latency with which everything signifiable is struck as soon as it is raised (*aufgehoben*) to the function of signifier').[26]

Commenting on the isomorphism of the money function with the phallic function, Goux maintains that 'The phallus is the general equivalent of objects, and the father is the general equivalent of subjects, in the same way that gold is the general equivalent of products.'[27] And, like gold, which can only become money when it is '*fetishized* and subsequently *symbolized* and *idealized*', the father can only fulfil the role of the Law, of the sovereign arbiter of conflict 'as long as he is … kept at a distance'.[28]

What do we observe in the paternal register but that the mediation of the father is possible only to the extent that what functions as father is excluded from the world of other individuals, that is to say, is *killed*, functions only as the 'dead Father,' who rules only provided that he is separated from the group of people, that is, expelled into transcendence?[29]

If the commodity is only a social relation between men which assumes, in Marx's description, 'the fantastic form of a relation between things', the patriarchal function is no less apparitional.[30] No wonder our money man must become a ghost. (Or, as one of the film's critics observed, 'there is not a great deal of difference between a banker and a dead banker'.)[31]

Ghost opens onto the white light of the past, the dust-covered upper reaches of Sam and Molly's new loft, in which it is just possible to discern the relics of a tailor's workshop – what very possibly may have been, given the loft's downtown Manhattan location, a turn-of-the-century sweat shop. Its date might be ascertained by that of the Indian Head penny Sam finds there: 1898. The sequence of national expansion and expropriation commemorated by the coin's image of the defeated native is recapitulated domestically in the first seconds of the film. Having broken through a false ceiling to discover virtually an additional storey's worth of space, the yuppie couple (aided by Carl) claim all they survey and excitedly debate both its use and exchange value.

This is gentrification as manifest destiny. It literalizes the theme of upward mobility, the trajectory which will eventually take the hero to heaven, and nationalizes his identity. Here I differ with Judith Mayne's reading of the film's racial inscription, whose 'near-infantile' imagery of a white heaven and black hell, is permitted, she argues, by making 'Oda Mae virtually the only character in the film who speaks of race'.[32] Although no white character specifically refers to African-Americans, Sam complains of his anxiety in pitching to his bank's Japanese clients, and in ethnically laden terms: 'I can't very well tell them my Swedish pompom girl jokes.' And far from going unmarked, Sam, Molly and Carl's race is spectacularly displayed at the film's opening, when they emerge from the gloom of the unconverted loft in strikingly white workclothes and dust masks. (Their mock-Stakhanovite poses could be seen, however, as an attempt to appropriate an imaginary aesthetics of physical labour, notably muscular definition, from the actual workers who once laboured in the loft.) This marking is particularly detailed with regard to the hero's status as a white middle-class American man. It is not difficult to see Sam Wheat, with his amber waves of hair, as

Uncle Sam, the US male (living just opposite the Post Office, working on a street draped in the Stars and Stripes). And like other white American men in the movies of this particularly paranoid period, Sam is under siege – by Japanese businessmen, Puerto Rican muggers, phallic women, and, most of all, by his own destructive double, Carl, another fair-haired banker who attempts to take Sam's place with Molly.[33]

When the mugging commissioned by Carl goes wrong and Sam is shot, he becomes the victim of the injustice traditional to the ghost story. But it is through the everyday injustices that are the coinage of this story that Sam is able to take his revenge. Most significant is his domination of the reluctant black woman, whose body is possessed by this white man (to the tune of 'Unchained Melody'), made into his medium of access to Molly, just after he demands that she give him money. In an attempt to verify his presence to the sceptical Molly, who has been warned by the police of Oda Mae's convictions for fraud, Sam expropriates the sum of a single penny. 'Tell her it's for luck,' he commands Oda Mae, recalling the couple's earlier discovery of the 'good omen' of its nineteenth-century predecessor in the loft. Invisibly propelled by Sam, the penny rises up the surface of the door dividing the two women. On it is stamped the heroic image of another dead white man, Abraham Lincoln, famed for emancipating the nation's slaves and subsequently suffering his own assassination. (Moreover, Honest Abe is the prototypically unpretentious figure of the nation, 'the pattern American' in Hawthorne's phrase, 'directness and plainness and principle' in Leo Braudy's elaboration).[34]

The image of this coin seemingly rising under its own power, indeed, that of a dead man's head ascending, conforms to the uniquely spectral status which Marx ascribed to the movement of money: 'The independent existence of the exchange-value of a commodity is here a transient apparition, by means of which the commodity is immediately replaced by another commodity.... Hence, in this process which continually makes money pass from hand to hand, the mere symbolic existence of money suffices.'[35]

Murdered for money, Sam becomes what money is – 'a transient apparition', a ghost. ('In order, therefore, that a commodity may in practice act effectively as exchange-value, it must quit its bodily shape.')[36] If he will ultimately go to heaven because he is 'good' (a moral distinction here characterized by an All-American artlessness – sleeping through *Macbeth*, cherishing his ugly TV chair, abjuring romantic declarations), he's also got the 'goods' of an exceptionally prosperous life. In English, as Lacan reminds us in his seminar on *The Ethics of Psychoanalysis*, the meaning of the plural 'goods' (i.e. property, wares, commodities) is opposed to that of the singular (i.e. something conforming to the moral order of the universe). This is not the case in French, he argues, which allows *les bons* both a moral and an economic meaning (the righteous *and* the valuable). Trading on his native tongue, Lacan moves from the compatibility of the economic and moral good in the French plural to their non-opposition in an ethics grounded in power. The philosophical basis for this ethics is Kant's *Critique of Practical Reason*, which challenges Bentham's utilitarian pleasure principle (that the law should be directed at securing the greatest good for the greatest number) by arguing that good defined as well-being, or pleasure, is merely an object of sensation, not of reason. In other words, feeling good is not necessarily good. On the contrary, Kant argues, in setting itself against our inclinations, the moral law often produces pain.

What has all this to do with our yuppie ghost? Let's look at *the good*, which Bentham would describe as *the useful* in its beneficial capacities (use values, in Marx's terms) and at *goods*, which are private property, good not in their utility (although they may well be useful), but good as objects of personal ownership, and therefore of power. 'To exercise control over one's goods is to have the right to deprive others of them,' Lacan warns, quoting Proudhon's 'All property is theft.' 'The domain of the good is the birth of power.'[37] Following Kant's ethical observation, that the law is not founded on the good, but the good founded on the law (the law isn't there to do you good, but you're only good if you obey it), Lacan argues that the moral law separates good will from any beneficial consequence. In that respect, the law is empty, grounded in no use or pleasure except the *jouissance* of its own exercise. Or, as Molly replies to Sam's question about what all their loft space is *for*: 'Just space.'

This ghostly space is the founding unit of value in this story, the reason people buy lofts, the nothing for which they toil, the *ex nihilo* which secures their signifying chain. It is both the origin of ambition and its merciful release: the white-out into which Sam blissfully merges at the film's conclusion. Where that other famous banker of the cinema, George Bailey, gratefully chooses castration over extinction at the end of *It's a Wonderful Life*, the already 'unmann'd' Sam finally accedes to oblivion – perhaps because, unlike George, he is required to surrender so little in the move from one very large space to another.[38] Where George is schooled in the slogan under his father's portrait – 'All you can take with you is that which you've given away', Sam tells Molly as he rises aloft, 'The love inside – you take it with you.'

How appropriate, then, that Sam characteristically – and, as he insists, sincerely – expresses this love with the word 'ditto' (a term of acquiescence to which Molly finally acquiesces, and echoes, in her reply to Sam's parting declaration). 'Ditto', an Italian dialect past participle of *dire*, 'to say', has been employed in English since the seventeenth century to say something without saying it, to say, literally, that whatever it is has already been said, is 'the aforesaid'. And 'ditto', of course, is typically abbreviated by two dots or quote-marks enclosing … white space.

If this makes it the ideal signifier for the exhausted endearments of the Hollywood romance, it also corresponds to the purely mediating function that Goux ascribes in a later essay to the 'post-traditional phallus'.[39] Where the ancient predecessor of that phallus functioned as a token of exchange, the badge proudly worn by the young male initiated into the incest taboo and its compensations (renounce your kinswomen and receive a bride from another family), now, Goux argues, the phallus is only *logos*, a signifier of entitlement, but no guarantee of it. (Just being a man won't get you a woman, although it might, as Goux points out, permit you to apply for a *'mortgage* on a possible, though entirely indeterminate, woman.')[40] The reference to finance is not beside the point: as Goux stresses, the cessation of the formal exchange of women between clans (like that of barter in general) made the phallus even more like money, a signifier of value in the abstract, exchange value.[41] Underwriting it, Goux reminds us (echoing Lacan echoing Kant) is the law, which the subject must obey because it is the law, not because it offers any reward for that obedience.

Detached from the utility of reciprocity, the phallus takes on the talismanic significance of 'pure mediation'[42] 'just as the financial sign is nothing but the indefinite inscription and circulation of a debt by means of accounting'[43] – the ghostly millions which appear and disappear from Sam's computer screen. As for speech, it too is subsumed in the aforesaid of 'infinite substitution', 'ditto' in reply to 'ditto'.

This returns us to the peculiar success of this troubled romance. Its ending, and that of Goux's essay on the phallus, leaves me with a morbid interpretation. If Sam's early retirement is just another example of what Goux calls the 'accelerated entropy' of our age, we might regard his ascension into heaven as a manifestation of a masculine death drive, the ultimate upward mobility of the male professional, the final sacrifice required to redeem the moribund prestige of the phallus.[44] The attraction of *Ghost* might then be, not that of a love which unites its central couple beyond the grave, but the annulment of all such entanglements, and most of all, in the case of the white male subject, that of the self.

As for *Ghost*'s medium, a final postscript: the success of this film and the subsequent *Sister Act* briefly made Whoopi Goldberg the highest-paid actress in Hollywood, a remarkable achievement for a black performer and an extraordinary one for a black woman 'known to be combative and unglamorous'.[45] If her character in *Ghost* is connotative of the congealed labour represented by the African-American subject, she soon became that apotheosis of the commoditized individual, the bankable star, reputedly the first actress able to 'open' a movie. Although Goldberg eventually yielded this primacy (to Demi Moore, among her successors), she remains a key figure in Hollywood while retaining her 'outsider' image. This precarious position is perhaps best represented in her hosting of the Academy Awards, in 1994 and again in 1996, a mediating role which has not traditionally gone to a movie star, but to a stand-up comic-cum-talk-show host (from Johnny Carson to David Letterman to Billy Crystal) capable of the required monologues and ad-libs. (Goldberg has hosted both TV charity specials and her own TV talk show.)

Before the 1996 Awards ceremony, Jesse Jackson, noting that only one of the 166 nominees was black (short-film director Diane Houston), urged those attending to wear the Rainbow Coalition ribbon in protest against the under-representation of African-Americans in the film industry. Quincy Jones, the Awards' black producer, readily concurred. Goldberg did not. Instead, she compered the proceedings in a ribbonless black velvet gown by Donna Karan and diamond jewellery said to be worth ... four million dollars. Her opening monologue ridiculed the plethora of ribbons donned at the ceremony for political causes (including one she designated as being for 'gay rights', presumably the AIDS ribbon), remarks which can, of course, be read as criticizing the sanctimony of those who wear their loyalties on their lapels, and then only once a year. 'You don't ask a black woman to buy an expensive dress and then cover it in ribbons', she added, neatly declaring her own political loyalties in the process.[46] This combination of hipness and conservatism seems totally consistent with Goldberg's cynical and sentimental role in *Ghost*, which can be seen to refute the old Hollywood stereotype of the superstitious black subject, rolling her eyes in terror at some imagined spectre, while ultimately endorsing New Age belief – albeit in a spirit of nothing very much at all. You may not laugh, but I suspect that this expert mediator did. All the way to the bank.

Notes

1. Terry Castle, *The Apparitional Lesbian* (New York: Columbia University Press, 1993), p. 241, fn.6: 'When Sam indeed begins "speaking through" Oda Mae, professing his love, the effect is peculiarly homoerotic: as if Oda Mae were speaking for herself instead of the ghost. The fiction of ghostly return, in other words, somehow licenses an uncanny "bodying forth" – onscreen – of female-female eroticism.'

2. Judith Mayne, *Cinema and Spectatorship* (London and New York: Routledge, 1993), pp. 149–50.

3. Iain Johnstone, 'Haunted by a Light Vessel', *The Sunday Times*, 7 October 1990, Section 7, pp. 8–9.

4. William Parente, 'Soul-Less Ghost', *The Scotsman Weekend*, 6 October 1990, p. III.

5. Judith Mayne also describes Goldberg's function in *Ghost* as that of 'mediator – between the audience and the improbability of the film, between the widely different stylistic reference points of the film', in *Cinema and Spectatorship*, p. 151.

6. Anton Antonowicz, 'Ghostbuster', *The Daily Mirror*, 19 September 1990, p. 15.

7. Richard Dyer, *Heavenly Bodies: Film Stars and Society* (London: British Film Institute, 1987), pp. 138–9: 'Through slavery and imperialism, black people have been the social group most clearly identified by and exploited for their bodily labour. Blacks thus became the most vivid reminders of the human body as labour in a society busily denying it.'

8. See Homi Bhabha, *The Location of Culture* (London and New York: Routledge, 1994).

9. bell hooks, *Reel to Real: Race, Sex and Class at the Movies* (New York and London: Routledge, 1996), p. 94.

10. Michael Atkinson, 'Video', *The Guide*, 7–13 December 1996, p. 115.

11. Michael Rogin, *Blackface, White Noise* (Berkeley, Los Angeles, London: University of California Press, 1996), p. 9. But 'Whoopi', as her profiles often note, also suggests the joke cushion and its simulated

flatulence, an emission which is racialized in *Ghost* when 'Rita Miller' tries to cover a fluffed line in the bank scene by explaining that she's got 'gas'.

12. Tania Modleski, *Feminism without Women: Culture and Criticism in a 'Postfeminist' Age* (New York and London: Routledge, 1991), pp. 131–3.

13. Judith Mayne, *Cinema and Spectatorship*, p. 143.

14. Joseba Gabilondo, *Cinematic Hyperspace: New Hollywood Cinema and Science Fiction Film – Image Commodification in Late Capitalism*, PhD Dissertation in Comparative Literature, University of California, San Diego, 1991, p. 204.

15. Lotte Eisner, *The Haunted Screen* (Berkeley: University of California Press, 1969).

16. Geoffrey O'Brien, *The Phantom Empire* (New York and London: W.W. Norton, 1993).

17. Maxim Gorky, as printed in the *Nizhegorodski listok* newspaper, 4 July 1896, and signed 'I.M. Pacatus', translated by Leda Swan, in Jay Leyda (ed.), *Kino: A History of the Russian and Soviet Film* (London: George Allen & Unwin, 1960), p. 407.

18. See Jacques Derrida, *Specters of Marx*, trans. Peggy Kamuf (New York and London: Routledge, 1994), p. 10: 'Let us call it a *hauntology*. This logic of haunting would not be merely larger and more powerful than an ontology or a thinking of Being.... It would harbor within itself, but like circumscribed places or particular effects, eschatology and teleology themselves.'

19. Ian Christie, *The Last Machine: Early Cinema and the Birth of the Modern World* (London: British Film Institute, 1994), p. 18, argues that 'film-makers started offering their customers short interludes, often titled *A Kiss in the Tunnel*, to splice into the over-familiar phantom rides'.

20. Michael Rogin, *Blackface, White Noise*, p. 73.

21. Michael Rogin, *Blackface, White Noise*, p. 75.

22. See also Miriam Hansen, *Babel and Babylon: Spectatorship in American Silent Film* (Cambridge, Mass. and London: Harvard University Press, 1991), p. 39, for a commentary on this film.

23. See Terry Castle, *The Apparitional Lesbian*, especially pp. 60–2, and Diana Fuss, 'Introduction' to her edited collection, *Inside/Out* (New York and London: Routledge, 1991).

24. Jean-Joseph Goux, 'The Phallus: Masculine Identity and the "Exchange of Women"', *differences*, Spring 1992: 40–75, p. 59.

25. Karl Marx, *A Contribution to the Critique of Political Economy* (New York: International Library, 1904), p. 168.

26. Jacques Lacan, 'The Meaning of the Phallus', in Juliet Mitchell and Jacqueline Rose (eds), *Feminine Sexuality* (London: Macmillan, 1982), pp. 74–85, p. 82.

27. Jean-Joseph Goux, 'Numismatics', *Symbolic Economies* (Ithaca: Cornell University Press, 1990), pp. 9–63, p. 24.

28. Jean-Joseph Goux, 'Numismatics', p. 18.

29. Jean-Joseph Goux, 'Numismatics', pp. 17-18.

30. Karl Marx, *Capital*, Vol. I (London: Lawrence & Wishart, 1974), p. 77.

31. Iain Johnstone, 'Haunted by a Light Vessel', p. 8.
32. Judith Mayne, *Cinema and Spectatorship*, p. 152.
33. See, in particular, *Falling Down* (1992), for its own elegiac treatment of the doomed white middle-class American male, and its own coin motif.
34. See Leo Braudy, *The Frenzy of Renown: Fame and Its History* (New York and Oxford: Oxford University Press, 1986), pp. 495–7.
35. Karl Marx, *Capital*, Vol. I, p. 129.
36. Karl Marx, *Capital*, Vol. I, p. 105.
37. Jacques-Alain Miller (ed.), *The Seminar of Jacques Lacan, Book VII, The Ethics of Psychoanalysis 1959–1960* (New York and London: W. W. Norton, 1992), p. 229.
38. See Kaja Silverman, *Masculinity at the Margins* (New York and London: Routledge, 1992).
39. Jean-Joseph Goux, 'The Phallus: Masculine Identity and the "Exchange of Women"', p. 70.
40. Jean-Joseph Goux, 'The Phallus', p. 67.
41. Gayatri Chakravorty Spivak, 'Ghostwriting', *Diacritics* 25:2 (Summer 1995) 65–84, p. 78, fn.25, denounces Freudo-Marxian 'psychoanalytic radical chic' analogies, singling out the simile 'money is like the phallus'. In reply, I submit this *Ghost*.
42. Jean-Joseph Goux, 'The Phallus', p. 68.
43. Jean-Joseph Goux, 'The Phallus', p. 72.
44. Jean-Joseph Goux, 'The Phallus', p. 73.
45. Tasha Colin, 'Making Whoopi', *Daily Mail,* 24 November 1992, p. 7.
46. Quoted in 'Black Protest Fails to Disrupt Ceremony', London *Evening Standard*, 26 March 1996, p. 5.

8

The Postcolonial Ghost Story

Ken Gelder and Jane M. Jacobs

Let us begin by noting that Australia's postcolonial condition is for the most part a consequence of claims made upon it – land claims, compensation claims, and so on – by its Aboriginal people.* It would be possible to describe Aboriginal people at this point in Australia's modern history as *charismatic*, in their capacity to mobilize forces much larger than their 'minority' status would suggest. When a claim is made on a sacred site, this feature is especially apparent: a government can look forward to losing millions of dollars through legal procedures that invariably bring together a 'smorgasbord' (as one newspaper described it) of interest groups over a protracted period of time. In this climate, Aborigines certainly continue to receive sympathy for what they do not have – good health, adequate housing, and so on – and yet at the same time they draw resentment from white Australians because they seem to be claiming more than their 'fair share'. We have elsewhere described this double-headed view of Aborigines as 'postcolonial racism' – a form of racism which sees Aborigines as lacking on the one hand, and yet appearing on the other hand to have too much: too much land, too much national attention, too much 'effect'.[1] It is surely a strange irony to hear white Australians these days – including some maverick Federal politicians – describing Aborigines as more franchised, more favoured, than they are. The benign side of this kind of racism works itself out in various polemics by white Australians which turn to Aboriginal spirituality as a way of healing a non-Aboriginal malaise.[2] Again, Aborigines are seen to have what we do not have: spirituality, sociality, charisma, cohesion: something extra.

We can nominate two important precursors which speak to this strange modern predicament. The sociologist Emile Durkheim, in

The Elementary Forms of the Religious Life (1915), drew an intimate connection between spirituality – religion – and sociality, using available material on Australian Aborigines to illustrate the point. For Durkheim, 'primitive' religion provides the paradigm for modern society in the sense that it establishes a notion of the *social* – so that, from a certain point of view, the 'primitive' and the modern ('the man of to-day') are more alike than one might at first imagine. Durkheim describes modernity in terms of 'the development of luxury', as if it stands in a kind of superstructural relationship to the more 'elementary' features of the 'primitive'.[3] Yet even this distinction is compromised, as when he notes that 'primitive' religion can itself be a 'luxurious' thing: 'it is not equivalent to saying that all luxury is lacking to the primitive'.[4] So modernity is seen to have something extra, something more than the 'primitive' – which is lacking. And yet there is this concession which suggests that the 'primitive' does not lack, that it, too, has that something extra which otherwise defines modernity. The paradox of this position is nicely expressed in Durkheim's subsequent description of 'the lower religions' as 'rudimentary and gross'.[5] At first glance, such a description would seem simply to stabilize the 'primitive' status of Aboriginal religion. But in fact these two words flatly contradict each other. 'Rudimentary' means 'undeveloped' or 'elemental', and maintains this sense that 'primitive' religion is not modern. But 'gross' means 'luxuriant' or 'flagrant' or 'excessive': it has quite the opposite effect. In other words, this description suggests lack and plenitude *at the same time*, both distinguishing the primitive from the modern and yet allowing it to overflow *into* modernity on the grounds that it, too, can be a 'luxurious' thing. We can write the following equation for this strange paradox: the 'primitive' is (not) modern. And this is not dissimilar to the contradiction that underwrites postcolonial racism: that one (i.e. a minority culture, Aborigines) can lack and have that 'something extra' at the same time.

Our second precursor for thinking through this strange paradox is Sigmund Freud's influential essay, 'The "Uncanny"' (1919), published just four years after Durkheim's *The Elementary Forms of the Religious Life*. Freud's concern is also with the (dis)entanglement of the 'primitive' and the modern, the past and the present. It is addressed primarily to the psyche, but it also speaks directly to the question of one's place in the world, attending to anxieties which were symptomatic of an on-going process of realignment in post-war Europe. It is well known that Freud elaborates the 'uncanny' by way of two German words whose meanings, which at first seem diametrically opposed, in fact circulate through each other. These two words are: *heimlich*, which Freud glosses as 'home', a familiar or accessible place; and *unheimlich*, which is unfamiliar, strange, inaccessible, unhomely.[6] An 'uncanny' experience may occur when one's home – one's place – is rendered somehow and in some sense unfamiliar; one has the experience, in other words, of being in place and 'out of place' *simultaneously*. This happens precisely at the moment when one is made aware that one has unfinished business with the past, at the moment when the past returns as an 'elemental' force (and let us signal our interest in ghosts here through this word: 'elemental') to haunt the present day. Freud's 'uncanny' can be applied directly to conditions in postcolonial Australia, in particular after the Mabo decision in 1992 and the subsequent anxieties about who might come to own what. An Aboriginal claim to land is quite literally a claim concerning unfinished business, a claim which enables what should have been laid to rest to overflow into the otherwise 'homely' realm of modernity. In this moment of decolonization, what is 'ours' is also potentially, or even always already, 'theirs' – an aspect of the ongoing recovery of Aboriginal identity in the modern scene of postcolonial Australia. The past returns to the present as the thing which was lacking but which – when it does return – then functions as that 'something extra'. An Aboriginal claim for land or for a sacred site (especially when it happens to be rich in mineral deposits) is often represented quite literally in this way, as something the nation cannot afford: a 'luxury'.

We have elsewhere used an evocative word to describe this return and the effects it generates, a word lifted from a footnote in Jacques Derrida's seminal essay 'Différance' (1968): *solicit*. Here, Derrida alerts us to some of the meanings embedded in the kind of structure which involves one thing (e.g. the past) soliciting another thing (e.g. the present) – when *solicit* is taken as an activating verb.[7] But let us give a fuller picture of this word's activating possibilities here. It can mean, firstly, 'to incite', 'to allure', 'to attract' – definitions which rightly draw attention to the seductive features of Aboriginal spirituality, sociality, and so on for many modern non-Aboriginal Australians. But there are other, less benign meanings embedded in this word: 'to disturb', 'to make anxious', 'to fill with concern'. We can also cite a more dramatic definition of *solicit* given by Derrida's translator: 'to shake the whole, to make something tremble in its entirety'.[8] Let us note that an Aboriginal claim for a sacred site, for example, can indeed work to 'shake' the entire country, to unsettle the regulative, homely economies of a 'settler' nation. One could equally as well read this force in a positive way, of course, as a way of inducing the kind of realignment of power that accompanies decolonization. In this context, we should remember the more obvious meaning of the word *solicit*: 'to conduct (a lawsuit)', 'to press or represent a matter', 'to transact or negotiate'. This is a real feature of Aboriginal claims to land and sacred sites in Australia, which are always conducted through the law courts and which precisely involve transactions and negotiations – between the one and the other, the past and the present, Aborigines and modernity.

Let us just indicate some of the uses to which the 'uncanny' can be put in the context of postcolonial Australia. We often speak of Australia as a 'settler' nation – but the 'uncanny' can remind us that a condition of unsettled-ness folds into this often taken-for-granted mode of occupation. We often imagine a (future) condition of 'reconciliation', and indeed, a great deal is invested in the packaging of this image as a means of selling it to the nation – but the 'uncanny' can remind us of just how unreconcilable this image is with itself. It is not simply that Aboriginal and white Australians will either be reconciled with each other or they will not; rather, these two possibilities (reconciliation; the impossibility of reconciliation) co-exist and flow through each other in what is often a productively unstable dynamic. Another, not unrelated, binary structure at work in contemporary Australia can also be mentioned here. In relation to Aborigines, modern white Australians can either be innocent, in the sense of not actually having participated in the earlier horrors of colonization, in the traumas of the past; or they can be guilty, in the sense that even to be postcolonial is not to be free from these past horrors, which ceaselessly return to haunt us. How implicated *are* postcolonials in the past? Paradoxically enough, the appeal to innocence casts white Australians as 'out of place', uninvolved in those formative colonial processes; while one's participation in what is sometimes cynically called 'the guilt industry' would render white Australians as in fact too involved, too embedded *in* place in the sense that every one of them, even the most recent immigrant, automatically inherits the (mis)fortunes of Australia's colonial history. In postcolonial Australia, however, it may well be that both of these positions are inhabited at the same time: one can be both innocent ('out of place') *and* guilty ('in place'). And this is entirely consistent with postcoloniality as a contemporary condition, whereby one remains within the structures of colonialism (with all its attendant horrors) even as one is temporally located beyond them or 'after' them. An Aboriginal claim for a sacred site is, as we have suggested, a salutary reminder that the past is always a matter of unfinished business. We may 'innocently' imagine that there is no place for Aboriginal sacredness in a modern secular nation. But in fact it seems – to some commentators, at least – as if sacredness is potentially *all over the place*, as if the nation has (reluctantly? willingly?) given itself over to the unleashed requirements of a previously diminished minority culture – as if it is ceaselessly being *solicited*, seduced, shaken up, taken to court.

The features we are describing here are, of course, by no means peculiar to contemporary Australia. Speaking broadly, this sense of modernity as a form of 'unsettled settledness' – as an 'uncanny' thing – is experienced only too often elsewhere in the world. When a nation (especially when it is imagined as 'one nation', to use a phrase commonly invoked both in Australia and in Britain) engages with others – indigenous people, immigrants, separatists – a sense of national identity is both enabled and disabled. The presence of 'foreigners at home' can intensify a nation's investment in the idea of a national 'self' at the very moment at which such an idea is traumatically unsettled. Julia Kristeva's book, *Strangers to Ourselves* (1991), is a meditation on this problematic which draws, inevitably perhaps, upon Freud's seminal essay. A nation's engagement with 'foreigners' leads her to offer a definitive structure for modernity built around the tension between *union* and *separation* – what in Australia would be 'reconciliation', and the impossibility of reconciliation.[9] The problem here involves the fact that boundaries which might have distinguished the one from the other are no longer tenable or even recognisable. For Kristeva, a certain anxiety results which stems from the difficulty of disentangling what is one's 'home' from what is not one's 'home' – what is 'foreign' or strange. As Kristeva notes, Freud's uncanny speaks to this anxiety directly:

Freud wanted to demonstrate at the outset, on the basis of a semantic study of the German adjective *heimlich* and its antonym *unheimlich*, that a negative meaning close to that of the antonym is already tied to the positive term *heimlich*, 'friendly *(sic)* comfortable', which would also signify 'concealed, kept from sight', 'deceitful and malicious', 'behind someone's back'. Thus, in the very word *heimlich*, the familiar and intimate are reversed into their opposites, brought together with the contrary meaning of 'uncanny strangeness' harboured in *unheimlich*.[10]

In fact, *unheimlich* is further glossed by Freud as meaning 'withdrawn from knowledge', obscure and inaccessible – as well as untrustworthy.[11] It is worth noting that these have been available characterizations of Aboriginal relations to the sacred, where secrecy is often associated (by mining companies, by government officials, etc.) with deception. But even a racist charge of deception is open to the uncanny effect since it is spoken in a structure which can never be subjected to any definitive kind of verification. If Aborigines say that a sacred site is here, and a non-Aboriginal 'expert' says that this sacred site is somewhere else – which is the way some claims about sacredness fall out – what you actually get is two sacred sites for the price of one! The latter claim, in other words, by no means disproves the former – nor can it ever hope to do so in any 'settled' way. In this context it is worth recalling that Freud himself had noted, '*heimlich* is a word the meaning of which develops in the direction of ambivalence'.[12] Kristeva's strategy is to internalize and individuate this ambivalence, as a means of coping with it. We should, she suggests, come to terms with the 'stranger in ourselves': 'The foreigner is within us. And when we flee from our struggle against the foreigner, we are fighting our unconscious – that "improper" facet of our impossible "own and proper"'.[13] So Kristeva draws a connection between a 'foreigner' and the 'improper' unconscious which solicits one's sense of a 'proper' self, i.e. one's sense of property. It would be worth noting, however, that her advocation of a psychic coming-to-terms with the 'foreigner' within us all is in itself a 'reconciliatory' gesture which would remove the kinds of ambivalence that inhere in the uncanny. But there is no need to wish 'improper' anxieties away – at least in the postcolonial context, where they may well have productive effects.

Australia may itself have been a 'foreigner at home'. At least, this is the account given by Ross Gibson in his book, *South of the West: Postcolonialism and the Narrative Construction of Australia* (1992). For

Gibson, Australia has been 'a duplicitous object' for the western world in the sense that it is both 'demonstrably a "European" society' (i.e. familiar) and yet also 'fantastic and otherworldly' (i.e. unfamiliar):

> Westerners can recognise themselves there at the same time as they encounter an alluringly exotic and perverse entity, the phantasm called Australia. Westerners can look South and feel 'at home', but, because the region has also served as a projective screen for European aspiration and anxiety, Australia also calls into question the assumptions and satisfactions by which any society or individual feels at home.[14]

The sense of this last sentence may not be entirely clear, but overall Gibson seems to be saying that – from the externalized position of the westerner – one can imagine being 'in place' in Australia only through the realization that one is also 'out of place'. Gibson in fact invokes the uncanny in his description (although it is an un-acknowledged invocation): Australia is 'both strange and familiar, in other words, an enigma'.[15] The problem with this book, however, is that although it is prepared to indulge this image of Australia as an 'enigma' to the rest of the world (a view which, in our opinion, would need some qualifications since it sounds like a variant on the Australian 'cultural cringe'), when it looks at Australia from *within* it produces an image of the country which is, in the first instance at least, far from uncanny.

Gibson is aware of the mythical teleology of 'settler' Australia, which fantasises about 'reconciliation' or (using Kristeva's word) 'union' – where a colony 'would gradually "belong", it would eventually be "in place", and it would cease to be a colony'.[16] However, he yearns for this teleology himself from time to time, especially – as it happens – when he is drawn to consider Australian landscape poetry:

> It is the development of this sense of subjective immersion in place, this ability to place and to think oneself in systems of settlement other than the acquisitive process of conquistadorial survey, that might be a reason for optimism as the third colonial century commences in the South Land.[17]

Oddly – through the 'subjective' space of landscape poetry – Gibson creates the possibility of being 'at home' in Australia, a possibility he had disavowed elsewhere. Even more oddly still, he maps out a route through which settlers can actually become, at some kind of final moment, *indigenous*. He can do this because in spite of his book's subtitle, he does not address the concept of post-colonialism at all.[18] Indeed, Aborigines themselves (the actual indigenes) barely feature in his discussion. Gibson's homely space, however, is not *entirely* bereft of otherness, as this long passage on a notorious outback Australian techno-military installation suggests:

> But this is not to say that everyone has redefined their under-standing of their place in the landscape. The more militarist attitude, which sees the continent as a foe to be brought to rule, still ranges abroad. The submerged domes of Pine Gap are obvious talismans: white Australians' (mythically induced) sense of the untouchability of the geographical centre has been turned to military advantage: what better place to locate unknowable technology than the arcane heartland where Nature preserves the most occult of mysteries? It is a canny [i.e. not uncanny!] ploy. Whereas white Australia has traditionally looked for security *from* the landscape, a black magic promises to turn the world upside down by maintaining that there is security *in* the landscape.... When the land becomes so otherworldly that only a 'masonic' class of technocrats can administer it, the conquistadorial class has taken its project to its end point....[19]

What Gibson produces here, strangely enough, is an image of a sacred site. We are directed to 'the submerged domes of Pine Gap' at the 'geographical centre' of Australia – rather than, say, to Uluru (Ayers Rock). This installation is made 'otherworldly'; it is secretive and 'masonic', returning us to Kristeva's gloss on *unheimlich*. It uses (in a strange invocation of the 'primitive') 'black magic'; it is unset-tling to Gibson's yearning for homeliness-in-the-nation. There is an irony in noting that this particular sacred site – for all its 'primitive' features – is indeed a *modern* one. And in fact it is modernity itself which produces the uncanny effect for Gibson's ideal of settlement, a modernity which is uncomfortably underwritten by globalized, 'militarist' capital. Indeed, what we have with Gibson's image of Pine Gap is a textbook case of the uncanny effect whereby, through an act of repression, Pine Gap appears unfamiliar to Gibson precisely because it provides him with an image of modernity which is *all too familiar*. So Pine Gap is to Gibson what (in his account) Australia is to the rest of the world: 'Both strange and familiar, in other words, an enigma'. Of course, if, under modernity, Australia were able to be settled through any form other than capitalism, then it might truly *be* an enigma! By imagining an Australia divorced from globalized capital, Gibson gives us a nostalgic structure where one can be 'subjectively immersed' in the former in order to remain alienated from the latter. In this arrangement, it is not that Australia is an 'enigma' to the west, but the other way around.

When she thinks about one's relations to the 'foreign', Julia Kristeva wonders what kind of response might be forthcoming: 'To worry or to smile, such is the choice when we are assailed by the strange; our decision depends on how familiar we are with our own ghosts.'[20] We might well ask, how familiar is *Australia* with its own ghosts? Who 'smiles' at them and who 'worries' about them? Let us turn, as a way of thinking through this issue, to a genre of writing which tunes into the landscape in a very different way to the kind of poetry which Ross Gibson had privileged: the Australian ghost story.

Certainly the ghost story in Australia is a minor genre, a *marginal* genre. To recall Durkheim's telling phrase, the ghost story is 'rudimentary' (an 'elementary' form, something less than literature, even something 'primitive') – and yet there is also something 'gross' or luxurious about it, too. These contradictory characteristics are built into the sensationalism of this genre. Many Australian ghost stories are 'over-the-top', hysterical, histrionic, spectacular, overflowing, meandering, 'creaky', indulgent: all this unfolds through the constraints of a minor genre. Australian ghost stories are also generally site-based and there is often an implied connection between a haunted site and a sacred site, as in William Sylvester Walker's evocative story, 'The Evil of Yelcomorn Creek' (1899).[21] But these stories do not respect the localness of their sites; they are never constrained in this sense. Instead, they show how their sites work to influence or impress people who are always passing through – people who take the effects of those sites elsewhere when they leave (as they usually do), spreading them across the nation. So the Australian ghost story is built around a local site, but dramatically extends the influence or reach of that site. It produces a site-based impression which spirals out of itself to effect, or affect, one's sense of the nation's well-being. Indeed, one's sense of the nation's well-being may well be disturbed by the impression one has of a local, haunted site, as if a supposedly 'marginal' thing can account for far more than its marginality would suggest.

A haunted site and a sacred site may, then, share certain features – and of course, the latter can also be associated with death, or with burial, and with the various powers which death (or the disturbance of the dead) has unleashed. A haunted site may appear empty or uninhabited; but in fact, it is always *more* than what it appears to be. To settle on a haunted site is to risk unsettlement, a postcolonial condition which acknowledges (rather than suppresses) the fact of previous, albeit displaced, inhabitation. The postcolonial ghost story is thus often quite literally about 'the return of the repressed' – namely, the return of the 'truth' (or a 'truth effect') about colonization. To dwell on a haunted site may produce a particular kind of postcolonial 'worrying'; it is always better to pass through and, as we have suggested, the haunted site, like the sacred site, can spread its influence rather than restrict it simply to its precise location. We can think of Uluru as an example; the number of visitors who are drawn to it, pass through it and carry its effects away with them would suggest that tourism is not entirely inconsistent with sacredness in its modern form.

In Australian postcolonial ghost stories the haunted site is known primarily through its *effects*, which, because they are not always restricted to a locality, may touch Aborigines and non-Aborigines alike. This is not to say that these sites do not have a cause, a reason why they are haunted. After all, the ghost story often depends upon an explanation of original causes. But the postcolonial ghost story tends to give more emphasis to effects rather than causes, to the impressions received by others from a haunted site which does not quite belong to them. Ghost stories are traditionally *about* possession; one takes possession of a haunted house and is possessed in return; all this happens on a property which is usually imagined as malevolent and overwhelming. But the postcolonial ghost story speaks more directly about *(dis)possession* through its emphasis on visiting or on passing through. The point about the postcolonial ghost story is that possession is there to be negotiated – whereas in the traditional ghost story there is no negotiation. Its haunted site is in this sense more 'open' and liable to be spread, so that there is less of a distinction between the site itself and what is beyond the site. This is what we mean by the postcolonial ghost story: it is an 'elementary' or 'rudimentary' form of expression which is enacted in the midst of modernity, and which is capable of producing 'gross' or luxurious effects that are unsettling in the sense that they overflow their location to speak uncannily to the nation's modern conditions.

Australia has a ghost of its own, of course: the bunyip. There have been a number of stories, usually by non-Aboriginal writers, which have located the bunyip in swamps or waterholes and represented the creature as frightening, often foreboding death – as in Rosa Campbell Praed's 'The Bunyip' (1891). Praed's evocative story, which may be more exactly designated as 'late colonial', gives us a creature who is heard rather than seen: this particular ghost only signifies itself aurally, as a sound. The sound works both to spread this haunted site and to confuse its origins: 'Though we tried to move in the direction of the voice, it was impossible to determine whence it came, so misleading and fitful and will-o'-wisp-like was the sound.'[22] So the haunted site in this story is all over the place. Just as it is without origins, so the bunyip also seems to have no cause; Praed is simply concerned with the effect this creature has on those settlers who pass through the bush. As Praed so beautifully puts it in her story – in a way that recalls Kristeva's 'smiles' and 'worries' – the bunyip 'deals out promiscuously benefits and calamities from the same hand'.[23] Let us just pause over this adverb 'promiscuously' for a moment. It offers the possibility, already suggested by the term *solicit*, that the haunted site – like the sacred site – is at least potentially an overflowing, luxurious thing which can reach across place indiscriminately. Praed's bunyip gives expression to these features, for it suggests that one cannot refuse it; the thing takes effect and draws you in, for better or worse, whether you like it or not (which is why this story is not *quite* post-colonial).

The settlers in Praed's story have yet to become 'homely', because they have been following a 'dray, loaded with stores and furniture for the new home to which we were bound'.[24] In other words, these settlers are still unsettled, and their talk about 'eerie things' speaks directly to that condition. In a certain sense they contribute to their haunting and their own unsettlement, since the bunyip is animated when they talk it up ('as we talked a sort of chill seemed to creep over us').[25] The creature 'promiscuously' emanates its aura through the bush, touching the settlers, preoccupying them, and forestalling their homely impulses. Far from being 'subjectively immersed' in the landscape, they are at least for the moment out of place or *displaced*. The bunyip becomes a figure for displacement, in effect, and in this sense it has a modern function.

We can contrast this with a later, more explicitly postcolonial ghost story told by an Aboriginal man to the well-known Australian anthologist and poet, Roland Robinson. In the first part of Percy Mumbulla's narrative, also titled 'The Bunyip' (1958), this creature – which in Praed's story had been simultaneously 'promiscuous' and evasive – is now monogamous and attached. The bunyip here belongs to a 'clever old-man', an Aboriginal elder. It is known or familiar, rather than unknown, and it is empowering rather than unsettling. Mumbulla's narrative suggests that the Aboriginal clever-man derives his power directly from this bunyip:

> This old fellow had a bunyip. It was his power, his *moodjingarl*. This bunyip was high in the front and low at the back like a hyena, like a lion. It had a terrible big bull-head and it was milk-white. This bunyip could go down into the ground and take the old man with him. They could travel under the ground. They could come out anywhere. They could come out of that old tree over there.[26]

Here, the Aboriginal clever-man and the bunyip travel together with outcomes which are already difficult to predict. It is not an issue of origins here, so much as a question of destination: there is no telling where the bunyip will end up. The description of this bunyip is worth noting, and aspects of it are repeated later on: 'That's when I saw the bunyip. He was milk white. He had a terrible big bull-head, a queer-looking thing.'[27] The creature here is both exotic ('like a hyena, like a lion', 'queer-looking') and local; it seems to be both imported and indigenous. It is obviously associated with cattle, which would have frequented waterholes where bunyips are found, with attention drawn to its 'milk-white' features. So in a certain sense, this bunyip is produced by colonization and embodies some of its features – the whiteness, the cattle-like anatomy, and so on.

Later, the Aboriginal clever-man argues with his sister, who was 'as clever as he was'. They magically cause each other's deaths through the resulting power-struggle – at which point the bunyip detaches himself and continues on his travels. So in the first part of the story, the bunyip was in a settled relationship to its Aboriginal host, albeit in the framework of an unsettled geography (mobility, unpredictable outcomes, etc.). It leaves only when that settled relationship breaks down through the mutually inflicted deaths of the brother and sister, deaths which the bunyip seems helpless to prevent. In the second part of the story, the bunyip is set free and in the process takes on a much more active function. At one point, he arrives unannounced at the home of an Aboriginal family:

> My old dad was smoking his pipe by the chimney. Mum heard the bunyip coming, roaring. The ground started to shake. He was coming closer. He came out of the ground underneath the tank-stand. Went over to the chimney and started rubbing himself against it. He started to get savage. He started to roar. Mum told Dad to go out and talk to him in the language, tell him to go away, that we were all right. Dad went out and spoke to him in the language. He talked to him: 'We are all right. No one doing any harm. You can go away'... Every time Dad spoke to him, he'd roar. My old-man was talking: 'Everything is all right. Don't get savage here'.[28]

The narrative shows how this second Aboriginal man is now obliged to negotiate with this creature, to calm him down. The bunyip needs to be told that no one is 'doing any harm' to this family, and that as a consequence his powers are not required. This Aboriginal family, in other words, does not *want* to play host to this bunyip: it now functions as an unwanted guest, whose concern for the welfare of the family (much like modern, paternalistic bureaucracies) is drastically misplaced. We might even say, *out* of place, since this bunyip has an 'unhomely' effect on what is clearly now a 'homely' (i.e. domesticated) scene. This is rendered in the story by having the bunyip appear to become 'primitive' – a feature which in this context unsettles this Aboriginal couple, and they send it away. At the same time, as we have noted, the descriptions of this bunyip clearly draw attention to the creature's modern characteristics: far from being 'primitive', it is quite literally an introduced or imported species.

A number of contradictions are thus mobilized in this story. The bunyip is a 'milk-white' thing that is metaphorically connected to cattle, those very things that signify the dispossession of Aborigines as cattle-based properties expanded across the country. And yet a creature which is so animated by colonization is nevertheless, initially at least, shown to contribute to Aboriginal empowerment. Later on, however, the creature becomes wilder, more 'savage', producing not empowerment so much as unsettlement. This savagery unsettles not the white settlers as the bunyip had in Praed's story, but Aboriginal people: the narrator's homely mother and father. In fact, as we have suggested, this bunyip now quite literally has an *unhomely* character – turning up unannounced at their homestead, roaring wildly, suggestively rubbing himself up against the chimney, and so on. The creature itself is highly unsettled, highly mobile, marauding, his whereabouts now even more difficult to predict than before: 'He travels around, up and down the coast.... He's even been seen in Victoria, at Lake Tyers Mission.'[29] So the second part of this strange story unleashes the bunyip to produce unsettling effects not on whites this time, but on Aborigines. And this seems to be because it now signifies two contradictory things: the 'primitive', from which this modern, homely Aboriginal couple has dissociated itself; and the post-colonial, which – precisely because it is itself a modern thing – shakes up (i.e. *solicits:* the sexuality implicit in this word is evident in the bunyip rubbing himself up against the chimney) the Aboriginal couple's home under the pretext of concern and demands their attention. And, of course, there is no essential contradiction here: the modern can indeed seem 'savage' enough, although this no doubt depends on who is looking at it. This couple are thus caught in the middle of such a contradictory movement between the 'primitive' and the postcolonial. It unsettles them, certainly; but we should pay attention to the way in which this Aboriginal couple engage with the bunyip as a matter of course. If nothing else, the later part of this strange story shows these Aboriginal characters *keeping* their place – and their sense of place – through direct negotiation.

We have said that the Australian ghost story is a minor or marginal genre. Australian writers and film-makers have not yet spectacularized this genre, as the United States has, through big-budget movies such as *Poltergeist II* (1986) – which is about a settler family inhabiting a new house built upon an apparently empty site which turns out to be an Indian burial ground – a site which is reanimated in order to move the family on (but where to?). Nevertheless, there have been several quite recent interventions in the genre, two of which we would like to discuss in some detail: Tracey Moffatt's *BeDevil* (1993), and Margot Nash's *Vacant*

Possession (1996). These have both been prize-winning films: *BeDevil* won an award for best sound at the Festival of Fantastic Cinema in Barcelona and was nominated for the Un Certain Regard section of the 1992 Cannes Film Festival; while *Vacant Possession* won the Special Jury Prize at the 1996 Creteil Women's Film Festival. They are both films about hauntings, and they are used here mostly as points of contrast. Nash's film shows its protagonist Tessa returning as an adult to her childhood home in Botany Bay – an 'original' place of modern Australian settlement. The film focuses on this dilapidated homestead and the traumas that had unfolded there. In particular, Tessa as an adolescent girl had fallen pregnant to an Aboriginal boy who had lived nearby. Tessa's racist father violently (savagely?) intervenes in their affair, and she runs away, abandoning her mother and sister in the process. This dreamy film shows how Tessa then becomes increasingly reconciled to the people – and the place – she left behind. Indeed, reconciliation is precisely what this film is all about: it speaks quite self-consciously to the national condition, using Tessa's homestead as an image of Australia itself. People ceaselessly pass through it; it is an 'open' place, full of visitors, ghosts and memories, some of them bad, some of them uninvited. But the ghosts in particular are ultimately benign: they unsettle only in order then to produce the kind of 'subjective immersion' that Ross Gibson had found in his landscape poetry. Tessa is finally reconciled to her home and to her father, her sister, the ghost of her mother, and the neighbouring Aboriginal family. The film works patiently towards a Gothic climax which provides a suitably 'wild' background for the storm before the calm with which the movie closes. The smooth, reassuring jazz music score keeps this theme intact: everyone finally gets on together, in this ultimately untroubled fantasy of homeliness. The theme of 'vacant possession' – a theme which would otherwise have spoken to the kind of postcolonial condition we have outlined here – is dropped in favour of a theme of fulfilment, where Tessa rests securely in the fact (i.e. the fantasy) that she finally 'belongs'.

Tracey Moffatt's *BeDevil* works somewhat differently. On the whole, this film – which presents three quite separate ghost stories – was reviewed in a perplexed way. According to Robin Films' publicity flyer (wittingly or unwittingly), this is a film 'where the unexplained happens', rather than the unexpected – which set the tone for *BeDevil*'s reception. In particular, it was seen to be indulgent and unnecessarily obscure, features often attributed to a minor genre, as we have noted. Unlike *Poltergeist*, for example, these stories did not privilege the explanation of the hauntings; and unlike *Vacant Possession*, they did not even seem to offer a coherent narrative *about* the hauntings. Interestingly, Moffatt – an Aboriginal film-maker – did not seem particularly interested in drawing upon Aboriginal burial sites: the stories generally do not have this connection to the horrors of colonial history, although they do occasionally construct some kind of affective relationship to it.

In fact, the point to make about these three stories is that all the ghosts in them are *modern*; this film does not reanimate some premodern imaginary or return to some colonial trauma. The first story, called 'Mr Chuck', is built around a swamp haunted by the ghost of a black American soldier from the Second World War. The second story, called 'Choo Choo Choo Choo', refers back to the ghost of a young white girl killed on a railway track. The third story, called 'Lovin' the Spin I'm In', shows a townscape haunted by a young Aboriginal couple who broke with traditional law in order to marry. In each of these stories there is again little interest in how the ghosts came to be where they are, or even in how they came to die. The interest is almost completely in the effects they have on those nearby or on those passing through. In the process, the issue of possession is never fully resolved: these are ghost stories which *refuse* the fantasy of reconciliation.

The stories – all three of them – go on to show the modern-ness of conditions which build up around these haunted sites. Thus in the first story, a cinema is built over the swamp which contains the body of the dead black American soldier. The bubbling swamp looks as though it might contain a bunyip – but the emphasis now is solely on the ghost's introduced qualities (the black American soldier does not belong; he was just visiting), not his indigenous qualities. We can very well see this moviehouse on a swamp as another version of Ross Gibson's militarist Pine Gap – in that it, too, activates an aberrant form of 'black magic' in the country! This story self-consciously puts cinema itself in the frame of modernity – and in the frame of 'elementary' effects which can be passed on (to the viewer). The film itself is implicated in the process of haunt- ing, in other words; for Moffatt in particular, who relies on sound and music and choreography rather than dialogue, film is a highly affective (we might even say, a luxuriant, indulgent) form of media.

Moffatt's ghost story suggests that the haunted swamp, if left to itself, would have no effects. It is precisely because the cinema has been built upon it that the swamp comes to life. So cinema has both a modernising function and an elemental function, and they combine in this film to produce the haunting. At one point, as a means of closing a white suburban woman's narrative of the events, the camera relocates itself to rise up into the air, to give a number of wide-screen panoramic landscape shots showing 'settled' Australians at their leisure – at the beach, riding bicycles, playing cricket, and so on. The story thus overflows its boundaries, to give a view of the modern nation at play – then it returns to the localness of the haunted site and the cinema which has been built upon it. The movement away from the site and towards the nation, then back to the site again, works to implicate the one in the other. This is the uncanny effect of the film, since it folds the haunted site into a 'familiar' location, and in doing so it makes that location appear strange. This produces an equation for ghost stories which we can list as follows: the site is (not) the nation. This would distinguish this film from Nash's *Vacant Possession*, which is all too ready to make Tessa's homestead a thing of national significance. Moffatt's film, on the other hand, both suggests a resemblance and refuses to allow that resemblance to settle.

There is in fact a striking contrast between the introverted traumas of the haunted swamp and the 'innocent' fun of Australians-at-their-leisure. Those Australians are allowed to go about their business, in a kind of unconscious state of bliss. But let us draw attention to the musical sequence which accompanies the camera as it rises up into the air. In contrast to the smooth jazz score in Nash's film, the music here is sharp and shrill – and in the background, almost inaudible, are the sounds of chains being rattled and a man shouting, 'Get up!' This is a rare moment in *BeDevil*, when there is an affective connection back to colonialism and colonial trauma, involving the forced clearing of Aboriginal people away from land that is now being enjoyed by modern, leisured Australians. Obviously, it works to undercut the innocence, and the familiarity, of that panoramic sequence of Australians at play. But at the same time, it remains as a background feature of that sequence which one might very nearly not hear (as we did not in our first viewing of this film). The 'innocence' of the sequence is almost preserved, in other words – *but not quite*. We can return to our earlier point about the enmeshing of innocence and guilt here, since the sequence casts postcolonial settlement through the mutuality of these positions: that the leisured or 'luxurious' activity of modern Australians is played out in a postcolonial field in which implication can be cast both ways (depending, of course, on one's 'position').

The central character in this ghost story is an Aboriginal boy, who is drawn to the site. There is no sense that he is drawn to it because of the dead black American soldier; rather, it is the cinema which attracts him. The film seems to explore the ambivalent effects of cinema – ambivalent in the sense that, as an image of modernity, it brings with it gains and losses. Cinema itself signifies leisure and luxury, for example, and seems oblivious to the traumas that bubble beneath its surface. In an earlier sequence in the story, the boy climbs inside the empty cinema and begins to slash the seats with a knife in an act of fetishized revenge (against the cinema itself? Against the modernity of the cinema?). Towards the end of the film, he breaks into the cinema and falls through the wooden floor, catching his legs; and it is at this point that the body of the dead black American soldier finally rises up from the swamp below – as if the desecration of the cinema has brought him to life. The story enacts an uncanny reversal, since – if this was a sacred site for Aboriginal people – desecration would unleash certain powers. But the swamp is not connected to Aboriginal burial, but, rather, to the burial of a black American soldier. The boy is desecrating a cinema, not an Aboriginal sacred site. The uncanny reversal lies precisely in this fact: an Aboriginal boy is desecrating something *modern* (as opposed to a non-Aboriginal boy desecrating something premodern or something connected to colonial trauma). This desecration suggests an ambivalent relationship to modernity, however, since modernity is certainly being rejected here (one hates it, resents it) and yet it is also being *animated* in the process. Thus, the American soldier might well stand as an image for the film itself, which rises up to engulf the boy – who, later on as an older man, is shown cutting into his own flesh. The film structures this ambivalence, showing Aboriginal characters to be unsettled by the various modern ghosts which haunt the stories, so that in this sense it compares a little with Percy Mumbulla's story 'The Bunyip'. At the same time, it wants to spread the effects of modernity across a larger canvas – other, non-Aboriginal characters are unsettled, too. In the process, the film also wants to *relish* its modern-ness – which is why it recreates it as an 'image' so painstakingly and so adoringly (for example, in the glowing 1950s *mise-en-scène* – the costumes and the 'look' especially – of the first story).

The modern-ness of these stories is also reflected through the number of narrators involved in the telling. Again, Aboriginal *and* non-Aboriginal narrators are implicated here – the film seems to carry with it a multicultural agenda which demonstrates that knowledge about ghosts is not private but shared (potentially by everyone). In fact, knowledge is not only shared, it is also mobile: it travels. Narrators often talk about a haunted site from somewhere else – from a suburban home, for example. In 'Choo Choo Choo Choo', we only hear about the haunted railway siding after the Aboriginal narrator has travelled to another site. So the effects of the hauntings are spread, both across cultures and across place: the sites, in other words, spiral out of their location even as they remain where they are. The final image of the third story, 'Lovin' the Spin I'm In', seems to reflect this, with a car spinning around on its axis, always apparently about to leave but still held by the force of the haunting. It seems as necessary to go elsewhere as it does to remain in place – and this is because to be 'in place' is already, uncannily, to be 'out of place'.

'Lovin' the Spin I'm In' is a story about a spirit who *possesses* a place: it anticipates Nash's topic of 'vacant possession'. It begins with two property speculators, one Asian and one European, coming into town to negotiate a deal over a 'disused' warehouse. But the warehouse is inhabited by Emelda, a Torres Strait Islander, and the ghost of her son and his lover. Now, the son and his lover are already dispossessed: they had, through their elopement, violated traditional law and were banished from their traditional land (and Emelda follows them). So the warehouse is both their place and not their place (since they are 'out of place'): in this sense all three Torres Strait characters act out a modern predicament. Another equally 'foreign' mother, a Greek neighbour – who narrates part of their story – tells her own son that the Islanders 'are not from around here'. By telling her son about these characters, knowledge itself becomes 'out of place', not quite a secret and not quite public: 'It is not for you to know', she says; and then she adds, '... well, perhaps you could know'. The Greek boy is attracted to the warehouse and, while there, the ghostly Aboriginal lovers appear and enact a choreographed dance. The warehouse begins to grip him, to *solicit* him; it 'overheats' (with the lovers' fiery passion?); and at the moment of climax, the property speculators return. The story seems to blend the romance of the boy's erotic waking dream with the anti-romance of off-shore development interests – both of which are driven by desire. So an 'indigenous' claim on place is bound up with the interests of globalized capital: this story never surrenders to Ross Gibson's nostalgia for a divorce between the two. And this binding up of a (dis)possessed site with the interests of a marauding, globalized capital is what produces the uncanny effect. The flow of this effect is by no means one-way. Certainly, capital can produce further, traumatic dispossessions (and in this story, Emelda is once again moved on). But the haunted site – again, like the sacred site – can unsettle the interests of capital in return. The mutuality of conflicting desires which build up around a site can, indeed, put the entire nation in a 'spin'.

We have wanted to highlight the genre of the Australian ghost story because of its potential in relation to Australia's postcolonial condition. We can think of this genre in terms of an entangled kind of haunting, which gives expression to unsettlement (or, displacement) in both Aboriginal and white Australians alike. This may well be because of the paradoxical arrangement of difference and sameness in Australia – which that word 'alike' may too easily smooth over. 'Ghosts' cannot function in a climate of sameness, in a country which fantasizes about itself as 'one nation' or which imagines a utopian future of 'reconciliation' in which, as in Nash's film, all the bad memories have been laid to rest. But neither can they function in a climate of difference, where the one can never resemble the other – as in a 'divided' nation. A more 'promiscuous' structure in which sameness and difference impact upon each other, spilling over each other's boundaries only to return again to their respective places, moving back and forth in an unpredictable, even unruly manner – a structure in which sameness and difference embrace and refuse each other simultaneously: this is where the 'ghosts' which may cause us to 'smile' or to 'worry' can flourish.

Notes

*   Some of the arguments in this essay can also be found in a different form and context in Ken Gelder and Jane M. Jacobs, *Uncanny Australia: Sacredness and Identity in a Postcolonial Nation* (Melbourne: Melbourne University Press, 1998).

1.   Gelder and Jacobs, 'Uncanny Australia', *UTS Review* 1, 2 (1995), 150–69.

2.   See, for example, David J. Tacey, *Edge of the Sacred: Transformation in Australia* (Melbourne: HarperCollins, 1995).

3. Emile Durkheim, *The Elementary Forms of the Religious Life*, trans. Joseph Ward Swain (London: George Allen and Unwin: 1976), p. 6.
4. Durkheim, *Elementary Forms of Religious Life*, p. 6n.
5. Durkheim, *Elementary Forms of Religious Life*, p. 8.
6. Sigmund Freud, 'The "Uncanny"', in *The Pelican Freud Library: Art and Literature*, vol. 14, ed. Albert Dickson (Harmondsworth: Penguin Books, 1987), pp. 342–7.
7. Jacques Derrida, 'Différance', *Margins of Philosophy* (Hertfordshire: Harvester Wheatsheaf, 1982), pp. 1–27, 16. See also Ken Gelder and Jane M. Jacobs, '"Talking Out of Place": Authorizing the Sacred in Postcolonial Australia', *Cultural Studies* 9, 1 (1995): 150–60.
8. Derrida, 'Différance', p. 16n.
9. Julia Kristeva, *Strangers to Ourselves*, trans. Leon S. Roudiez (New York: Columbia University Press, 1991), pp. 171–3.
10. Kristeva, *Strangers to Ourselves*, p. 182.
11. Freud, 'The "Uncanny"', p. 346.
12. Freud, 'The "Uncanny"', p. 347.
13. Kristeva, *Strangers to Ourselves*, p. 191.
14. Ross Gibson, *South of the West: Postcolonialism and the Narrative Construction of Australia* (Bloomington and Indianapolis: Indiana University Press, 1992), p. x.
15. Gibson, *South of the West*, p. xii.
16. Gibson, *South of the West*, p. 72.
17. Gibson, *South of the West*, p. 18.
18. Reviews of Gibson's book have been quick to make this point. See, for example, Alan McKee, 'What is Postcolonialism?', *Screen* 35, 3 (Autumn 1994): 311–15.
19. Gibson, *South of the West*, pp. 91–2.
20. Kristeva, *Strangers to Ourselves*, p. 191.
21. See William Sylvester Walker ('Coo-ee'), *When the Mopoke Calls* (London: John Long, 1899); reprinted in Ken Gelder (ed.), *The Oxford Book of Australian Ghost Stories* (Melbourne: Oxford University Press, 1994).
22. Rosa Campbell Praed, 'The Bunyip', in Gelder (ed.). *Australian Ghost Stories*, p. 108.
23. Praed, 'The Bunyip', p. 103.
24. Praed, 'The Bunyip', p. 105.
25. Praed, 'The Bunyip', p. 106.
26. Percy Mumbulla, 'The Bunyip', in Gelder (ed.), *Australian Ghost Stories*, p. 250.
27. Mumbulla, 'The Bunyip', p. 251.
28. Mumbulla, 'The Bunyip', p. 250.
29. Mumbulla, 'The Bunyip', p. 251.

Part III
Spectral Culture

9

The Machine in the Ghost: Spiritualism, Technology and the 'Direct Voice'
Steven Connor

9.1   DESUBLIMATING THE SÉANCE

It is routinely claimed that Victorian spiritualism is the expression of a widespread dissatisfaction with the materialism of nineteenth-century science, industry and social and political thought, an assertion of the transcendence of spirit, as a principle of moral, religious and even political renewal, in an objectified world of inert things and blindly mechanical processes. 'No group of people more zealously threw their energies into the effort to discredit materialism than the men and women who endorsed spiritualism in the second half of the nineteenth century', writes Janet Oppenheim.[1] And yet few commentators on spiritualism, whether in the nineteenth century or the twentieth, have failed to notice the odd and sometimes rather grotesque mimicry of materialist language and modes of thought that characterizes not only Victorian spiritualism but perhaps also Victorian supernaturalism in general. For the Victorians as well as for us, spiritualism became stubbornly indissociable from its vulgar repertoire of apparitions and phenomena: rappings, ringings and other unexplained sounds and voices, waftings of fragrance, tilting and rotating tables and similarly vagrant furnishings, 'apports', or the telekinetic transport of objects, through to the various forms of materialization, in the ectoplasmic extrusions of spirit hands, spirit fingerprints and, finally, the 'full materialization', of spirit-figures who walked about the room, socialized and sometimes even flirted with the members of the séance; there were also the more spectacular *coups de théâtre* associated with mediums like Daniel Dunglas Home, such as the famous Ashley House levitation, in which witnesses swore that Home floated out of the window of a room overlooking Victoria Street and back in again through an adjacent window.

As Janet Oppenheim has demonstrated so well, the 'other world', in the senses both of the supernatural realm believed in by Victorian spiritualists and the alternative social sphere constituted by spiritualist culture itself, was closely entangled with the official and everyday world, not least in the edgy but abidingly intimate relations between the practices of spiritualism and the earnest investigations of the Society for Psychical Research. Spiritualism was not so much endangered as driven by the demand for empirical evidence, since the entire purpose and function of the séance was to provide, time and again, manifest and unignorable proofs of the reality of human survival and the capacity for communication between this world and the next. Similarly, the repeated drama of unveiling or exposure which became associated with the investigation of spiritualism is oddly duplicated by the rhetoric and practice of unveiling or revelation within spiritualism. Spiritualism shared with its opponents the language of investigation, evidence, exhibition and exposure, and the séance was seen by spiritualists themselves as a kind of laboratory for the investigation of the spirit world, a stage on which to unveil or bring to light hitherto concealed mysteries. Indeed, spiritualism also shared with its materialist adversaries an impatience with supernatural explanations of its phenomena. Annie Besant defended her surprising embrace of theosophy after a lifetime of secularism with the claim that 'the repudiation of the supernatural lies at the very threshold of Theosophy',[2] a sentiment with which Charles Maurice Davies concurred in 1874 in declaring that 'Spiritualism has no such word as Supernatural' and Florence Marryat echoed even more emphatically in 1894 in asserting *'There is no such thing as super-nature.'*[3]

Commentators on spiritualism, among both its sympathizers and enemies, were alternately amused and embarrassed by this affinity with materiality, not to say materialism. It is this affinity which makes for the uniquely comic nature of the Victorian séance, the impossibility of separating the hair-raising thrills provided by spiritualism from its more giggly side. Alex Owen correctly observes that the mood of the séance was often far from solemn, and could be downright hilarious;[4] but one can go further than this, to suggest that, for the Victorians as for us, the meaning of spiritualism has something essentially to do with its irresistible tendency to collapse into comedy. The recent dignification of spiritualism as a subject of serious enquiry by cultural historians risks distorting its subject in so far as it allows one to forget, or, as it were, forget to take seriously, the shrieking silliness of the whole business. Seeing spiritualism steadily and seeing it whole means recognizing its entanglement with facticity, fraudulence and farce. So there is a certain appropriateness in the fact that Henri Bergson, the theorist both of the spirit and of the comic, was himself for a short time the President of the Society for Psychical Research.

Of course, there was also resistance to the 'naturalization' of the spiritual. Many spiritualists themselves tried to divert attention away from the crass thrill-seeking of spiritualism's apparatus and special effects. Theosophists, who, as Janet Oppenheim has shown, relied upon certain aspects of spiritualism to a large degree, also distanced themselves from the sensationalism of the séance, and the cheapness of its gratifications.[5] Sophia de Morgan, in *From Matter to Spirit*, an account of ten years of spiritualist activity and guide for novices, carefully distinguished the stages in which mediumship is developed, separating the 'earlier and most material forms of mediumship' such as rapping and table-moving, which 'do not seem to be susceptible of any great change or refinement', from the more developed inward manifestations such as clairvoyant vision and the hearing of inner voices.[6] In a similar way, the Society for Psychical Research came to concentrate on the less easily exposable and more intriguing forms of mental mediumship such as hypnotism, automatism and telepathy rather than the more dubious displays of physical phenomena. The Society for Psychical Research is at one with those more doctrinal or theoretical spiritualists who preferred to elucidate the underlying meaning of such phenomena rather than to dwell upon their material nature or effects, whether that meaning be the revelation of universal spiritual principles, or the psychological insights into existence of the subliminal self towards which Frederic Myers pressed. I find a curious tendency, even among the most distinguished cultural historians of spiritualism, such as Janet Oppenheim and Alex Owen, to replicate this slightly embarrassed move away from the crass substance of spiritualism to its significance. Janet Oppenheim explicates spiritualism in terms of its relations to urgent and earnest disputes in nineteenth-century theology, science and philosophy, while Alex Owen, though she aims specifically to treat 'spiritualism and its phenomena "on their own terms"'[7] (xviii), nevertheless also ends up sublimating the particularities of spiritualist practice in her account of its sexual-political meanings.

I propose by contrast a slower, more sluggish way of reading spiritualism; an interpretative desublimation, if you will, which resists the dignifying impulse of allegory, by which spiritualism can be read in terms of what it signifies or shadows forth about the nature of late Victorian society. Rather than seeing spiritualism as the enactment of theology or sexual politics by other means, I try to make out what might be called a cultural phenomenology of its acts and enactments, its affects, practices and embodiments – an act of analysis that must start from the principle of trying to understand what séances were *like*. Such a cultural phenomenology will involve paying close attention in particular to the properties and dramaturgy of the séance, that essential and defining scene of spiritualist operations, in order to seize the logic of its spectacle and sense the phenomenology of its phenomena. Such a mode of analysis will therefore need to be curious, not only about the drives, wishes, fears, and so on, which were at work in spiritualist displays, but also with the nature of the ostensive drama itself. To borrow two key terms of spiritualism itself, I intimate the advantage of reading manifestations and materializations in terms of the acts of making manifest and making material that they constitute.

Clearly, my concern is therefore with what Freud called 'psychic reality', the reality of what is believed to happen and what is represented as happening in the séance, rather than with the truth or fraudulence in themselves of the claims made on behalf of such phenomena. But I am uneasy about the unconditional indemnity against falsification that this may appear to give my argument and therefore wish to make its conditions of disproof quite plain here. Although in principle it might still appear persuasive even if the truths claimed on behalf of spiritualism were actually established or establishable, my argument is rooted at the deepest level on the presumption that no particle of such claims – that spiritualist phenomena are evidence of the continued personal existence of individual beings after death, and of their capacity to communicate with us – is in fact true. The establishment of the truth of spiritualist beliefs would be enough to collapse my argument. But this is less to do with any particular weakness in my argument than with my conviction that, if spiritualism were thus true, *nothing* in the way of rational investigation and argument would any more count for much. We would no longer be in the kind of world in which such activities had any purchase or power. We would no longer be in any kind of world inhabitable by the beings we have come to know as human at all. I am not among those for whom this last is an exhilarating prospect.

In what follows, I have two linked purposes. First of all, I will suggest that the séance is the scene for the creation and exploration of a new kind of collective bodily experience. I will need to investigate the relationships between vision and voice acted out in the séance, in order to establish that the phantasmal body of the séance is constructed in and through auditory-vocalic space, which it is difficult to reconcile with the envisioned or explicated space which is taken to have become dominant through the nineteenth century. Secondly, I will explore the more-than-casual connections between the scene of the séance and the imaginary desires and demands occasioned by emerging forms of communicative technology, and especially the auditory-vocal technologies of the telephone, the gramophone and the radio. In its secession from the condition of scopically explicated space, the phantasmal body of the séance predicts and resists the relativized or virtual body allegedly being brought into being for the first time by postmodern communicative media. But I conclude by suggesting that the very form of spiritualism's resistance, its attempt to rehabilitate the body of the voice against the disembodiments of contemporary acoustic technologies, must itself borrow from the forms of bodily reparation which already belong to those technologies.

9.2 SÉANCE AND THE SONOROUS

The nineteenth-century séance was caught between the competing demands of experience and evidence. With the establishment of the photograph as the measure of objective truth during the second half of the century, the séance was orientated more and more around the need to produce visible traces, as the reality of manifestation became measured against the possibility of recording. Transient and uncapturable forms of spiritual manifestation yielded place more and more to what could yield unmistakable evidence. The knockings and table-turnings turned into automatic writings; the smells and sounds became the 'apports' physically delivered into the space of the séance by performers such as Mrs

Guppy, who, not content with simply lobbing flowers into the laps of her sitters, specialized in the materialization of fruit and vegetables (Georgiana Houghton thought that her tendency to 'eat the manifestations' was a 'a great weakness'.)[8] With the advent of 'full materialization' later in the century, in the form of spirits who moved around the room and held converse with members of the séance independently of the person of the medium, there were many more opportunities to produce the seemingly unimpeachable testimony of the photograph. It is hard for one attempting to reconstruct the phenomenology of the séance not to be influenced by its photographic iconography, with all those stayless, absurdly swathed figures blotted on to the scenes of the séance by the crudest kind of double-exposure. Spirit-photography is the form of the séance's submission to the domination of the eye and its prosthetic technologies. In spirit photography, otherness is made visible and familiar, and the unmasterable event of the manifestation becomes the fixed and manipulable record.

But the organization of the séance around the expectation and possibility of the photograph or the photographable can easily obscure the dominance in it of non-visual experiences. As they sat in the darkness or semi-darkness, the members of the séance would see much less than they would touch, taste, smell and, most importantly, *hear*. Walter Ong suggests that the difference between a visual-typographic perspective and an oral-aural perspective is the difference between being in front of and being in the midst of a world. '*Sound situates man in the middle of actuality and in simultaneity, whereas vision situates man in front of things and in sequentiality*', writes Ong.[9] The 'acoustic space' in which the oral-aural individual finds himself, Ong continues, is 'a vast interior in the center of which the listener finds himself together with his interlocutors'.[10] The scene of the séance, with its dim light, and its emphasis on shared responsibility and community of sensation, emphasized the inhabitation of this shared interiority. The experience of heightened and attentive listening which is so central a part of the experience of the séance renders the participant at once passively exposed to and intimately enclosed within a shared space of audition which can perhaps be interpreted in the light of the infantile experience of the 'sonorous envelope' or bath of sound analysed by Didier Anzieu.[11] The diminution of sight also loosened the alliance between the dominant senses of hearing and sight and encouraged liaisons between hearing and the proximity senses, of touch, odour and taste.

It is assumed that the séance was for summoning ghosts. I do not think that this was its primary purpose. The primary purpose of the séance was not to evoke beings from another world, but to enact the hypothesis of a different kind of body in this world. The excited passivity of the séance characteristically produced sensory intensification, and a condition in which, as the medium Elizabeth d'Esperance describes it, thoughts were on the point of becoming things:

> the loss of physical power seemed to intensify that of the senses. Distant sounds, beyond hearing at other times, became perfectly audible; a movement of any of the sitters sent a vibration through every nerve; a sudden exclamation caused a sensation of terror; the very thoughts of the persons in the room made themselves felt almost as though they were material objects.[12]

With this intensification came a sense of the enlargement of the body's forms and limits. This is centred on the body of the medium, whose role was not so much to provide a channel for other entities, as to exemplify a bodily condition of fluidity and transmissibility as such. The body of the medium was extensible, exorbitant, and, to borrow a word employed in the 1820s to advertise the performances of the ventriloquist Monsieur Alexandre, 'ubiquitarical'.[13] The dream logic of the séance establishes a close relationship between the various appearances and manifestations – the slate-writing, the sudden cascades of fragrance and flowers, the mysterious touches and mobile sounds – and the receiving/transmitting apparatus of the medium. Georgiana Houghton records a remarkable séance with Mrs Hardy and Mrs Guppy, in which the spirits enlisted the substantial person of the latter for a vigorous game of levitational musical chairs in the dark:

> Mrs. Ramsay, whose seat was next to hers, said, 'Oh! be still and quiet, for Mrs. Guppy is *gone!*' In about a minute she said in a faint voice, 'Where am I?' and she *was* within the circle, but they must first have entranced her. But again she was lifted up, and now in her normal condition, for she spoke several times, and her voice was heard close to the ceiling. Suddenly she was placed on Mrs. Burns's lap, but was quickly removed, and was carried swiftly round and round the circle, her dress whisking against us, brushing firmly against Mr. Sergeant Cox (who was seated next

to me) and myself, and at one time I took hold of her foot above the level of my head; then for an instant she was on my lap, and next, at my request, on the lap of the friend by my side. She described it as the most delicious feeling of *dangling*. They afterwards floated Mrs. Hardy in the same manner, then Mrs. Guppy again, and they then seated her on the floor by the side of Mrs. Hardy in her chair.[14]

The medium's corporeal indeterminacy suggests a uterine fantasy of the maternal body: the members of the circle are enclosed within an imaginary interior space provided by the body of the medium. The association of spiritualist phenomena with the enclosure of the home, and further enclosures within the home – the séance room, the joined circle of hands, the recess, or darkened cabinet into which the medium retires – assists this construction of an imaginary maternal cavity.

And yet this containing body also itself provides a manipulable bodily content: Georgiana Houghton remarks, regarding an earlier séance in Mrs Guppy's home, that 'the room ... was, so to speak, *full* of Mrs. Guppy, so that there was plenty of her atmosphere to be gathered for their [the spirits'] purposes'.[15] The medium's imaginary body both furnishes and suffuses the space of the séance. The imaginary body of the medium is 'utopian' (literally, 'of no-place') precisely because it is exorbitant and superfluous to customary space: rather than existing in space, it is itself a kind of space. As such, it promised and modelled a form of collective body, capable of putting forth new parts and appurtenances: dissevered hands, legs and heads were common appearances in the séance. These parts were, of course, made up of ectoplasm, the semi-transparent, plastic pseudo-substance exuded from the body of the medium or formed from the collective psychical resources of the circle. The doctrine of the ectoplasm allows for the dissolution, transformation and re-forming of singular actual bodies.

The suffusive body of the séance is also a body characterized by the mobility of sound, in its influx into the interior of the body, and its passage outwards again into the world. (A little later on, in the twentieth century, ectoplasmic materialization itself would be explained by reference to a theory of matter vibrating at different rates.) Where the optical body is an anatomy unfolded to the eye, which allows it to be clearly differentiated from its outside and from other bodies, the phantasmal body of the spiritualists is a transmissive or connective medium; it is experienced in terms not of the relationship between interiority and exteriority but in terms of passage between them. For all of the startling visual apparitions of the séance, its tendency is to replace a visual body with the fundamentally auditory/acoustic phenomenology of the sonorous body.

9.3   THE DIRECT VOICE

One of the less often remarked ways in which the 'other world' of spiritualism became entangled with the 'real world' of science and progress was in its mirroring of the communicational technologies of the second half of the nineteenth century. For some years after spiritualism began its career in 1848 with the 'Rochester Rappings' experienced in a house in Hydesville, New York, the principal means of communication with the dead was the system of usually alphabetic knocks, which had slowly to be decoded by the sitters. No more literal parallel to the digital system of the electric telegraph could be imagined. In 1858, Charles Partridge had already published his account of spiritualist experiences under the imprint of the 'Spiritual Telegraph Office'; and, as one might expect, the spirits soon began themselves to communicate in morse code.[16] When in 1871 a spirit circle in Cincinnati, working with the mediumship of a Mrs Hollis, received messages in morse, it prompted them to incorporate a telegraphic instrument into their séances. The spirits claimed to have invented telegraphy in advance of its invention in the human world (one wonders quite what *for*), and indeed to have given unseen encouragement to its inventor and developers. Although this encouraged hopes that 'the time is not very distant when telegraphic communication between the two worlds will be as much established as it now is between Louisville and Cincinnati',[17] spiritual telegraphy made considerable demands on the spirits' powers of organization and engineering. It was necessary, for example, to find and retrain a deceased telegraph operator in the spirit world, whose efforts would need to be supported, as on earth, by a 'band of electricians to sustain the community spirit, while he handles the key of the instrument'.[18] Nor was it possible for the spirits simply to commandeer the telegraph instrument placed in the centre of the circle; first of all, it was necessary to materialize a 'battery' to power it.[19]

During the 1860s and 1870s, there was a series of what Alexander Melville Bell, phonetician and father of the inventor of the telephone, called systems of 'visible speech', which enabled the direct transformation of acoustic signals into visual form – including, most notably, the phonautograph, an apparatus which translated sound vibrations into patterns traced on smokeblack, and which was instrumental in Alexander Graham Bell's experiments with telephony. This might parallel the automatic writing and 'direct writing' practised by mediums during this period, both of which dispensed with the requirement for the members of the séance to decode the spirit messages. Then in 1876 and 1877 came the near-simultaneous invention of the telephone and the phonograph. As we will see, both of these technologies, and especially the former, quickly entered the language of spiritualism: the effect was both further to 'materialize' spiritualism itself and to highlight the ghost-liness of the new technological power to separate the voice from its source, either in space, as with the telephone, or in time, as with the gramophone.

There is a deeper relation between the evolution of ghost phenomena and the developing logic of technological communications. For both involved the move from somatic to telematic processes of relay, as effects and manifestations that took place in or through the physical person of the medium – the easiest of these to produce being the production of the voice of the spirits by the medium's own vocal organs – were replaced by manifestations separated from the medium's body. The two forms of climax were the 'full materialization' brought about most spectacularly by mediums like Florence Cooke, who, in the person of 'Katie King', moved around the room, conversed with sitters, sat on their knees, tickled them, and so on, and, secondly, and less often remarked, the phenomenon of the 'direct voice', which is to say, a voice which speaks independently of the medium's vocal organs. In the direct voice, the phenomena must be thought of as being facilitated rather than produced by the medium, who acts as a telephonist rather than as a telegraphist, making the connection rather than herself interpreting the signal. Often, in 'direct voice' manifestations, the spirits would employ a trumpet (resembling a speaking-trumpet or megaphone rather than the musical instrument), or even a series of trumpets, which might be placed in the room at a distance from the medium. The trumpet served both to amplify the voice, and to change its position: trumpets would be moved telekinetically through the air and round the room. The use of this property led to the mediums who specialized in this mode of manifestation becoming known as 'trumpet mediums'. The spiritualist use of the trumpet was probably first suggested by the use of speaking trumpets for the deaf, as well as Biblical uses of the instrument as a sign of spiritual warning and revelation, rather than by the characteristic amplifying horn of the phonograph and later the gramophone. But the technique of making spiritual voices audible comes increasingly to cohere with the technological means of amplification. In the mediumship of Pearl Judd in New Zealand in the 1920s, the direct voice was first achieved by means of a phonograph horn rather than a trumpet.[20]

Partly because of its resemblance to the rapidly familiarized experience of communication by telephone, the direct voice came to be seen as conveying a sense of the presence of spirits superior to that obtainable through visual phenomena. The daughter of W. T. Stead, journalist and vigorous propagandist on behalf of spiritualism, recorded her father's views on the superiority of the evidence of the voice over evidence afforded to the eye:

> I have seen my son materialise before my eyes; but why should I wish particularly to see him? That I hear from him is certain. We used to talk to each other by means of the telephone. I knew his voice, believed what he said. It was enough. I did not see him; I heard him. So now.[21]

After his death on board the *Titanic*, W. T. Stead himself made contact with 'Julia's Bureau', the room he set up in his house in Wimbledon for spiritualist meetings. His daughter defies the most sceptical reader to resist the evidence of 'his living, vibrating, unmistakable ego' provided by his voice.[22] The medium who conveyed the voice of Stead was Mrs Etta Wriedt, and another participant in her séances in the same year testified in similar terms to the irresistible power of the voice to compel the sense of presence: 'I felt I was being brought closer than ever before to the dead; there was a sense of face-to-face conversation, a steady, continuous stream of speech, not fugitive and streaky, but robust and direct.'[23] Recording his experiences with a direct-voice medium called Estelle Roberts, Hannen Swaffer remarks similarly on the power of these spirit-utterances heard in the dark to suggest 'not merely a voice, but a living man or woman'.[24] Indeed, the very power of the direct voice could induce a sense of derealization of the listener, as is suggested by the following playful-creepy exchange recorded by Maurice Barbanell:

> 'We can't see you,' I said to one spirit voice, heard regularly.
> A laugh came.
> '*Why, you must be dead,*' was the amused answer.[25]

I have suggested that nineteenth-century séances tended to reassociate vision and tactility. The experiences of the direct voice in spiritualism often seem by contrast to involve a disavowal of the body's own speaking apparatus, and a discrimination of speech from the experience of touch. Edith Lecourt has suggested the importance of oral experience in infantile vocalization, the 'sonorous cavity' of the mouth being established both as 'the site of a rich sensory experience in which *the association between touch and hearing* has ... a particular importance' and as the means of a sonorous differentiation of the self and not-self, since it is 'through the presence or absence of motor and tactile participation that sounds produced are differentiated from sounds external to the self: first fundamental advance on the sonorous plane in the establishment of the boundaries of the self'.[26] Lecourt goes on to argue that the achievement of articulatory distinctness establishes an equivalence between spirituality and the diminution of touch in the audio-tactile ensemble:

> One notices, for example, people who speak 'as though without touching themselves', no more than hinting at the touch of articulation (as when one tries to speak with a full mouth or with something hot in it), and, at the opposite end of the scale, those who produce a verbal porridge, thereby maintaining a permanent and undifferentiated contact.
>   It also so happens that religion, as in India, characterizes divine sound by the peculiarity of not originating in a contact, an 'untouched' sound, which gets its purity from this dissociation.[27]

Some nineteenth-century productions of spirit voices are represented as non-oral, as ventriloquial in the etymological sense of being produced by processes which bypass the organs and processes of bodily speech. Georgiana Houghton writes that, during one vocal manifestation, 'there was a pause, during which I felt my mouth very firmly shut; and I was then spoken of and through, "Her lips are closed as to prophecy for the present, but the time shall come when they will be opened to declare the Will of the Lord."[28] Paradoxically, the closing of the bodily mouth is here the occasion and condition of a power of spiritual utterance which seems to be a performative disproof of what is actually said in it.

The direct voice which came to maturity from the late nineteenth century onwards involves an intensification of this experience of 'untouched sound'. It brings about a striking reduction in the substantial presence and participation of the medium, as the transformations effected in and on the body of the medium in nineteenth-century spiritualism give way to transformations in the environment effected through the medium but without markedly affecting her. The direct voice tends to involve a marked diminution of bodily stress and excitation, as for instance in this description of the powers of Mrs Etta Wriedt by W. Usborne Moore:

> Unlike the gifts of poesy, art, oratory, or song, it demands from her no effort; and, with proper precautions, it causes no strain upon her physical constitution. To exhibit it, all she has to do is to sit passively in a chair, preferably in pitch darkness. It is, indeed, difficult to know what her personality has to do with the phenomenon, for she never goes into the trance condition, and talks naturally throughout.[29]

Rather than providing a channel or habitation for the spirits and their voices, the medium is placed in the position of the switchboard operator. We might also see this transition in terms of the changing roles of the telegraph operator and the telephonist. The transmission and decoding of a telegraph required the active participation through bodily and mental action of the operators at either end of the message. By contrast, the telephone signal was routed through the body of the switchboard operator, whose function was simply to facilitate a connection, to 'put the caller through' (though this very passivity required a set of phatic protocols and disciplines of response). The odd positivity of the word 'telephonist', which allows one for a moment to conceive of the switchboard operator as actually making the call, actually highlights her reduced role as a simple quasi-mechanical relay.

If the increased passivity of the female medium in the facilitation of the direct voice corresponds to the generalization of the passive female function as telephone operator, the increasing technolo-gization of the phenomenon, along with the reputation it gained for being the most technically demanding form of mediumship, seems from the First World War onwards also to have encouraged the increased identification of male mediums with the direct voice. J. Arthur Findlay experimented with John C. Sloan; H. Dennis Bradley celebrated the achievements of the American direct-voice medium George Valiantine; Lucy Chauncy Bridges recorded her experiences with the direct-voice medium Peter Clarke and the most well-known British exponent of the direct voice in the years after the Second World War was Leslie Flint.[30] The most famous exception to this, Mina Stinson Crandon ('Margery'), confirms this pattern in that she was also the most spectacularly bodily of twen-tieth-century mediums; her productions of the voice of her control, her deceased brother Walter, were accompanied by a range of phenomena – convulsive trance, spectacular feats of telekinesis and materialization – which are rather anachronistic in their extrava-gance. Another exception to the identification of the direct voice with male mediums actually serves to confirm the conventional associations between women and bodily subjection to the invading voice. James Crenshaw's *Telephone Between Worlds* tells the story of a Californian medium named Richard Zenor, who allegedly discov-ered and displayed his powers as a direct-voice medium early in life. At around the age of 12, however, Zenor began what Crenshaw calls 'a new and rarer phase of mediumship', in which, instead of being conveyed through a trumpet, voices began to be heard emanating from his own lips. Where he had previously been able to remain fully conscious as a trumpet medium, the production of voices through his person required him to lapse into trance. The result of this reversive feminization is that Zenor is said to have become 'a telephone link between two worlds, the instrument whereby those no longer clothed in the physical garment, as we know it, could speak naturally and directly to those left behind'.[31] The pattern thus seems to be that bodily dispossession requires the suspension of consciousness, whereas the quasi-technological production of the direct voice is seen as an extension or modality of consciousness.

It is tempting to see in this a recapitulation of the movement in the history of the practices of ventriloquism from female to male: I have written elsewhere about the move from the female experience of being physically possessed and spoken through by the divine or demonic other which is characteristic of oracular and ecstatic speech (for example, in the utterances of the pythia at Delphi and in the history of glossolalic utterance from Montanism through to the revivals of the phenomenon among the Camisards in the early eighteenth century and in the congregation of Edward Irving in the 1830s) to a male practice of ventriloquism as a secular entertainment, in which the ventriloquist speaks through the body of another.[32] This pattern seems to be confirmed by the fact that the quasi-technologization of vocal manifestations in the direct voice makes it possible for the male medium to discourse with the voices he produces, the medium participating, as it were, in the message, where the appropriation of the vocal apparatus of the medium allowed discourse only between the spirit and the other sitters.

The more 'direct' the voice, then, the more indirect the agency of the medium becomes. We would be right to expect that the massive intensification of broadcast and recording media after the Second World War, along with the developments of the techniques of radio astronomy, would result in further dissociations of the voice from the person of the medium. In 1964, a Swedish writer named Friedrich Jürgenson published a book in which he claimed to have recorded 'voices from space'. He followed this up with claims to have made contact with the dead through the direct use of radio and microphone.[33] Konstantin Raudive, a Latvian psychologist, set out to replicate Jürgenson's experiments. In the book he published in 1968, *Unhörbares wird hörbar* (*The Inaudible Becomes Audible*), he claimed that, by combining various means of recording, including providing input into a tape-recorder from radio receivers tuned to the white noise between channels, microphones recording in a silent room, and diodes, with enhanced playback, he too had been able to capture and converse with voices which he assumed to belong to the dead. Raudive's discovery caused a small media sensation, especially in Britain, after the publication of the translation of his book.[34] There are some interesting new features of this new mode of appearance of the voices of the dead. We can see this as an extension of the cooling, dematerializing movement shown by spiritualism as a whole. In Raudive's experiments the receptiveness of the medium and the evocative ritual of the séance are replaced by the diode, or microphone, and the tape-recording apparatus, and the quasi-technological ritual of the séance gives way to a wholly technological procedure.

The actual voices obtained by Raudive also exhibit some

interesting new features. Where the direct voice had previously acted as the guarantee of the survival of their owners' personality wholly unchanged after death, the new voices from the ether were sometimes characterized by striking linguistic disturbance, speaking, not in the language they used in their lives, but in an unstable compound of different languages. It is as though the orderly traffic of previous spirit communications had now become subject to the pressures of late-twentieth-century communications, with the airwaves thronged with messages of different kinds from different cultures and languages. As compared with the small, congenial and culturally homogeneous companies of spirits summoned by earlier direct-voice séances (in which the Irish and the Red Indians were welcome because they knew their place), the 70 000 or so voices accumulated by Raudive constitute a jammed overload that makes the cosy conversations of the previous generation of spiritualism seem an impossibility. If there could be a postmodern spiritualism, then this might well be it. As might be expected, however, Raudive developed various ways of limiting, controlling and personalizing this heteroglossolalia. Spirit controls established themselves and helped to filter the flood of posthumous vocal traffic (though in the manner of disc jockeys or air traffic controllers, we may surmise, rather than that of the genial compères of a previous dispensation) and he and Peter Bander devised methods for asking and answering questions.

In this movement away from the physical person of the medium and the dissolution of the corporeal community of the séance, the development of direct voice can therefore be shown to redouble the ghostly dematerialization of the voice effected by modern technologies, but I want now to consider the ways in which the séance nevertheless worked against this tendency, offering corporeal rehabilitations of the voice. To begin with, it is clear that the séance continues to associate the voice with an ensemble of kinetic sensations and effects. Among the purposes served by the trumpets in direct-voice mediumship, for example, was that of providing the voice with spatiality and direction, as well as supplementing the disembodiment of the voice with touch. The unnamed writer of an article in *The Direct Voice*, a short-lived journal established in 1930 to explore and publicize the phenomenon which provided its title, describes the energetic movements of the trumpets during a séance conducted with the medium Maina L. Tafe:

With regard to physical phenomena, the writer has witnessed the following: levitation of as many as three trumpets at once, all illuminated with a band or dots and crosses. Touches with the trumpet have been numerous especially on the face and head; several times with as many as three trumpets at once, which were whisked round the circle from sitter to sitter at considerable speed.[35]

Touching with the trumpet in this way appears in almost every other account of trumpet séances I have read. In many of them, the touches seem to be intended to suggest the inhabitation of a discontinuous body, the form of which was both dissolved and subtly renewed by the pattern of nudges, pokes and palpations:

Someone would be lightly touched on the point of the nose, another on the top of the head, another's hand would be touched, and so on – never a hard knock. At request, any part of the body would be touched without a mistake, without any fumbling, a clean, gentle touch....[36]

The relationship between voice and touch established in the trumpet séance is helpfully glossed by Didier Anzieu's investigation of the role of sound and the voice in forming both body-image and ego-image in early infantile experience; Anzieu stresses that the voice of the parent or carer does not merely accompany the enclosing and defining caress, but is as it were its sonorous form. For the baby, auditory and tactile impulses are still closely associated, and thus the parent's voice provides as it were the shape of the infant's self. Anzieu surmises that patients suffering from a damaged or disturbed sense of ego may have been subjected to the experience of rough, discordant or invasive voices in early life.[37]

As well as reassociating the voice with movement and sensation, the experiences of the direct voice also aimed to preserve or restore some of the corporeality of the voice itself. Many direct-voice séances acted out ritual compensations for this technological spectralization of the voice. The records in *The Direct Voice* of a séance with Mina Crandon, as 'Margery', demonstrate the attempt to recorporealize the mechanical voice. Mrs Crandon sat behind a curtain in front of which were arranged four speaking-trumpets. Mr Walter, a member of the circle, was appointed to operate the Ediphone, a dictating machine supplied by the Edison company for the purpose. Since the trumpets were levitated and moved through the air as the spirit-voices spoke through them, it was necessary to ask permission of the spirit-controls to hold the trumpet in position close to the mouthpiece in order to ensure proper recordings. The mechanism whose purpose was to make possible the abstraction and capture of the disembodied voice – the further disembodiment of the disembodied – hereby became transformed into a surrogate body. Mr Walter reported that, holding the trumpet against the microphone,

> he could feel the vibration of the 'voice', which appeared to come from the *center* of the trumpet. Also, when one of the trumpets with the larger apertures was used he said that he could feel *warm breath on his hand*.
>
> This tallies exactly with my own experience when operating the machine on different occasions, when my hand became quite hot and moist from the breath of the voice that was speaking through the trumpet; indeed, a truly remarkable experience.[38]

If the spirits employed breath, this implied the existence of other spirit-organs. Writing in 1894, Florence Marryat defines the direct voice not as voice produced independently of vocal apparatus as such, but rather 'when spirits speak to you with a thorax and gullet of their own, instead of using the organs and speech of a medium'.[39] That Marryat means this quite literally is plain from her account of an interchange with Charlie, the spirit control of the direct voice medium Mr Rita:

> Charlie indulged now in a little amicable 'sparring' with me, because, hearing how loudly he spoke in the direct voice, I asked him if he had materialised a perfect throat and gullet. He replied that he had. 'And have you a tongue and teeth, and everything pertaining to the mouth and throat, Charlie?' I continued. 'Put your forefinger out as far as you can, Lady No Death,' he replied [a reference to Marryat's book, *There Is No Death*], 'and I will show you if I have.' I did as he desired me, and a hand met my finger in the dark and guided it to a mouth. It was an enormous mouth – a perfect cave of Adullam, where you might have hidden seventy prophets. 'Isn't that a mouth,' demanded Charlie of me, 'and a very fine mouth too?' I acquiesced in his decision. 'Well, put your finger right in it,' he continued; 'don't be afraid, I won't

bite you – and tell them what you feel.' I put my finger in the mouth, and felt all round it carefully. The interior was moist and smooth like the mouth of any mortal. I could feel the palate and the tongue, which seemed also very large. Then I made a tour of the gums, which felt swollen like those of a teething baby, but there were no teeth. I told the circle just what I had felt, adding: 'You must be very young, Charlie, since you have not yet cut your teeth.' 'Yes,' he answered, 'it is about time I cut them, I think. Don't you agree with me?' And with my finger still in his mouth, all the teeth sprung into existence both of the upper and lower jaw, and Charlie gave my finger such a bite that I called out and withdrew it.[40]

Later explanations and experiences of the vocal apparatus necessary for the direct voice are less colourful, but most of them insist both on the materiality of the process of voice production and on the necessity for the spirits to materialize a 'mask' of vocal organs for them to speak through.

Usually the mask of ectoplasmic vocal organs also remained invisible, but an exception to this too is offered in the Margery mediumship, which, as we have seen, combines highly technical investigation with the most archaic and grotesque bodily fantasies. The most remarkable fruits of Walter's willingness to cooperate with the investigators were his successful efforts to materialize in visible form first hands, then a larynx and, finally, an entire, if disgustingly shrunken-looking talking head, photographs of which alleged materializations survive. An interesting sign of the embrace of technological ways of thinking about the dissociation of the voice is the consistent use in the official report of the case for the *Proceedings of the American Society for Psychical Research* of the term 'teleplasm' in preference to the term 'ectoplasm', to describe the substance used by Walter to materialize these forms. The term 'teleplasmic' had first been proposed and used by F. W. H. Myers in 1890, in preference to the term 'telesomatic', to describe the transmission of bodies.[41] In this substitution of terms, an essentially parturitive conception, of a substance exuded directly from the body of the medium, or from the collective body of the séance (*ectoplasm*, from the Greek *ekto-*, outside, seems to imply a movement from the inside to the outside), has yielded, under the suggestive pressure both of spiritualized terms like telekinesis and telepathy and of more familiar technological terms like the telegraph and the telephone, to the idea of a substance not merely stretched or extended, but transmitted over distance. The experience of speech transmitted through mute and nonhuman substance seems to have suggested the idea of substance itself made transmissible in the service of speech. Although later science-fiction fantasies of the transportation of the human body will borrow from technologies for transmitting visual information – examples might be *The Fly*, the 'beaming' technology employed in *Star Trek*, or even Willy Wonka's transporting television in *Charlie and the Chocolate Factory* – the fact that long-distance transmission belonged, until the development of television, to the technologies of sound (the cinema involved localized projection rather than transmission), made for a close association between acoustic experience and the sense of the teleplastic malleability of the body.

9.4   CONCLUSION

In twentieth-century spiritualism, the voice became the most important form of embodiment and manifestation for nonembodied entities: it was at once the most powerful and the most versatile form of witness to the unseen. In this, spiritualism draws deeply on the experiences of modern acoustic technologies, both telephonic (transmissive) and phonographic (reproductive). Spiritualism attests and contributes to the ghostliness of these new technologies, even as it also deploys them in its strangely enthusiastic struggle against the supernatural, to affirm the materiality, the manipulability, the *technicality* of the unseen. Perhaps it is itself a kind of new technology, a way of at once raising and laying spirits, of exorcizing the immateriality of the otherworld. In its phenomenological commentary on the technologies of the dissociated voice, the direct voice of spiritualism restores to vocality the substantiality and the sense of living presence which were in danger of being stripped away by contemporary technologies. It gives voice back to the body and the body back to the voice. Palpable without being visible, the direct voice joins to the traditional authority of the voice without a visible source the warrant of hapto-sonorous corporeality. As such, far from asserting the transcendence of spirit against the technological materialism of the twentieth century, spiritualism should be seen as a renewed ceremony of reparation for the disembodying effects of acoustic technologies.

But in compensating for the technological emaciation of the voice, the séance also discloses and depends on the reparatory reifications which are already effected by such technologies. The séance in fact doubles, or ghosts, the structure of hapto-sonorous hallucination which made the technologies of the telephone, the gramophone, the radio and the tape-recorder, along with all their contemporary refinements, so comfortable and familiar from the outset. For the disembodiments effected by contemporary technology have become familiar to us, in the intimate ease with which we are addressed by voices without source, and the ways in which we assimilate and are assimilated to the objects and apparatuses of vocal transmission (to the point where we find it easy to conceive of telephonic implants in our bodies). Perhaps it is this easy inhabitation of disembodiment to which the séance refuses to consent, even as it borrows and consolidates such effects. Thus it is vital that the process of speaking through and with the technological apparatus provided by the séance should continue to involve the struggle against impediment and obscurity. This sense of the mutual resistance of voice and its technological vehicles is itself an attempt to maintain a dual resistance in spiritualism: a resistance firstly to the absolute identification of the voice and its vehicles, with the consequent impossibility of marking a distinction between a voice and that of which it is the voice; and secondly a resistance to that intolerably close coherence between spiritualism and the technologies which it employs as its vehicles. This might explain the peculiarly persistent anachronism of the technologies borrowed by the séance. The fact that these imaginary technologies are always slightly out of date, slightly awkward and klunky (the levitating trumpet, the talking heads and larynxes, the joining of the cat's-whisker diode to the tape-recorder in Raudive's experiments), works to maintain the guarantee that the direct voice is the product and expression of a transformative kind of *work*. But, for all its efforts to enact the work of the voice against materiality and mechanism, the séance keeps letting us hear, despite itself, the workings of the machine in the ghost.

Notes

1. Janet Oppenheim, *The Other World: Spiritualism and Psychical Research in England, 1850–1914* (Cambridge: Cambridge University Press, 1985).

2. Annie Besant, *Why I Became a Theosophist* (London: Theosophical Publishing Society, 1891), p. 17.
3. Charles Maurice Davies, *Heterodox London: Or, Phases of Free Thought in the Metropolis*, 2 vols (London: Tinsley Brothers, 1874), Vol. 2, p. 41; Florence Marryat, *The Spirit World* (London: F. W. White, 1894), p. 34.
4. Alex Owen, *The Darkened Room: Women, Power, and Spiritualism in Late Nineteenth-Century England* (London: Virago, 1989), p. 54.
5. Oppenheim, *The Other World*, p. 165.
6. Sophia de Morgan, *From Matter to Spirit: the Result of Ten Years' Experience in Spirit Manifestations, Intended as a Guide for Enquirers* (London: Longmans, Green, Longman, Roberts and Green, 1863), p. 57.
7. Owen, *The Darkened Room*, p. xviii.
8. Georgiana Houghton, *Evenings at Home in Spiritual Séance: Welded Together By a Species of Autobiography*, 2nd Series (London: Trübner and Co., 1882), p. 14.
9. Walter J. Ong, *The Presence of the Word: Some Prolegomena for Religious and Cultural History* (Minneapolis: University of Minnesota Press, 1981), p. 28.
10. Ong, *The Presence of the Word*, p. 164.
11. Didier Anzieu, *The Skin Ego*, trans. Chris Turner (New Haven: Yale University Press, 1989), pp. 157–73.
12. Elizabeth d'Esperance, *What I Know of Materialisations from Personal Experience* (London: 'Light' Publishing Co., 1904), p. 19.
13. Handbill in Harry Price Collection, University of London.
14. Houghton, *Evenings at Home in Spiritual Séance*, 2nd Series, pp. 224–5.
15. Houghton, *Evenings at Home in Spiritual Séance*, p. 13.
16. Charles Partridge, *Spiritualism: Its Phenomena and Significance (Spiritual Telegraph, Tract No. 1)* (New York: Spiritual Telegraph Office, 1858).
17. N. B. Wolfe, *Startling Facts in Modern Spiritualism* (Cincinnati, no. pub., 1874), p. 256
18. Wolfe, *Startling Facts*, p. 250.
19. The links between telegraphy and spiritualism are more than analogical. Janet Oppenheim notes, for example, that 'while Cromwell Varley, an electrical engineer of some renown, was busy with the Atlantic cable, his wife developed her gifts of trance utterance, clairvoyance, and automatic writing' (*The Other World*, p. 9). Richard Noakes of the University of Cambridge has explored the close interest that Varley himself took in spiritualist phenomena, and use of electrical calibration to record them and prove their reality: 'Tying the Unseen with Electricity: Victorian Science and the Naturalisation of the Supernatural', paper given at the *Victorian Supernatural* conference, University of North London, 26 November, 1995.
20. Clive Chapman and G.A.W., *The Blue Room: Being the Absorbing Story of the Development of Voice to Voice Communication in Broad Light With Souls Who Have Passed Into the Great Beyond* (Auckland: Whitcombe and Tombs, 1928), p. 51.
21. Estella W. Stead, 'My Father (W.T. Stead) and Spiritualism', *Nash's*

Magazine VI (1912), p. 552.

22. Stead, 'My Father', p. 545.

23. Testimony of James Robertson, reported in W. Usborne Moore, *The Voices: a Sequel to 'Glimpses of the Next State'* (London: Watts and Co., 1913), p. 176.

24. Hannen Swaffer, 'Preface' to Maurice Barbanell, *The Trumpet Shall Sound* (London: Rider and Co., 1933), p. 9.

25. Swaffer, 'Preface', p. 10.

26. Edith Lecourt, 'The Musical Envelope' in *Psychic Envelopes*, ed. Didier Anzieu, trans. Daphne Briggs (London: Karnac, 1990), p. 215.

27. Lecourt, 'The Musical Envelope', p. 216.

28. Georgiana Houghton, *Evenings at Home in Spiritual Séance: Prefaced and Welded Together By a Species of Autobiography* (London: Trübner and Co., 1881), p. 78.

29. Moore, *The Voices*, pp. xvii–xviii.

30. *Behold I Live*, compiled by Lucy Chauncy Bridges, from *Tape-Recordings* (London: Regency Press, 1966).

31. James Crenshaw, *Telephone Between Worlds* (Los Angeles: DeVorss and Co., 1950), p. 6.

32. I sketch this history briefly in my '"Jigajia... Yummyyum... Pfuiiiiiii!... Bbbbblllllblblblblobschb!" "Circe"'s Ventriloquy', in *Reading Joyce's 'Circe'*, ed. Andrew Gibson (Amsterdam: Rodopi, 'European Joyce Studies', No. 3, 1994), pp. 101–6 and at length in my *Ventriloquies: a Cultural History of the Dissociated Voice* (Oxford: Oxford University Press, 1999).

33. Friedrich Jürgenson, *Rösterna från Rymden* (Stockholm, 1964); *Radio- och mikrofonkontakt med de döda* (Uppsala: Nyblöms, 1968).

34. Konstantin Raudive, *Breakthrough: an Amazing Experiment in Electronic Communication with the Dead*, trans. Nadia Fowler, ed. Joyce Morton (Gerrards Cross: Colin Smythe, 1971). The story of the media affair is judiciously told by Peter Bander, a psychologist who gave up his lecturing job to work with Colin Smythe in publicizing and investigating Raudive's claimed discoveries, in *Carry On Talking: How Dead Are the Voices?* (Gerrards Cross: Colin Smythe, 1972).

35. 'Some Twentieth-Century Mediums: 1. Miss Maina L. Tafe', *The Direct Voice* 1 (1930), p. 13.

36. J. Arthur Findlay, *An Investigation Into Psychic Phenomena: a Record of a Series of Sittings with Mr. John C. Sloan, the Glasgow Trance and Direct Voice Medium* (Glasgow: Society for Psychical Research, 1924), p. 11.

37. Anzieu, *The Skin Ego*, pp. 169–70.

38. 'Voices Recorded in the Séance Room' (no author named), *The Direct Voice* 3 (July, 1930), p. 82.

39. Marryat, *The Spirit World*, p. 138.

40. Marryat, *The Spirit World*, p. 277.

41. *Proceedings of the Society for Psychical Research* (1890), p. 669.

10

Angels in the Architecture: the Economy of the Supernatural

Clive Bloom

10.1 THE NEW OCCULT

Despite the importance of science and technology in the Western world and the advances of rational thought across the last two hundred years, a general belief in the paranormal is both widespread and deeply felt.[1] Horoscopes, clairvoyancy and spiritualism all command a large audience and have a special place in the popular imagination. The paranormal and the occult are fascinating areas which hold rich material for the student of cultural studies and popular sociological beliefs, and both offer fields which have yet to be explored but which have immediate appeal. This essay asks the questions 'what cultural and historical factors allow irrational belief to flourish in an age of technology?' and 'what apparently arcane beliefs are the *products* of a technological modern society – products of both progress and paranoia?'

The more one thinks about the supernatural, the more one is struck by both the increasingly complex web of connections the topic suggests, connections that refuse to be disentangled, and the very real sense that there is no topic to be discussed at all (ghosts? the supernatural?). If there is a topic, it is not that of an eternal return, but rather the narration of a progressive and inclusive modernity in which supernaturalism is an integral part – both marginal *and* essential.

We may state the problem in terms of a certain grammar or logic upon which the very nature of the debate might rest. Let us say that this is a debate in which the predicate seems to have slipped its subject, and that this predicate has increasingly identified a subject only in terms of its own procedures as a predicate. Ghosts exist because we determine them as ghosts – narrate them into 'life'. In a subject such as this, the proper object of our debate must be that which is spoken of in terms of its mode of speaking instead of discussing the veracity or otherwise of that which does the speaking, its origination or significance. What is significantly missing in this grammar is an appropriate place for the copula. Here the determining quality of the connection between subject and predicate is itself not simply occulted, but occluded by the necessary tensions between the two. The question posed by this occlusion of the copula takes us to the heart of our quest. We are not here dealing with the nature of a reality awaiting its revelation. This is not about the nature of things nor about the grounds of knowledge but rather we are concerned with the nature of perception.

It seems to me that one must refuse any debate on grounds which accept any equivalence between the ideas of occultists on the one hand and science on the other, not because there may not be the occasional similarity (usually merely coincidental), but because such a debate can only end in stalemate. On these grounds the epistemological debate was one that was already redundant before the fact. This is the reason why each and every book on spiritualism, occultism, UFOs, reincarnation, near-death experiences, parapsychology, and visits from ancient space gods always claims the authority for a new and universal dispensation based on the premise that every tenet of accepted science and technology must be radically rethought within the occult framework of the new apocalyptic vision of the individual writer or cult representative. The foundation of almost every work in these various genres is the acceptance of *illumination* as a higher and more efficacious means towards the penetration of the order of nature and the inherent nature of things.

This seems not, therefore (at least initially), to be a debate between faith and reason, but rather two forms of logic based on quite unrelated conceptual systems without any equivalence. Indeed, most writers in these occult genres insist upon the conspiratorial nature of both conventional science and established religion which (against the evidence of history) have worked together in order to *conceal* a set of truths they only dimly understand but which they, nevertheless, fully comprehend would destroy their power should such truths be revealed to a wide public. I will return later to the logic behind revealed or illuminated knowledge, but for the moment it must suffice to point out that there remains a continuum which leads from spiritualism to theosophy and from these two to the techno-occultism of extraterrestrialism or ley-line investigation. We will see that, despite disclaimers by a number of writers and spiritualists, there remain sufficient correlations between groups to talk of a popular mentality (or more properly and correctly) of a popular perceptual mapping which consists of numerous routes and connections within which individuals locate their own hermetic system or supernatural experience.

In debates such as this we must separate the nature of the experiences described by spiritualists and others from a belief in any system they might espouse, but we must accept as genuine (hoaxes excepted) the nature of the experiences themselves. I mean by this that these experiences are undoubtedly *in* the world if not of it and that although these experiences are of a material nature (by which I mean an actual individual was the subject of the experience – maybe its author) they can be neither understood nor verified outside the matrix of subjectivity. The moment of *encounter*, if it is to be understood at all, is a moment of *hallucination*, but it is not pure *delusion*. To say 'I saw my mother a moment ago' is not the same as saying 'I saw my mother (who died last year) a moment ago'. These are statements belonging to different registers, but the second statement may be a correct account of an encounter inexplicable in terms of reference to the universe of the first statement. Empirical evidence offers no refutation of evidence in this second encounter.

If science emphasizes effect (not self-based) then 'magical' encounters emphasize affect (where subjectivity is a necessary corollary of determination: the self as conduit). Magical encounters are suffused with an overabundance of affect where a 'fact' in the world is determined by the presence of subjectivity and then returned as effect. All such magical hallucination aspires then to the condition of an *event* in which excess of subjectivity (conditioned by the limits of 'self') returns from 'elsewhere'. Thus the constellation: I am alone or I am chosen as a witness, I am not alone but among a world of strangers, or I am being persecuted by strange creatures: I am therefore a special messenger of the witnessed signs. Such hallucination and its experience 'in the world' aspires to the condition of history and yet is excluded not only by outside derision but by its own incapacity to conform to historical determination (nor yet to the theological determination of the miraculous – of which it falls short). Excluded from history although experienced as an event, the supernatural is relegated by its own processes and procedures to pseudo-history and the marginal *confronting* history, incapable of being incorporated within it. Supernatural experience occurs *within* history but lacks significance: the effort of becoming an event is too great for the weight of its signification, leaving it only mere anecdotal status.

Moreover, there is a decided lack of social obligation in such encounters, missing the proprieties of ordinary procedures and ordinary social action. And yet, is not all this also a type of over-flowing of the banal ('just as I got to sleep ...', 'we were on a lonely road going home ...', 'I awoke suddenly ...') which returns trans-fixed and dislocated? It is this dislocation that makes the hallucination an event but prevents it from becoming history. Instead all is determined by a certain *scenario*, a theatre of staging, witnessing and participation at once cerebral and visceral. This scenario, according to its script, setting and direction, creates a framework whose dynamic tends towards zero: a trajectory out of time altogether into the ritualistic and mythic – already somehow anticipated by its text. What script, what text might this be?

Such psychic texts begin with the relationship between individual pronouncements and experiences and the systems within which they locate themselves. Often psychics will manifest materials which appear determinedly random and chaotic. However, all psychics rationalize their experiences within specific otherworldly systems which are themselves neither chaotic nor random. These coherent maps of elsewhere are rarely the product of unique individual explorations even though the experiencer may believe that to be the case. It is much more likely that these individually experienced explorations consciously or subconsciously belong to a long and clearly delineated history of psychic development that stretches back into the origins of modernity which we may locate in the mid-nineteenth century. This *historical* development must be viewed as a cultural phenomenon into which individuals insert themselves as psychic (however unwillingly).

In such a way the occult map has been subject less to being revealed over time than *constructed* into a coherent system of generations of psychics building upon their knowledge of each other's work. The subject is definable by its history as a history of perception. This is its reality, not that of a charting of an elsewhere found by illumination. Here is a different history of the modern. Any history of our topic must inevitably be intimately involved with the history of the supernatural. My contention is that spiritualism *represents a decisive break* in such a history. This may be viewed as a revolutionary leap from an essentially archaic, religious belief system concerned with the limits of sin and redemption to one that was in most of its features materialist, religiously ambivalent or agnostic, and in many of its more theorized aspects engaged in an aggressive debate with Darwinism or the consequences of Darwinism.

The new dispensation of an essentially rationalized supernatural was believed both to go beyond and to explain religion and science. Although this advance was supposedly based on 'natural law' and a type of spiritualized universal mechanics, it was founded on one central dogmatic assertion: *survival after death* – something absolutely accepted as proven beyond doubt through the increasing activities of mediums. The meaning of this new area of speculation is summed up in a sermon preached after the death of the actress Anny Ahlers (who died in suspicious circumstances in 1933). The sermon was given by her husband:

> I believe that we can and do have communication, in God's providence, and under God's care and protection, with those who have gone on before.... If we believe in religion at all, we know that the unseen state is a reality. The subject can be approached from the point of view of faith or from that of science. By blending the two, the faith of the one is strengthened and the science of the other is helped.
>
> Spiritualism proves that those who pass on are subject to growth, and that they advance sphere by sphere upwards and onwards. At first, a spirit is earthbound. Gradually, he *[sic]* goes on and becomes acclimatized to the unseen. After learning he goes on until at last he becomes a leader and a teacher. Spiritualism is a science, not a speculation.

Such emotional evidence is 'confronted' and 'investigated' by later writers who significantly display their credentials for integrity in affidavits and supposedly impartial forewords supplied, as often as not, by doctors or clergymen. This, for instance, is the Reverend Weatherhead's foreword to Paul Beard's book, *Survival of Death*, first published in 1966 and subsequently reissued in 1988:

I commend this book enthusiastically because it is quite outstanding as a discussion of the evidence for and against the human survival of death. The Christian Church has offered affirmation and consolation. Spiritualism has offered alleged communications. Mr. Beard offers evidence with a quality of analytical detachment, which, to my mind, is exactly what is so badly needed. In the end he regards the evidence as sufficiently conclusive *to warrant belief in survival*, but he examines every possible alternative interpretation of the phenomena and is never woolly, or afraid of where his investigations may lead. He concedes every possible claim that telepathy and clairvoyance may account for many alleged 'messages from the dead', but he finds a *residue* in the evidence for which the most intelligent and *reasonable* explanation is that of survival.

No reader can fail to be convinced of the author's complete integrity and fairness, or of his ability and insight [emphasis mine].

Reverend Weatherhead predicts,

'Psychic Research' will yield most enriching discoveries if it is explored by those who bring to it the kind of mental discipline and ability to examine evidence which is shown by scientists in material fields like biology, physics, chemistry and astronomy.

It is here in the 'residue' that 'survival' is proven as a matter of 'reasonable explanation'.

For Hannen Swaffer, one of Britain's leading early advocates of spiritualism and in whose second volume of memoirs the sermon appears, the knowledge gained through spirit communication is as significant as that of Galileo, Darwin or Oliver Lodge. Unlike science, spiritualistic knowledge aims to provide a particular form of ontology based on the conjunction of personality and death. In this model of evolution death is demoted to a peculiarly minor stage of life:

Death does not say farewell to man as an individual; death heightens his individuality; death is one more rung in the ladder of his individual evolution and he emerges from death as an individual with his consciousness intact, with his memory in no way impaired, with all the faculties of mind and spirit ready to give him a larger service, because they are freed from the limitations of a physical body with its cramping, restricting, five poor senses.

Such statements are nowadays reiterated by self-styled experts in near-death investigations which have gained a respectability usually withheld from psychic investigations proper. The message remains essentially the same, however. This, for example, is Melvin Morse MD (one of the best known near-death gurus), in his introduction to Betty J. Eadie's book, *Embraced by the Light*, a work to which we will have cause to return and which is rather unusually but significantly dedicated to 'my Lord and Saviour Jesus Christ'. Here is Morse:

> *Embraced by the Light* is not just Betty Eadie's story of dying during surgery and coming back to life, it is actually a journey into the meaning of this life. I remember a young boy who said to his parents after surviving cardiac arrest: 'I have a wonderful secret to tell you – I have been climbing a staircase to heaven'. That young man was too young to explain what he meant. This book contains that same wonderful secret. It is not a secret about life after death: it is a secret about life.

This central paradoxical proposition, at one stroke, demotes the miraculous nature of resurrection to the level of the banal and at the same time enhances the mundane so that it becomes immanent with the godhead. As the supernatural becomes normalized so the banal (our ordinary lived existence) becomes miraculous, hence Rosemary Brown, a medium who has spent many years transcribing the 'current' musical compositions of 'Liszt', 'Beethoven' and latterly John Lennon, tells us reassuringly that

> Clairvoyance, the sighting of spirits, is in no way a frightening or 'ghostly' occurrence. To me, the spirits who appear are as unthreatening as any corporeal visitor, and like them they will sit chatting on the sofa or stand casually by the piano while I play.

Hannen Swaffer, quoting Silver Birch (the guide of medium Maurice Barbanell) completes the paradox through the message,

> In man, this cosmic spirit, this life force, is individual. Man is an individuality, a spark of divine fire; man is an integral part of the

infinite intelligence that some call God, and I, the Great Spirit of life.

Such radical re-evaluations of life (given to the world by ethereal spirit guides speaking through entranced mediums) point to a wholly new cosmological pattern of reference and a wholly new cosmography in which it is now possible to find 'embedded in the evidence for survival [amid] a number of baffling, worthless and disconcerting features' (Beard) proof of a cosmic order in which the dead will, under the directions of ancient and wise guides, play a part on the world stage in order to bring about a new enlightenment in a troubled century.

No wonder that *only* this special knowledge (which is constantly contrasted with the dogma and assertions of religion and science, and which supposedly deals only in facts) is also a divinely ordained form of consolation:

> And [religion] will fail everyone who requires, not assertion but knowledge, and who, when 'faith' fails him, demands facts. Those, only Spiritualism can give. For it rolls away the stone of death. It bridges the gulf between the two worlds, enabling them to unite in love in service to mankind. (Swaffer)

It is this message of *consolation* that unites the early mediums of New York State with the later theorizing of Madame Blavatsky, the spirit messages of Sir Arthur Conan Doyle and White Eagle, the work of mediums such as Doris Stokes, Doris Collins and many others as well as a whole range of ufologists, ley-liners and eco-occultists. Medium Rosemary Brown puts it thus, 'The next world is very similar to ours, only infinitely more beautiful'; Ann Walker wrote her book to prove that spirit guides are real and that, 'families and loved ones [are] with us always'; Betty J. Eadie to show that 'our deaths are also often calculated to help us grow'; Doris Collins to prove 'survival of death'; Peter Redgrove, eco-occultist and mystic feminist in his 1980s version of this message, *The Black Goddess and the Sixth Sense*, opens his book with the somewhat alarming statement that 'I've always known we are surrounded by invisibles', and in accepting the reality of life beyond death, sees this as just one manifestation of a new Gaia consciousness or '[a] wonderful communion and continuum which joins the whole world'. Linda Williamson in her book *Mediums and Their Work* even states that mediumistic activity heralds 'New Age Consciousness'.

10.2   THE ORIGINS OF CONTEMPORARY OCCULTISM

The decisive break in the history of supernaturalism that occurred with the advent of spiritualism may be conveniently and, indeed, is usually dated to the year 1848. While revolution disturbed Europe, John Fox, his wife, Margaret, and daughters Margaret and Kate moved into their new home in Hydesville, New York State. Within weeks the family had become the victims of strange rapping noises. One night, one of the daughters challenged the phenomena with the words 'Do as I do, Mr. Splitfoot' (the reference to the devil was soon conveniently forgotten) after which time the sisters became the centre of, and the controllers of, the weird phenomena.

It might have been expected that the happenings at Hydesville would have quietly passed into one of the more bizarre backwaters of history, especially since the sisters both made and then retracted statements about fraudulent practice, but this was not to be the case, for their own brand of mysticism and inspiration was steeped in the peculiarly hysterical and histrionic atmosphere of American religious practice and participated in the millennialism and apocalyptic imagination of New York State particularism. On precisely the day of the first Fox phenomena it was claimed by 'The Seer of Poughkeepsie', Andrew Jackson Davis, a self-taught healer and mystic, that a voice had spoken to him, proclaiming 'Brother, the great work has begun.' At once, the Fox sisters and their small house had become the centre of a cult and they had found their John the Baptist.

It is beyond the scope of this essay to document the extremely rapid rise in spiritualist activity in America during the latter half of the last century. Suffice it to say that by the 1850s there was a positive epidemic – a rage – for spiritualistic phenomena and that mediumship flourished on both sides of the Atlantic, from Emma Britten to the Bang Sisters of Lily Dale near Buffalo and from them to Daniel Dunglas Home, whose feats of levitation inspired Henry Sidgwick and Frederick Myers among others to found the Society for Psychical Research in 1882. From a quite different starting-point Mary Baker Eddy had in 1879 founded the first 'Church of Christian Scientist' whose ambiguously and oxymoronically named belief system became the other part of the evangelical appeal of spiritualist belief. By the early twentieth century Lily Dale had become spiritualism's largest summer camp, its focal point the now moved and resurrected cottage of John and Margaret Fox!

All this activity in the realm of this new supernaturalism (the term was retained until the Second World War when it was replaced by discussion of the paranormal) might have remained at the level of popular superstition and arcane parlour tricks – might have remained simply a fashionable scandal – had it not been for the fortuitous conjunction of a certain expression of nonconformist belief, Christian Science and Theosophy. With these, the new occult gained its creed and its geography and it was into these that believers were able to insert their own personal and idiosyncratic narratives.

Helena Petrovna Blavatsky, usually known as Madame Blavatsky, began her rise to fame after visiting the Eddy farm in Vermont in 1874. With some psychic ability and much personal presence she was taken up by one Colonel Olcott and together they formed a 'Miracle Club' followed by the Theosophical Society, which she founded in 1875 with William Quern Judge. Inspired first by the mysterious entity 'Tuitit Bey', Blavatsky moved on to India where further inspirational entities led her to complete an occult cosmography described in *Isis Unveiled* (1877) and *The Secret Doctrine* (1888). Again, it would be too difficult in an essay of this nature to detail the beliefs of theosophists, but what can be said is that theosophy's immense success at the end of the last century was due in part to its own internal logic, which,

> sought to replace the *belief system* of the Christian religion and the *knowledge system* of modern science ... with a spiritual knowledge that was free from associations of guilt and which did not carry within it a moral imperative. Theosophy transmuted scientific knowledge into an echo of spiritual knowledge.

The powerful combination of nonconformist religion mixed and matched with theosophical or similar doctrines created a new area of popular culture – essentially modern, American and plebeian, which found a quick and easy acceptance in Britain. It is this Anglo-Americanism which has dominated the modern occult and which has been determined independently of European groups who themselves often owed their ideas to this side of the Channel. Indeed, it often merges and subsumes independent European

Romantic magical and spiritual traditions which appear to develop outside the model described here and which yet, when investigated more closely, are tied to developments that may be considered broadly Anglo-American, or which are associated with European émigré culture.

After the First World War, for instance, belief in spiritualism grew extremely rapidly and the uncertain inter-war years gave much space for groups to flourish. It was in this atmosphere in 1936 that the mysterious Parisian group the *Fraternité des Polaires* transmogrified into the White Eagle Lodge and it was from this source that Sir Arthur Conan Doyle spoke his message of love and universal brotherhood from 'the other side' having been in life the acknowledged spokesman of Anglo-American spiritualism and the owner of the Psychic Bookshop down the road from Westminster Abbey.

A full history of modern supernaturalism would be a considerable task. I have offered enough background, I hope, to show that there is a clear internal history to the subject *(made by occultists for themselves)* from which many branches have sprouted, from mediumship to near-death experiences and from paranormal investigations to ancient-spaceman theory. There is now an occult literature on 'biology' (Karl Ernst Krafft; Kenneth Ring); 'psychology' (Chet B. Snow); 'evolution' (Ernest Hackel; Frederick Spencer Oliver; 'Tuella'); 'history' (Ernst Zundel); 'archaeology' (Edgar Case, Erich von Daniken); 'geology' (Alfred Watkins; John Mitchell; David Icke; Immanuel Velikowsky); art (Rosemary Brown); physics (Charles Fort); geography (William Scott-Elliott; Augustus Le Plangeon; Charles Berlitz); ecology (Peter Redgrove). All this does not include internal crossovers within such study (e.g. UFOs and near-death experiences) nor the purely occult, magic ceremonial or spiritual work available. Lines cross and re-cross; for example, Erich von Daniken claimed to have written his works out of a state of 'extra-sensory perception' (using various 'books' including *The Book of Mormon* and *The Book of Ezekiel)*, the name of which he calls *espern*; and that his books were written as much by *illumination* as by investigation. In *The Gold of the Gods*,

> Daniken quotes from the Book of Dzyan, which he describes as 'a secret doctrine ... preserved for millennia in Tibetan crypts'. The original text, of which nothing is known, not even whether it still exists, was copied from generation to generation and added to by

initiates, without informing his reader that the book of Dzyan was the authority claimed by Blavatsky for her Secret Doctrine, and was unknown to the world prior to her invention of the manuscript that could only be read by the 'inner light'. (Quoted in Morris).

Before we situate this history within a wider cultural history, it might be useful to give a flavour of the mélange of ideas provided by occult and mediumistic experience.

Betty J. Eadie's *Embraced by the Light* is a classic account of a near-death voyage and its paranormal narrative closely follows the general script prescribed for almost all such journeys:

1. At the point of death, the dying person hears a loud and disturbing noise, seemingly in his own head, which may take the form either of buzzing or ringing.

2. He begins to move at high speed through a long dark tunnel. (Occasionally movement takes place through a passage or a cave, or either up or down a well or staircase. The space is generally confined and usually dark.)

3. At this point it is usual to see an extremely bright light marking the end of the tunnel. All accounts of this light emphasize its brilliant but non-dazzling quality.

4. The experient may then feel himself to be outside his physical body, frequently suspended in a horizontal position above it looking down on his physical shape.

5. The traveller emerges into the light and is overwhelmed by a sensation of peace and loving-kindness.

6. He may now meet with friends and relatives, whose function appears to be both welcoming and reassuring.

7. A warm shining being is generally encountered who shows him in instantaneous panorama his past life, with its strengths and weaknesses.

8. At some later stage he comes to a barrier, a frontier post of sorts, which he must pass to go into the next phase of existence. If his earthly body is revived by resuscitative methods and he has to return to it, however, this is the point at which he must turn back. (Forman).

Eadie's account smoothly unites orthodox Christianity, theosophy and extraterrestrialism and she moves from an encounter with Jesus to a visit to the garden of Eden and a vision of a celestial being suggestive of the Virgin Mary. On the way we are given insights into the concepts of universal love, spirit guides and hierarchical places and finally led to scenes reminiscent of alien abduction narratives. Thus we move effortlessly from

> There was no questioning who he was. I knew that he was my Savior, and friend, and God. He was Jesus Christ, who had always loved me.

to,

> When we die, my guides said, we experience nothing more than a transition to another state. Our spirits slip from the body and move to a spiritual realm,

to,

> I saw a large machine similar to a computer, but much more elaborate.... I was taken to another large room similar to a library. As I looked around it seemed to be a repository of knowledge, but I couldn't see any books. Then I noticed ideas coming into my mind, knowledge filling me on subjects that I had not thought about for some time – or in some cases not at all. Then I realized that this was the library of the mind.... Some of the details of what followed *have been removed from my memory*, but many impressions remain. (Emphasis mine).

It is only in this library of the mind that Eadie can find the books only readable by the light of illumination (Blavatsky's *Book of Dzyan* (Zion?) or maybe Kenneth Grant's re-rendering as 'fact' of H. P. Lovecraft's *Necronomicon*), that have organized her own narrative in the first place and of which she personally is unaware. Christianity and extraterrestrialism are here blended in a way similar to that of Thelma Terrell ('Tuella'), who, like George van Tassel, claims contact with aliens of the 'Intergalactic Confederation', sometimes called the 'Interplanetary Space Command' whose commander is none other than Jesus-Sananda! All this is further enhanced in Eadie's narrative by a moral majority message on anti-abortion. We are told of one spirit, 'he had chosen to enter this world mentally handicapped'. For good measure, Eadie does not have an Indian spirit guide – she is herself the daughter of a Sioux Indian!

10.3 MADE IN THE USA: CORPORATE OCCULTISM

Here is the new dispensation: an infinitely benevolent universe whose founding principle is love and in which infinitely wise beings called guides help humankind to higher and higher levels of perfection in a preordained plan which yet includes free will. Above this Edenic panorama is the Christ figure – paradigmatic cosmic spaceman and formative idea behind a whole variety of Tibetan fraternities. The purpose of this miraculous panorama is the enlightenment of humanity, a humanity based on individualism, family values, the church and a communalism which embraces global humanity but which is ultimately determined by an absolute and mysterious subjectivity. It comes as no surprise that mediums as well as UFO abductees constantly stress their ordinary and often humble family origins as indeed do both Doris Stokes and Doris Collins. Equally many are affiliated to spiritualist churches, investigation groups, or both.

The scenario confirms in elaborate yet bizarre detail the desirability of ordinariness, home and family, re-establishing a single and radically conservative thought: we are all, as we always knew, important to the scheme of things. Moreover, the notion of the discovered 'fact' that no one dies but only 'passes over' completes the trajectory of the rationalist project in bringing the supernatural finally to heel under the inquisition of materialism. Andrew Jackson Davis, whose 'harmonial philosophy' was one of the foundation stones of modern spiritualist belief, argued as early as the mid-nineteenth century that mind or 'spirit' did not exist, only 'matter', as did J. R. Newton in Connecticut in the 1860s. Both Florence Nightingale and Harry Houdini were praised for their spiritual rather than material powers and their ultimate ability to unite both within a process of manifestation *in* the material realm. The anti-materialism of the American transcendentalists was a puny philosophy compared to one which made the very nature of material objects spiritual and thereby reconciled consumption with religious and scientific imperatives in an age of acquisition. Indeed, the coincidence of the language of Emerson with spiritualism is completely ignored by historians of American intellectual history.

I wish to end here with the briefest of comments on the cultural context of the material I have presented. Anybody who has read the many works in this particular canon knows one cannot top them for sensation or revelation. I shall not try to compete. What I should like briefly to suggest is that this new occultism is a key area, long neglected, of the popular imagination and a central feature of the modern sensorium. More specifically, I wish to assert modern spiritualism's 'Americanness', spiritualism as a product of an Americanized milieu, and as a peculiar instance of the coincidence of popular belief in the farms and villages of the East coast and European émigré theorizing and mysticism, which itself confronted, but was directed by, the new corporate culture of the western world, of which America was the leading example.

It seems to be no coincidence that the modern occult coincides in its origins and parallels in its development the rise of modern corporate business culture and its own struggle against entrepreneurial capital and individualist enterprise from the last quarter of the nineteenth century through to our own. While the concept of the corporation had existed since Tudor times it is only with the appearance of the American holding company that the 'occulting' of business really took place:

> In America the corporation would have a fertile new life. Since corporations, the creatures of government, could be made immortal and could be given whatever powers the lawmakers wished for them, popular leaders had long feared the corporation. Sir Edward Coke, seventeenth-century champion of common-law rights against a tyrant-king, warned that corporations 'cannot commit treason, nor be outlawed nor excommunicated, for they have no souls.' While Americans never succeeded in giving corporations a soul, they did see the corporation magically transformed in other ways. Corporations here would multiply as never before, they would spread over the land, and finally permeate every citizen's daily life. While the American corporation, a new species of old genus, was not without its own menacing features, it became (what Coke could never have imagined) the democratizer of property.... The corporation had many advantages over the enterprising individual.... A creature of the law, it was immortal.... Lawyers presided over the mysteries of corporation law.... Property became a new realm of the occult. (Boorstin).

Secret business trusts in the USA, when outlawed, metamorphosed in the hands of managing lawyers (of whom the chief magician was Rockefeller's Samuel C. T. Dodd) into the 'holding company' of which Standard Oil was the first in 1899. Far removed (at least on paper) from human (i.e. fallible) interference, the 'immortal' but 'soulless' corporation retained the same rights as actual humans but avoided the responsibilities. Here was a new *spectral* economic and legal body against which the popular and populist refusals of the last hundred or so years have been to little avail.

It is ironic that the topography of the supernatural is itself of a nature with the spectre of capital that it appears to oppose. It is no coincidence that as early as the 1840s (and exactly contemporaneous with the origins of spiritualism), Emerson could point out in his essay *Self Reliance* (1841, 1847), that

> Society is a *joint-stock company* in which the members agree for the better serving of his bread to each *shareholder*, to surrender the liberty and culture of the eater. The virtue in most request is conformity. (Emphases mine).

Nor is it a coincidence that 'whoso would be a man' in Emerson's philosophy 'must be a nonconformist'.

By uniting corporatism (communalism, hierarchy, order, and *management*) with individualism (spiritual egalitarianism leading to Christ-figure transcendence) the modern occult also reconciled guilt with redemption. The higher planes of the spirit world coincide with the management levels of the corporation; the spirit-guides help manage, teach and *benevolently* promote those climbing the hierarchy just as those might be helped in climbing the rungs of the business ladder; and the goal in both is secret knowledge and inner enlightenment when, on meeting the Chairman of the Board (both alien and familiar), we too are let into the inner sanctum among those secret books of accounts. It is no surprise that in both the corporation and the modern occult the guiding principles are those of law and management following from guidance and enlightenment. The 'Jesus Spaceman' hypothesis unites the Protestant work ethic with the *'guiltless'* alien visitor in order to take power back into the hands of the disenfranchised who nevertheless wish to (but can *never*) be incorporated in the spectral economy.

Even though Blavatsky was Russian, she learned her trade in New England – progressive, futuristic, individualistic, plebeian and democratic. Indeed, it was Blavatsky who promoted the idea that the Americans were the sixth root 'race' *(sic)* of the descendants of Lemuria. This popular dispensation which constantly 'reduces' the political to the personal and yet elevated it thereby was nevertheless a *direct result* of the materialist enlightenment and the liberal imagination. As a supposed terminus for materialist inquiry spiritualism and modern occultism provided their own paradoxical version of materialism: the inability of the individual to die, and the inevitability of spiritual immortality. Humankind was again placed at the centre of the universe only if it submitted to the higher consciousness of cosmic pantheism and hierarchic universalism.

Spiritualism has not merely provided a suitable response to plebeian uncertainties about social change and mass society, nor has it been merely a paranoiac response to neuroses over the atomic bomb, the space race, the crisis over ecology, changes in genetic investigation and human surgery, or even the meaning of consumer objects, but instead it has been an active participant in shaping ideas over race, human reproduction and evolution, the meaning of history and the defining characteristics of individual identity. Modern occultism is not merely the 'other' of rationalist inquiry, rather it is itself the product of rationalism and a form of rationalism as dementia. Isn't it here that we find the crisis of the copula that I mentioned in my introduction? This is the mythic space of the modern and the stories told therein are our stories alone, a dialogue within and about our contemporary imagination, our own desires and our own inadequacies.

Note

1. The following sources provided material for this essay: Beard, Paul, *Survival of Death* (Tasburgh, Norwich: Pilgrim Books, [1966] 1988); Boorstin, Daniel J., *The Americans: the Democratic Experience* (New York: Vintage, 1974); Brown, Rosemary, and Sandra White, *Look Beyond Today* (London: Bantam, 1986); Case, Edgar Evans and Hugh Lynn Case, *Edgar Case on Atlantis* (New York: Warner, [1968] 1988); Collins, Andrew, *The Second Coming: a Terrifying True Story* (London: Arrow, 1994); Collins, Doris, *The Power Within* (London: Grafton, 1986) and *Positive Forces* (London: Grafton, 1990); Cooke, Ivan (ed.), *The Return of Arthur Conan Doyle* (Liss, Hampshire: White Eagle Publishing Trust, [1933] 1980); Eadie, Betty J., and Curtis Taylor, *Embraced by the Light* (New York: Aquarian/Thorson, 1992); Forman, Joan, *The Golden Shore* (London: Robert Hale, 1988); Grant, Kenneth, *Outer Gateways* (London: Skoob Books, 1994); Icke, David, *Truth*

Vibrations (Bath: Gateway Books, 1993); Lipstadt, Deborah, *Denying the Holocaust* (Harmondsworth:Penguin, 1994); Morris, David, *The Masks of Lucifer: Technology and the Occult in Twentieth-Century Popular Literature* (London: Batsford, 1992); Newton, Toynes, Charles Walker, and Alan Brown, *The Demonic Connection* (Worthing, Sussex: Badger Books, [1987] 1993); Randi James, *The Mask of Nostradamus* (New York: Charles Scribner, 1990); Redgrove, Peter, *The Black Goddess and the Sixth Sense* (London: Bloomsbury, 1987); Rose, Louis, *Faith Healing* (London: Gollancz, 1968); Sassoon, George and Rodney Dale, *The Manna Machine* (London: Sidgwick and Jackson, 1978); Schwartz, Bernard, *The Law in Armenia: a History* (New York: McGraw-Hill, 1974); Snow, Chet B., *Mass Dreams of the Future* (Crest Park, California: Deep Forest Press, 1989); Spencer, John, *World Atlas of UFOs* (New York: Smithmark, 1992). Stokes, Doris, *Voices in My Ear* in *The Doris Stokes Compendium* (London: MacDonald, [1980] 1988); Swaffer, Hannen, *My Greatest Story: Vol. 2* (London: Psychic Book Club, 1945); Von Daniken, Erich, *The Gods and Their Grand Design* (London: Souvenir, 1984); Walker, Ann, *Heaven Can Wait* (London: Excalibur, 1989). Williamson, Linda, *Mediums and Their Work* (London: Robert Hale, 1990).

11

The Other Side of Plato's Wall

Ralph Noyes

In a powerful short story published in 1924, 'The Wish House', Rudyard Kipling puts into the mouth of one of his Sussex characters the term 'Token' as a synonym for ghost. 'Token' has not yet made it to the *OED* with this particular definition, but we can assume that Kipling had picked up a good local word. 'Token' is rich in meanings, not least in suggesting that the ghost offers us something which is likely to prove of fleeting value (like token thanks) but can possibly be traded in for a minor benefit if we can find the right slot (like a *geton* for a hot shower at a French camping site or Monopoly money for a hotel in the Old Kent Road). But what, in fact, is the market value of the ghostly coinage? Does it amount to more than that token promise written on each banknote by the Chief Cashier to the Bank of England to pay the bearer on demand a certain sum in pounds, a promise the attempted enforcement of which will certainly lead either to the issue of further faery gold in the form of token paper or token discs, or to the summoning of a police officer? Why have these tokens been passed from hand to hand (from mouth to ear) for millennia past in all societies for which we have records? Why have so many writers of the greatest fiction decided to give them currency?

I must declare an interest. As a member for the Society for Psychical Research (the SPR, for convenience) I cannot myself ignore the evidence amassed by the Society since its foundation in 1882 that ghosts in their several forms (the term embraces more than one phenomenon and needs some discriminating definitions) are not only a common element of human experience but sometimes provide powerful tokens of their independent existence. But I make this declaration as a health warning, not as a programme. I don't need to propagandize for the SPR's material: it is readily available in the Society's library for anyone who wishes to study it. Instead, I would like to use the opportunity offered by the editors of this helpfully wide-ranging book to mull over the problems which confront all of us who are unwise enough to tangle with elusive occurrences. You need to be warned of my conviction that 'ghosts exist', but you can rest assured that I am far from understanding them. Despite the many ingenious suggestions which have been made by past and present members of the Society (people of the calibre of William Crookes, Oliver Lodge, Sigmund Freud, Henri Bergson, Maurice Maeterlinck, Andrew Lang, William James, Carl Jung among others) little is on offer by way of satisfying explanation for the man on the Clapham omnibus, let alone a developed theory which would seem to our scientific friends at all consistent with their increasingly successful endeavours to tell us how the world works in the realm of our familiar three-dimensional. In these circumstances, and within these tolerant covers, a fruitful way forward may be to examine the language in which ghosts have been reported, to relate the ghost to some other common phenomena which have tended to elude everyday certitudes, and to cast a cautious eye at the weird speculations which the hardest-headed of our scientific colleagues now feel compelled to introduce simply to make sense of the behaviour of mere matter.

The language is rich. 'Ghost' possesses a large range of synonyms, near-synonyms, cognates and related terms in all European languages, particularly as we come further north into regions of extended winter darkness: spirit, sprite, spectre, *geist*, *revenant*, poltergeist, visitant, *gespenst*, phantom, phantasm, *klopfgeist*, spook, *spuk*, shade, apparition, wraith, *erscheinung*, *doppelgänger*, together with a few rather disappointing terms in Latin and Greek and a gaggle of darkly sinister nouns in Scandinavian vocabularies. Students of non-European languages report a similar richness of terms, though with interestingly different emphases on ancestors, witches, magic, shamanic flight and, in some cases, gruesomely physical references to the 'living dead'.

Each of these different terms chooses to emphasize either a particular characteristic of the ghost or a common hypothesis about what it is. Among the persistent hypotheses which language reflects are that the ghost is something which *returns* (*Revenant*); which returns *deliberately* (Visitant); which sometimes returns *often* to a particular place or person (the Haunting Ghost); and which on occasion returns *malignly* (Poltergeist, Zombie). Underlying all such words is the tradition, persistent in common belief in all societies, that something in the nature of intelligence and personality survives bodily death. Under this tradition, ghosts are the returning dead. When the writers of fiction turn to the 'supernatural' it is almost invariably from the same tradition that they draw their plots and conjure their effects. It is a very rare ghost story indeed which imagines a *living* agent as the source of spookish activity. The only case which springs readily to mind is Edward Bulwer-Lytton's *The Haunters and the Haunted*, in which a house is grievously troubled by the 'occult' powers of a distant agent who possesses something akin to that mysterious phenomenon, electricity (only just beginning to be understood in Bulwer-Lytton's time and serving him well enough as the pseudo-scientific basis for his compelling piece of terror). For the most part it is the human dead who haunt ghost fiction (with a few non-human exceptions of the kind which preoccupied M. R. James).

It is an interesting paradox that the common perception of the ghost as a human who has survived death usually fails to bring the comfort which might be expected from such remarkably Good News. Ghosts are almost invariably feared, even when their intentions seem benign. Psychologists, anthropologists and other social scientists have offered some reasons. Their speculations are well summarized in a recent book by a member of the SPR, Rosemary Dinnage.[1] In her introduction to a series of taped interviews with a wide range of people about their perceptions of death, Dinnage reminds us of Freud's view that we have all, at some time or other, cherished less than wholly loving emotions about our near and dear: 'frightening fantasies of the dead as being hostile are a projection of our own hostility to them – hostility that we felt while they were alive, or anger at them for leaving us'. She reminds us also of Lévi-Strauss's comment that the living need to make a contract with the dead, so that 'in return for being treated with a reasonable degree of respect, the dead remain in their own abode ...'.[2] If that contract is not observed, the dead may well return, and their mood will not necessarily be friendly. Dinnage reminds us again that an almost instinctive response to the lumpen fact of the inert corpse is often one of pity for its deprived state, coupled with the fear of its anger. No wonder that humankind has so often buried grave-goods with the departed in the hope of giving comfort and diverting anger (a practice which has, in extreme cases, extended to the burial of wives, concubines and the whole of the – usually female – domestic establishment).

Fear of the ghost thus finds a degree of explanation in the brute facts of the human condition as analysed by scholarly minds. It is this fear which has come to colour the many other terms for 'ghost' which occur in all languages. When Marx identified 'spectres' 'haunting' Europe – meaning by 'spectres' something of which we should be afraid – his Dialectical Materialism was covertly drawing on a substructure of very *un*materialistic folk belief. He meant to cause some shudders (guilty or not as the case may be), but he was leaning upon supernatural solicitings of the kind which Engels roundly dismissed in the robustest of commonsense terms in 'Natural Science in the Spirit World' (discussed by Willy Maley elsewhere in this volume). Fearing the ghost, and allowing that fear to contaminate all other words by which the ghostly phenomenon is represented, comes easily enough if we take for granted the tradition that ghosts are surviving humans. This tradition may, of course, prove true. It is sensible to keep an open mind. The inveterate gambler, Pascal, suggested how we should place our bets (and we shall all find out soon enough). But in the rest of this essay, I would like to avoid all presuppositions and to examine the remaining words in the ghostly vocabulary in the hope of suggesting an unbiased approach. I shall therefore no longer be concerned with words like '*revenant*' or 'visitant', or any others which seem to tell us, *a priori*, what ghosts are. I shall be trying, instead, to adopt what has been called the 'phenomenological' approach, that is to say, 'a plain description of direct experience, free of prepossessions, speculations and theories'.[3] My main focus will be the question, 'what has been the direct experience of the ghost by ordinary people?'; and I will be examining those elements of the language which seem to offer 'plain description' without begging questions.

'Spirit' is interesting (and 'sprite' derives from it). 'Spirit' relates to 'respiration'; it has something to do with our invisible breath. Some of those who have experienced a ghost have clearly found it useful to compare the phenomenon with our 'insubstantial' air. It took until the late seventeenth century to discover that air is in fact a massively omnipresent substance which presses upon us at sea level with sufficient force to suspend a large column of mercury; it is very far from insubstantial. But, in our everyday experience, air is not noticeable; it is an entirely reasonable metaphor for something which makes little if any impact on most of our senses. Those who have used this metaphor may also have had in mind the ability of expired air to become briefly visible as a foggy dew in cold weather. 'Wraith' is not too far distant. Wraiths tend to coil breathily around tombstones.

'Spectre' is a word with a network of associations. It clearly has its root in the Latin *spectare*, to see, to perceive, to look at. It relates to 'aspect', 'prospect', 'spectator', and all such words which have to do with the faculty of sight. It includes 'spectrum' among its relatives, the terms used by Newton when he first used his prism in 1665 to cause a ray of sunlight to exhibit its seven-fold constituents. 'Spectral' is a derivative, sometimes employed to designate the elements of Newton's spectrum (which are also the elements of the rainbow), but far more often used, poetically, to stand in for the 'unreal', the 'insubstantial'.

'Shade' clearly has something to do with light, even if only as an object or agent which obscures illumination. But insubstantiality is its main characteristic: 'shadow' is one of its cognates, and we all know that a man who is frightened of shadows is frightened of everything (which means he is frightened of nothing 'real').

'Phantom' has the core meanings of 'illusion', 'unreality', 'vain imagining'. When we call a ghost a phantom we are making an ontological statement, we are doubting whether the ghost is 'really there'. ('Phantasm' is a close relative; its history is discussed below). Whereas 'spirit', 'spectre', 'shade' and their relatives attempt to be phenomenological ('what was the thing *like*?'), or epistemological ('in what manner did we apprehend it?'), 'phantom' already adopts an *a priori* position about what is and what isn't. It affirms that the ghost is not real. It is as tendentious – albeit in the other direction – as *'revenant'* and 'visitant'. Interestingly, it has (since the Enlightenment) spawned a greater variety of derivatives than other terms in the ghostly vocabulary. Most of these secondary usages carry the implication that what is described does not achieve the full range of robust characteristics expected of 'normal' experience by common sense: phantom limb, phantom pregnancy, phantom freight (a notional or token charge for delivery), phantom circuit (a trick performed by electrical engineers), phantom voters (a trick performed by corrupt regimes), a phantom of delight, phantom tumour, phantom larva (because transparent and nearly invisible), phantom orchid (because uncannily pale). The difference in flavour between these phantom usages and the usage of other spectral terms is apparent if we attempt some substitutions: Strindberg did not write *The Phantom Sonata*; Marx did not tell us that us that phantoms were haunting Europe; if we need assistance with our prose, we do not employ a phantom writer; the third person of the Trinity has never been called the Holy Phantom. The main interest of 'phantom' for natural historians lies in the indication it gives us that many percipients of the ghost have found it to be markedly different from tables and chairs, a phenomenological clue which is probably important.

'Apparition' is a relative newcomer, often used by people who wish to find some neutral term for the designation of the ghostly phenomena they propose to examine. Members of the SPR have made much use of it, probably in the hope of avoiding unnecessary polemics and encouraging fellow scientists to study the material dispassionately.[4] It is no more than a minor irony that 'apparition' (with its descendants, 'appearance' or even 'mere appearance') derives from Greek and Latin roots which relate to the faculty of sight and tend to imply that the other senses were not involved – characteristics possessed by the many other, more 'supernatural', terms whose occult baggage the SPR researchers were seeking to cast overboard.

I have left unexamined many of the other words which embody the persistent set of experiences which people the world over have called 'the ghost'. Further linguistic analysis could be made; it might fruitfully shape future research programmes. But my limited survey is perhaps enough to suggest some key factors: the faculty of sight tends to predominate; little, if anything, usually impinges on the other senses (setting aside some dubiously evidenced clanks and groans); the occurrence is brief, and it is 'independent' in the sense that the ghost comes and goes in its own time; nothing in the way of physical evidence remains after its departure (except possibly some broken dishes if the ghost has chosen to be a poltergeist). Faced with such a puzzling constellation of absurdities, we may well decide to return to our everyday certitudes. But if we have the folly to persist in our enquiries, even if only to assist literary criticism, it may be helpful to look for analogies. The rainbow is one of them. H. H. Price, Professor of Philosophy at Oxford and a sometime president of the SPR, once remarked, 'I have often thought that if rainbows, reflections, mirages, and the like had been less common than they are, philosophers would have denied their existence on *a priori* grounds'.[5] For centuries, the rainbow remained mysterious. It shares some characteristics with the ghost: brevity, independence of action, insubstantiality and the lack of any *post facto* evidence for its existence. It has the additional features of moving away from the observer as fast as he or she approaches it and of offering a lucky seven as the number of its colours. For most of human history the rainbow attracted a range of occult speculation. It was often seen as a message from supernatural beings, particularly when accompanied, as it often is, by Jove's thunderbolts. Crocks of gold were expected at the points where it visibly touched the earth. The impossibility of determining precisely where these points might be, and the failure of all travellers ever to reach the rainbow's end added to the uncanny reputation. It was a phantom if ever there was one.

When Newton first decomposed a ray of sunlight into its constituent elements by interposing a prism (one might be tempted to say that he had 'deconstructed' the sunlight if that term had not already been pre-empted for less physicalist enquiries) he also decomposed the rainbow. With the publication of the *Opticks* (which Newton postponed until 1704 when the spectre of the quarrelsome Mr Hooke, who had viciously assailed him at meetings of the Royal Society, had been laid to rest with the ghosting of the latter in 1703), no one could any longer expect crocks of gold from the rainbow, but its 'reality' as a phenomenon was placed permanently beyond doubt. And there was a wider gain. Not only had the seven-coloured wraith yielded to rational explanation, but a whole class of ghostly occurrences, including the great family of the mirages, had achieved a secure ontology. No longer was it necessary to entertain superstitious feelings for (or, on the other hand, to cast into the metaphysical limbo of not being 'really there') objects and events whose only fault consisted of appealing to fewer than the usual five senses. Only for poets and the makers of metaphors did something remain of the pale afterglow which the erstwhile supernatural never entirely loses. In the life of the imagination, rainbows still come and go, carrying intimations. And chasing them remains a handy term for occupations which the world considers idle.

The rainbow was lucky; there have always been plenty of them. Although they took centuries to understand, they were seen sufficiently often and by a large enough number of people, frequently in company with each other, to leave no doubt that they *happened*, however supernatural they might seem. But suppose, following H. H. Price's speculation, that rainbows had been a much rarer event.

Imagine some country in which rain does not fall more often than a dozen times in a century (let its inhabitants get their water from underground sources in the manner of Xanadu). Rainbows will not only seem as strange as they appeared to the Greeks and the Romans, their very occurrence will be disputed. There will be occasional reports from single witnesses who were travelling in the desert at the time; these reports may, with luck, be supplemented by a few cases of multiple-witnessing, some of them recorded, perhaps, even in the suburb of a city. Historical records may provide some dubious collateral. But the reports will be far too few and probably far too badly documented to convince determined sceptics that it wasn't all 'mere imagination'. Those among us who have a taste for fantasy fiction of the kind essayed by Johnson in *Rasselas* or Swift in *Gulliver's Travels* could readily take these initial conditions as the starting point for an extended narrative in which the population of Xanadu divides among believers and non-believers, pronouncements are made *ex cathedra* by priesthoods and scientific establishments, a few fanatics go to the stake, sturdy upholders of common sense achieve State honours, harmless eccentrics establish some 'New Rainbow Movements', and a maverick academic or two who cautiously assert that rainbows actually seem to happen are denied the renewal of their university contracts and/or research funding.

But we need not allow our imaginations to run to this degree of extravagance to recognize that phenomena persistently reported by the folk (including even academics) deserve serious study; that the absence of some parts of the usual range of sensory response is no argument for neglecting them; and that it is a *trahison des clercs* to dismiss them *a priori* by the lazy device of placing them in the *ad hoc* category of 'mere imagination' (or even, more shiftily, 'hallucination') without examining the evidence.

In 1886, four years after the founding of the SPR, its then Honorary Secretary, Edmund Gurney, published in conjunction with collaborators an extensive survey of one category of ghost, the 'crisis apparition'.[6] The crisis apparition is the reported appearance to a witness in visual form of a (geographically) distant relative or friend who is at the same time undergoing a traumatic experience, frequently that of death. Crucial to the scientific assessment of this phenomenon are such self-evident points as whether the witness had any reason to suspect a crisis in the distant subject; whether, in the event, the apparition coincided fairly closely with a real –

checkable – crisis; whether any ordinary means of communication could have conveyed the information of the crisis to the witness; whether other – checkable – information was also conveyed. Gurney *et al.* collected some 700 cases by an assiduity of correspondence and personal visits which can only leave us ashamed or admiring a century later. They established beyond reasonable doubt that, during the mid-to-late-nineteenth-century period which they were examining, the 'ghosts' of distant individuals in crisis were not infrequently seen by witnesses in circumstances which precluded 'normal' means of communication. They recorded cases in which the apparition was seen by more than one witness at the same time; and in several of their cases additional information of a very specific kind (checkable and checked) was also conveyed, for example, the precise and often bizarre circumstances in which the crisis had arisen.

Gurney *et al.* were working in conditions which were rather favourable, both to the occurrence of 'abnormal communication' and also to the *post facto* establishment that it had in fact occurred. In the period they were examining, the British had a remarkably far-flung empire. There could hardly have been a family in the UK which didn't have some nephew/uncle/lover/husband/friend finding his (not usually her) way in countries which were distant by a sizeable fraction of the earth's circumference – Canada, Australia, India, South Africa.... At the same time, the normal means of communication were elementary and slow – letters might take six weeks or longer to reach Britain by ship from the antipodes. The first of these factors (the far-flungness) rendered it likely that *if* 'anomalous communication' could occur, the British would be well placed to unearth it. The second factor (slowness of normal communications) made it relatively easy to ascertain that the witness(es) could not have acquired their information by 'normal' means. It was thus relatively straightforward (even if strenuously demanding by way of correspondence and other means of enquiry) for Gurney *et al.* to establish beyond reasonable doubt that something was going on which the conventional science of their time could not accommodate. The crisis apparition is far less frequently reported to the Society than hitherto. Among many possible explanations are: the decline of the British imperial involvement in other continents and, hence, the greatly reduced number of British who are likely to have a crisis overseas; and the swifter means of communication now available to us (fax and 'phone will tell within minutes if our near and dear are suffering, we don't need apparitions to keep us informed). But the material placed on record by Gurney *et al.* in *Phantasms of the Living* remains, with some 700 well researched cases, as a body of evidence which should not be ignored.

Gurney's choice of the term, *Phantasms*, as a major part of his title is interesting. 'Phantasm' relates to 'phantom', on which I have commented above. 'Phantasm' shares with 'phantom' the characteristics of delusion, illusion, the not 'really real'. In choosing 'phantasm', Gurney was leaning over backwards to avoid any presumption on the part of potential critics that he and his collaborators had been brainwashed into some premature and too simplistic ontology, for example the supposition that something like a quasi-substantial 'soul' or 'spirit' had emanated from Uncle Charlie to pay a final visit to the living. We need to remember that at the time of Gurney's studies the recently founded SPR, determined to preserve a neutral and scientific approach to its material, was in the process of making a decisive split with the many committed Spiritualists who had joined the Society. The last thing Gurney would have wanted was to sound like an unreconstructed Spiritualist, carrying all the baggage of the Spiritualist belief in a remarkably mundane afterworld, populated by remarkably unchanged simulacra of persons once living, and capable of contact in the form of remarkably ordinary (or portentously platitudinous) communications by way of those claiming mediumistic abilities. The Spiritualist belief-system and some of the indisputable and often startling data emerging from Spiritualist practice have since been the subject of much analysis and a degree of experimentation both by intelligent Spiritualists themselves and – notably – by the SPR.[7] But the early 1880s were not the time for this kind of analysis. Gurney's concern was to present the facts emerging from his 700 or so cases and to invite scientific attention to them without imposing unnecessary barriers by way of unexamined presuppositions. 'Phantasm' probably seemed to him to suit this turn, and it is also notable that the second part of his title was 'the Living'. He quite explicitly did not wish to tackle at that stage the question of whether the deceased – the 'really dead' – might also on occasion leave their calling-cards by way of a brief appearance to witnesses.

Faced with the massive evidence that apparitions of the living were a not-too-uncommon experience in the British population at large, Gurney *et al.* felt obliged to offer some guesses at what might be occurring in these cases. Searching for a preliminary hypothesis which would offer the least offence to common sense, Gurney plumped for an explanation in terms of telepathy, a term recently invented by one of his collaborators, F. W. H. Myers, to categorize the phenomenon of the apparent non-conventional response of one mind to another, for which a degree of independent evidence had already been collected by the Society. Gurney suggested that the witness became telepathically aware of the distant subject's distress and hallucinated an image of the subject. This attractively simple, parsimonious and not too spooky view ran immediately, however, into certain difficulties which Myers discussed within the covers of the book: for example, that an apparition was not always that of a subject in crisis (in some cases no reason whatever could be conjectured for the sudden appearance of Uncle Charlie, who remained in cheerful good health); that an apparition was some-times quite unknown to the witness (who was therefore unlikely to be having a telepathic response); that the apparition sometimes conveyed visual information which was not only unknown to the witness but was also unlikely to have been in the mind of the subject (for example, the precise details of an accident which had left the subject dying and unconscious); that an apparition was sometimes seen by several witnesses at once, including people quite unconnected with the subject; and that in these cases of multiple-witnessing the witnesses agreed in locating the apparition at a single point in space (some, for example, seeing it in profile and some head-on). Myers advanced these points as objections to Gurney's telepathic hypothesis and felt obliged to argue that some-thing with greater ontological status than that of a mere hallucination, however defined, had been present when the apparition was seen (something which perhaps possessed the onto-logical respectability of a rainbow? – though Myers did not suggest this analogy himself). The debate which took place between Gurney and Myers within the covers of *Phantasms of Living*, conducted on both sides with much ingenuity, ended in polite agreement to disagree. It was also a 'classical debate' in the sense that all later commentators on the problem of the apparition have found it desirable to take their departure from it.[8]

Gurney's attempt to confine his study to apparitions of 'the Living' also encountered problems. There were cases in which the apparition was clearly of a subject who had been dead for at least some hours when the witness saw it; and there were others in which the death was yet to come. As a fairly arbitrary device of methodology (*some* definition had, after all, to be adopted) Gurney *et al.* defined an apparition as being of a *'living'* subject if it was witnessed during a 24-hour period which encompassed 12 hours before and 12 hours after death in those cases (by no means all of them) in which the subject had actually died. It is doubtful whether any student of the subject has ever felt less than uneasy about this valiant attempt by Gurney *et al.* to set manageable limits to their field of enquiry.

Inevitably, the Society did not rest content with studying apparitions of 'the Living'. As earlier parts of this essay have reminded us, the folklore of all societies is far richer in supposed apparitions of the long dead than in those of the recently living. It was not long before the SPR turned its attention to the study of supposed *post mortem* apparitions (apparitions of those who had been dead for longer than Gurney's arbitrary upper limit of 12 hours). Much has been placed on record about these phenomena in the Society's *Proceedings* and *Journal*, and all of this material is readily accessible in the SPR's library and archives for those who wish to study it. For the purposes of this essay it is enough to say that the Society has amassed a good deal of not-too-bad evidence for such things as: the appearance to individual witnesses in visual and (more rarely) audible form of apparitions which claim to be the emanations of deceased persons whom the witnesses say they recognize; the appearance to witnesses at an allegedly haunted location of apparitions which are not recognized but which often claim to be the emanations of deceased persons (claims which plodding leg-work has not infrequently authenticated, at least in the sense that the study of parish registers, birth and death certificates, obituary notices, family records and the like seem to provide collateral); the occurrence of vigorous and sometimes violent physical effects for which the term 'poltergeist' is a convenient label and with which (notwithstanding the SPR's disposition to look for a living agent or 'focus' in such cases) there is often a claim by the manifesting entity that it is a deceased human. In many of these instances information is conveyed to the witness which it is hard to account for in conventional terms. A variety of hypotheses have been debated by the Society to account for these several phenomena.[9]

What, after all this, is *'the Ghost'*? 'The Ghost' has proved a powerful metaphor in many areas of human endeavour – literary, philosophical, anthropological, religious, socio-psychological. But

I've tried to suggest that 'ghost', *tout court*, is far too simple a word to embrace all those various synonyms and cognates which I've discussed above. Those several terms, reflecting a variety of linguistic embodiments which are detectable in all languages, should certainly not be condensed too readily into a single word with which to play literary or philosophical games. Still less can any unitary term be allowed to stand in for the rich variety of phenomena which have been soberly placed on record by natural historians of the kind represented by the SPR and kindred organizations. We need to know precisely what we're doing in any particular case before deciding to use 'spectre' instead of 'phantom', or 'zombie' instead of 'vampire', or 'apparition' instead of 'visitant', or 'ghoul' instead of 'phantasm'. And an organization which has scientific objectives must also be wary of adopting, too casually, any of these terms from the folk vocabularies, loaded as they are with implicit ontological presuppositions. We need, for the time being, to be as empirically inclined about 'ghosts' – as *'phenomenological'* – as we might wish our predecessors to have been about the rainbow (or, for that matter, meteorites, electricity and hypnotism, all of which attracted superstitious speculation and bluff commonsensical rejection in about equal measure). We still await our Newton in psychical research; no one has yet found the right prism by which to deconstruct the SPR's particular range of rainbows.

But the 'prism' is, of course, too simple a hope: ghosts are orders of magnitude more complex than rainbows or any other reducible phenomenon of human experience; something more sophisticated than mere technology will be needed to accommodate them to an enlarged understanding of how the world works. Psychical researchers have had a tendency to take their phenomena too literally. They have asked questions which they felt were 'scientific': 'was it really *there*?' Some of them have performed grotesquely physicalist experiments in the hope of answering naive questions of this kind. The case is recorded of an earnest researcher who sat by the bedside of his dying wife, seeking by an ingenious system of weights and springs to measure the loss of mass which the unhappy lady would undergo at the moment of death, a figure which he hoped would establish the weight of her departing soul or spirit (he obtained and published a rather small weight). In other cases researchers have ingeniously killed small mammals enclosed in sealed vessels in the hope of detecting the 'rays of energy' dispersed by the corpse as it gave up the ghost. Nonetheless, papers published by the Society have often tended to imply that the non-ordinary phenomena which they report, on good evidence and often with elaborate statistical safeguards, will not achieve ontological respectability – are likely to be rejected by sceptics as not 'really real' – unless wholly lumpen evidence can be provided and a wholly physicalist (five-senses) explanation can be given within the framework of a curiously old-fashioned interpretation of nineteenth-century (three-dimensional) physics. Some researchers behave as though, despite Newton, rainbows must be dismissed as 'unreal' because they move away from us as fast as we approach them and because crocks of gold are never found at the points where the bow intersects the horizon; and many seem to ignore altogether that the physics of the late twentieth century demands far more than the three dimensions of common experience to account for the behaviour of mere matter.

Poets and writers of imaginative fiction have not usually been thus blinkered; nor, judging from the tales they tell and the words they use, have the men and women on the Clapham omnibus for whom books and poems are written. Literature, even when not explicitly of the ghost-fiction genre, is filled with echoes and intimations of the 'supernatural'. Without having done the necessary research, I will wager that there is hardly an extant novel without some reference (however passing and dismissive) to spectral occurrences, and hardly a poem, even when written by other than metaphysical poets, which fails to intimate (however remotely) that we are creatures moving about in worlds unrealized. Writers, and the folk they write for, do not on the whole feel that they have to be Fundamentalists of an old-fashioned Materialist persuasion.

We cannot expect psychical researchers to become poets or fictioneers. They might, however, have something to learn from the many texts in which good writers have deliberately tackled the genre of the 'supernatural'. They would find, to begin with, that some of their epistemological and ontological problems ('Was the apprehended object really *there*?') have been agonized over by some of the best of writers. In *The Turn of the Screw* (1898) were Peter Quint and Miss Jessel mere hallucinations of the governess, or did they have some independent 'reality'? The question has been much debated. Henry James himself made contradictory statements about his intentions from one time to another. The text itself provides a powerful suggestion that the two ghosts were more than imaginary: the governess's description of them causes Mrs Grose, the housekeeper, to identify them at once with the Quint and Jessel, now dead, who once worked in the house. But how can we know that Mrs Grose was doing any more than attaching her own fancies to some hysterical perturbation in the governess, thus giving a spurious ontology to what might otherwise have passed off as a mere fit of the vapours? One wonders how Gurney and Myers would have debated the matter if a comparable case had come to the SPR (as many cases indeed did, if usually with less disturbing implications). It is not surprising that James described the story as 'a trap for the unwary'. We can take it virtually for granted that, as the brother of William James (President of the Society in 1894/95), he would have been aware of the work undertaken by the SPR since 1882. (Indeed, on one occasion Henry read, to a meeting of the Society, a paper which William could not himself be present to deliver.) As a master of ambiguities, Henry James would certainly have savoured the rueful ironies of now-you-see-it/now-you-don't which have haunted the best psychical research since the foundation of the SPR. *The Turn of the Screw* was perhaps not only a masterpiece of 'supernatural' fiction but also an oblique commentary on the dilemmas of those who seek to pursue rainbows in advance of a developed paradigm which might make rainbows more user-friendly.

In addition to finding that their perplexities are often shared by the writers of fiction, psychical researchers might learn something from the sense of the Uncanny which ghost narratives often convey. Gurney and his collaborators were struck (as later researchers have been struck) by the sheer ordinariness of the apparitions they were studying: there was little of the night side of Nature about them; they frequently appeared in broad daylight; as often as not, they presented themselves to witnesses as wholly solid for the brief moments of their manifestation; the alarm usually generated in the witness tended to follow the *disappearance* of the apparition and to be linked with an inference ('Something must have happened to Charlie') rather than with the occurrence itself. There was, in short, little of the spooky about them. Ghost fiction, on the other hand, frequently dwells on the feeling of the witness that something entirely weird is going on: scalps prickle, hair rises, shudders trouble the spine, and other physiological responses are reported which indicate not just fear but fear-with-a-difference, a disproportionate phobia rather than the rational alarm of being faced by a polar bear, an explosion on board the aircraft or a thug in an alleyway. The complex of feelings reported by those in the presence of the 'supernatural' is often summed up as being a sense of the Uncanny. Attempts have been made to explain or diagnose the peculiar flavour of these emotions, mainly by Freud and his followers. That faithful Freudian, Ernest Jones, elaborating on the master, suggested that we feel as Uncanny the threatened return to consciousness of repressed infantile incestuous desires.[10] Others, perhaps more fruitfully, have suggested that these emotions, unmistakable to all of us who have had them, even if only in bad dreams, reflect a dissonance between the course and content of Uncanny events and the expectations we have of the world in the light of our common experience: something grotesquely untoward is going on, and it shakes us to our animal core, fine-tuned as the latter is by evolutionary pressures to dealing with our usual three-dimensional. (It is difficult to give references for these latter views: they tend to be thrown out *en passant* in the course of works dealing with these matters. I am unaware of any sustained analysis, comparable to the work of the Freudians, which specifically addresses our phobic reaction to the 'supernatural'.) But whatever view we take of the attempts so far made to explain the sense of the Uncanny, psychical researchers have usually neglected it, and they may well be making a mistake in doing so. The sense of the Uncanny possibly contains an important phenomenological clue.

There is a third (perhaps more dubious) respect in which psychical researchers might find it profitable to examine ghost fiction. In ghost fiction the manifesting entity is often a great deal more loquacious than any ghost which has come the way of the SPR. The length at which Hamlet's father carries on has no parallel in anything reported in the scientific literature; and the instances could be multiplied. It may merely be that the need for dramatic effect causes good but scientifically uninformed authors to script their ghosts with lengthy texts (informed writers like Henry James know better: Miss Jessel and Peter Quint are as silent as most of the apparitions reported to the SPR). Or it may be that most writers, like most spiritualist mediums, wish to convey in accordance with the predominant folk-belief and the expectations of their customers, that the ghost is the reappearance of, or emanation from, a deceased human, speech being the most forceful means of making the point. But psychical researchers might well ask themselves why ghosts outside fiction are on the whole seen but not heard, whereas the deceased communicators at a séance are always heard but not seen (except in the very unghostly manner of the alleged and grossly physical manifestations which never stand the light of day).

Some conclusions can perhaps be drawn from these intersections of Life and Literature. For writers the ghost is a powerful metaphor with many overtones of the kind discussed earlier in this essay: its hold on the imagination comes with a money-back guarantee; it is a sure-fire means of evoking a constellation of emotions in the reader, particularly those of that special kind of dread which goes by the name of the 'Uncanny'. This could hardly be the case unless we common readers possessed an in-built readiness of response (just as most of us possess an in-built readiness of response to snakes, spiders and other forms of non-mammalian life). This response requires an explanation, and the Freudian *Just So* story fails to provide one (for this reader at least). Something far more deeply interfused seems to be in question than any threatened return of guilty thoughts from the nursery. The power and universality of the ghost in literature is not only very serviceable for writers, it also provides something of a promise to ghost-hunters that they are not wholly wasting their time.

From literature psychical researchers might, in addition, take the indication that they have tended to be too literal, too scientifically Fundamentalist, too inclined to treat the phantom as being 'real' (or not) depending upon its ability (or otherwise) to behave like tables and chairs and the other phenomena of common experience which successfully appeal to all five of our routine senses. The rainbow should have warned them against this simplistic view; imaginative fiction might give them a second chance. The human faculty of imagination – the faculty of making images – might serve as a powerful indication that man does not live by bread alone. A metaphor is, by definition, a figure of speech, not a figure of substance. Writers are free to invoke, by canny means, a response which lies deep in human nature; psychical researchers, as natural historians, must plod along with their attempts to describe Nature as they find it. What might illuminate them both is the recognition that figures of speech and figures of substance are possibly the same; that neither of them needs to defer cravenly to the currently received wisdom that only figures of substance possess a secure ontology; and that Plato was possibly right in describing the phenomenal world (the world which a now out-dated physics calls the only 'real' one) as being the mere shadows cast on a wall at the end of his celebrated cave.

In *The Walls of Plato's Cave: the Science and Philosophy of Brain, Consciousness and Perception*, Professor John Smythies draws on late-twentieth-century physics as well as a number of other disciplines to provide forceful arguments that we shall betray ignorance as well as naiveté if we any longer take as our touchstones the kind of bluff bulldogism which caused Dr Johnson to feel that he had refuted Bishop Berkeley by stamping his foot on a stone and exclaiming 'I refute it with my foot thus'; or David Hume to conclude that the laws of Nature had been finally understood at the time of publication of his *Enquiry Concerning Human Understanding* (1748) and that anything contravening them must be classed as 'miracles' and therefore regarded as superstitious nonsense, or Lord Kelvin to decide that almost everything in physics had been well established by the third quarter of the nineteenth century and that the intake of physics undergraduates to London University should therefore be tapered off, or contemporary neurologists to assert that a full account of human experience can be given in terms of their increasing (and spectacularly successful) understanding of the biology of the brain. Smythies deals with far more than these pedestrian incidents in the history of knowledge; his concerns are philosophical in the widest sense; it would be wrong to attempt a summary of this remarkably far-reaching text. It is enough to say that he leaves us less embarrassed than we might otherwise feel in suspecting that the findings of psychical researchers and the intimations of imaginative writers may – however counter-intuitive to brute common sense – find an entirely rational locus on the other side of Plato's wall.

I must end with a disclaimer. In common with all scientific organizations, the SPR does not demand that its members should adhere to any particular hypotheses; we are all free to express our individual views. By the same token, the Society has no collective doctrines, and none of us is entitled to speak in its name. The opinions expressed in this essay are solely those of its author.

Notes

1. R. Dinnage, *The Ruffian on the Stair* (Harmondsworth: Penguin, 1992), p. 8.
2. C. Lévi-Strauss, *Tristes Tropiques*, trans. John and Doreen Weightman (Harmondsworth: Penguin, 1992), p. 232.

3. See J. Poynton, 'Making Sense of Psi', *Journal of the SPR* 59:835 (April 1994), p. 403.
4. See, for example, G. N. M. Tyrrell, *Apparitions* (London: SPR, 1973), *passim*, and H. Hart *et al.*, 'Six Theories About Apparitions', *Proceedings, SPR*, vol. 50, part 185 (London, 1956), *passim*.
5. H. H. Price, *Thinking and Experience* (London: Hutchinson, 1969), p. 252.
6. E. Gurney *et al.*, *Phantasms of the Living* (London: Trübner and Co.: 1886). The initial edition is very rare; see also the abridged version, ed. Eleanor Sidgwick (London: Kegan Paul, 1918).
7. See, for example, A. Gauld, *Mediumship and Survival* (London: Heinemann (& SPR), 1982) and SPR Proceedings *passim*.
8. See, for example, G.N.M. Tyrrell, *Apparitions*; H. Hart, *et al.*, 'Six Theories'; and A. Gauld, *Mediumship and Survival*.
9. Bibliographical details of the Society's debates can be found in the volumes listed above.
10. Ernest Jones, *On the Nightmare* (London: Hogarth Press, 1931 and 1949), esp. pp. 343–50.

Index